Gender and Sexuality in Ghanaian Societies

Gender and Sexuality in Africa and the Diaspora

Series Editors: Besi Brillian Muhonja (James Madison University) and Babacar M'Baye (Kent State University)

Series Advisory Board: Nkiru Nzegwu, Achola Pala, Melinda Adams, Binyavanga Wainaina, Ashley Currier, Betty Wambui, Jane Rarieya, Olufemi Taiwo, Cheikh Thiam

Gender and Sexuality in Africa and the Diaspora publishes innovative, interdisciplinary research on intersections of gender, sexuality, and other political, social, economic, cultural, and geographic identity markers. The series has particular interest in groundbreaking scholarship on herstories/histories, elements and politics of gender and sexuality that center critical African and African diaspora thought and philosophies within global contemporary theoretical debates across the disciplines. Thus, manuscripts exploring gender relationships, queer identities, sexualities, masculinities, and femininities within both Africa and its diaspora in interdisciplinary contexts are highly encouraged.

Recent Titles in the Series:

Gender and Sexuality in Ghanaian Societies

Edited by

Martha Donkor and Amoaba Gooden

LEXINGTON BOOKS
Lanham • Boulder • New York • London

Published by Lexington Books
An imprint of The Rowman & Littlefield Publishing Group, Inc.
4501 Forbes Boulevard, Suite 200, Lanham, Maryland 20706
www.rowman.com

86-90 Paul Street, London EC2A 4NE, United Kingdom

British Library Cataloguing in Publication Information Available

Library of Congress Cataloging-in-Publication Data

Names: Donkor, Martha, editor. | Gooden, Amoaba, 1967- editor.
Title: Gender and sexuality in Ghanaian societies / edited by Martha Donkor
    and Amoaba Gooden.
Description: Lanham : Lexington Books, [2021] | Series: Gender and
    sexuality in Africa and the diaspora | Includes bibliographical references
    and index.
Identifiers: LCCN 2021043266 (print) | LCCN 2021043267 (ebook) | ISBN
    9781793628442 (cloth) | ISBN 9781793628466 (paperback) | ISBN
    9781793628459 (epub)
 Subjects: LCSH: Women—Sexual behavior—Ghana. | Patriarchy—Ghana. |
    Sex role—Ghana.
Classification: LCC HQ1816 .G46 2021 (print) | LCC HQ1816 (ebook) |
    DDC 305.409667—dc23
LC record available at https://lccn.loc.gov/2021043266
LC ebook record available at https://lccn.loc.gov/2021043267

Contents

Acknowledgments

Working on this book was a collaboration of love—across location, space, and time. Our history as friends and colleagues spans twenty-six years from when we first met each other as graduate students at the University of Guelph, Canada; Amoaba, a Jamaican-born Canadian, and Martha, a Ghanaian-born Canadian. We both currently reside in the US in different geographical locations and were able to use various virtual platforms to work on this edited collection. Special thanks to Dr. Babacar M'Baye who invited us to consider pulling together, in one place, research on Gender and Sexuality(s) in Ghana. We write this book for our daughters: Susan Appiah-Kubi, Niarra Gooden-Clarke, and NyAshia Gooden-Clarke. We offer the contents of this book to them, in hopes that they will continue to use their voices to disrupt rigidly fixed notions about gender and sexuality, ultimately opening spaces so they can be who they are in the world.

Introduction

Martha Donkor

In the introduction to her edited volume on sexuality, Signe Arnfred states simply, "The time has come for re-thinking sexualities in Africa."[1] The implication is clear: there had been a certain way of thinking about sexualities in Africa that obscured more than it revealed. For a long time, our understanding of gender relations, the nature of patriarchy, and sexuality in Africa, including Ghana, came through accounts written by European colonialists, missionaries, and adventurers/travelers. Some of the accounts were written by people who were not trained experts in anthropology or sociology but adventurers or affiliates of colonial enterprises who looked at Africa through Western eyes; thus, they had preconceived negative notions about Africa and looked for "evidence" to support such notions. For example, the English explorer Hugh Clapperton, who was generally positive in his descriptions of the peoples he encountered, noted that the women of Little Popoe (in West Africa) were "clean, well made, and for negroes, handsome."[2] One wonders what else Clapperton wanted or expected to see in the women of Little Popoe. Similarly, Ifi Amadiume referred to the work of Mrs. Leith-Ross, wife of a colonial official who was commissioned to study the Igbo after the Women's War of 1929. In the final publication of her research, Leith-Ross wrote that the Igbo were ignorant and undeveloped, among other characterizations.[3] Both Clapperton and Leigh-Ross's narratives demonstrate the kind of colonial imagination where Africa and its people are othered and Europeans placed on a hierarchy.

Colonial writers described African social systems in an oppositional framework to that of Europe. For instance, when they wrote that African social systems were primitive, then we want to simply ask: primitive in relation to whose? Colonial writers put Africa and Europe in a ranking order in which Europe occupied the top, superordinate position and Africa occupied the bottom. As Donkor observed in an analysis of colonial policies against miscegenation in Africa, Europe was everything that Africa was not. Europe was developed and progressive, Africa was primitive and backward; Europeans were civilized, Africans were savages; European women were chaste, African women could not control their libido. The negativity didn't stop with the achievement of independence by African countries. In the contemporary period, the spread of AIDS on the continent, female circumcision, and child prostitution have again thrust Africa on the negative trend of scholarly analysis of sexuality. The denigration of African gender relations and sexualities has in turn engendered a parallel impetus for scholars who want to reject Western negative depictions of Africans and their social systems and practices to set the record straight through contextual research.

From feminists who have challenged Western, mainstream feminist scholarship on the definitions of woman and theories of women's oppression, to anthropologists and sociologists who have interrogated colonialist depictions of African women's sexuality under patriarchy, there is what Donkor terms rescue and restore—that is, scholars must rescue and restore the body of literature that analyzes African women's experiences in their proper cultural contexts. Rescue and restore literature is decolonizing to the extent that it debunks and destabilizes the colonial hegemony of knowledge production about Africans. From edited volumes to single-authored books and thousands of articles on women, scholars, Africans on the continent and those living in the West have explored African women's lives from diverse philosophical, empirical, and theoretical perspectives. And like women living under patriarchy everywhere, these studies show that African women's experiences under patriarchy cannot be reduced exclusively to negative or positive impacts. Nor is it even sufficient to say that the truth lies somewhere in the middle for, as we will see later, African women's experiences, including their sexual behavior, are influenced by multiple and complex forces that do not lend themselves to simple negative or positive impact analysis.

One of the earliest and significant scholars on African women's gender and sexuality is feminist anthropologist Ifi Amadiume. In her book *Male Daughters, Female Husbands: Gender and Sex in an African Society*, Amadiume calls attention to the fact that Western feminists were wrong to essentialize precolonial African women's experiences and to impute on the women an enduring oppression under Africa's peculiar brand of patriarchy. As Kirk Hoppe rightly observes, "Precolonial African women were not an undifferentiated, exploited and powerless group in need of feminist rescue, and were disempowered, not elevated, by colonialisms."[4] Both Amadiume and Hoppe echo a central argument that Chandra Mohanty made in her seminal manuscript "Under Western Eyes." Mohanty criticized Western feminists who studied pockets of people and used the limited information to generalize about Third World women. She called attention to historical and material conditions that created the Third World and argued for contextual analyses that linked particular contexts to the global political economy. Without that critical contextualization, scholars stood the danger of glossing over the nature of the oppressions that Third World women, especially African women, experienced because of colonialism and the women's strategies to end their oppression.[5] African and other non-Western scholars are drawing attention to the falsity of the notion that African social institutions and traditions are impervious to change and African women's oppression is universal and absolute. Such characterizations of African women are contrary to the realities of the many and diverse societies and cultures that comprise Africa.

It is also worth observing that despite their theoretical reformulation of gender in the late twentieth century, Western feminist scholars continued to apply characteristics of femininity that imputed inferiority and powerlessness to African women in their bid to explicate the universal nature of women's oppression under patriarchy. That is, when Western scholars interrogated previous analyses of the gender binary as inadequate and restrictive in scope and understanding, they did not extend such analyses to African women. The "discovery" that gender is fluid implied that women's statuses and social interactions are dynamic. Incidentally, such dynamism didn't seem to apply to African women. Consider this observation by Danish agro economist and author Ester Boserup:

> Africa is economically the least developed part of the world. . . . It is also the
> part of the world where women's legal status is weakest: the woman has no adult
> status in family legislation and no legal right to support herself and the children,
> whom she must support but over whom her husband alone disposes.[6]

It is difficult for Donkor, as a Ghanaian woman, to recognize the woman Boserup described in the context of the late 1980s. African social systems are not frozen in time and thus impervious to change. Such generalizations are also problematic in that they do not take into consideration the great diversity of cultures in Africa. Examples abound in different African cultures that show that the gender binary based on biological sex is not set in stone. Gender roles can change based on age, religious, or political status. Amadiume, for example, uses the concept of the male daughter and female husband to challenge notions about a universal gender binary based strictly on biological sex.[7] Her study of the Igbo illustrates that feminine and masculine characteristics could be fluid and Igbo women as daughters could exercise power over wives and perform rituals on behalf of the patrilineage. Among the Akan of Ghana, the mythical *abrewa* (old woman) is the repository of wisdom to whom people go for advice in difficult circumstances. In ordinary day conversations, it is common for people to ask, in the face of stupid behavior, whether the person exhibiting such behavior did not have an *abrewa* in their home growing up.

Gender flexibility occurs as well in religion and politics. In her role as a mediator between the gods and the community, a priestess, regardless of age,

wields power, respect, and higher social status than most men in her community. Similarly, queen mothers among the Akan used to perform the spiritual
function of symbolically cleansing their communities to ward off disease
and other misfortunes when such phenomena occurred. Also, queen mothers'
status as political figures gave them tremendous power. Again, among the
Akan, a queen mother could (still can) assume the role of a male chief even
when there were male royals who could become chiefs. A notable example of
this phenomenon is Yaa Asantewaa, late-nineteenth-century queen mother of
Edweso in the Asante kingdom whose son, the chief, had been captured and
exiled by the British. Yaa Asantewaa not only assumed sole political authority
of the town but she also sat in the council of chiefs of the kingdom. Notably,
Yaa Asantewaa declared war on the British in February 1900 when the male
chiefs cowered in the face of British intimidation and humiliation to give up a
sacred relic of the kingdom. Lest anyone think that the actions of queen mothers like Yaa Asantewaa were unique, it should be noted that until the colonial
takeover, women's political power was widespread in many African societies.

The post-independence era opened new avenues for women to assert themselves or reaffirm the power they lost under colonial rule. With the onset of
market economies, women, not just queen mothers, acquired political capital
as powerful market women. Market women could organize to challenge colonial policies and they continue to be powerful power brokers in West African
countries. The Aba Women's war of 1929 stands as a testament to the power
that market women wielded in Igbo communities and how such power could
be deployed against the tyranny of colonial rule. Thus, when Mohanty interrogated Western feminist characterization of so-called Third World women
as oppressed and held under patriarchal bonds, she exposed a serious flaw
in Western feminist perceptions of non-Western women that African scholars continue to grapple with and debunk. Western feminist scholars lumped
African women together as a monolithic group regardless of markers that
distinguished one group from another.

The view of African women as an undifferentiated group has generated
tension between Western and African feminist scholars and activists on several issues. The Beijing Conference on women in 1995 exposed the fissures
between African and Western feminists on the matter of sexuality in Africa.
Western participants at the conference pushed to name female circumcision as mutilation and hence oppressive. In turn, African delegates accused
Western participants of cultural imperialism. African feminists and activists
called out white feminists for their "savior mentality" and to leave African
women to identify sources of their oppression and deal with those sources
on their terms. Among African feminists, so-called lesbian politics drew
sharp contrasts in their ranks. Some claimed lesbianism was foreign to Africa
while others looked for evidence in female relationships to establish the fact

that lesbianism was not exclusive to the West. Thus, in attempts to challenge Western scholarship on African women's sexuality, tensions have occurred in a multilayered fashion that, inadvertently, has enriched scholarship on African women and sexuality.

Before these tensions among feminist scholars regarding the nature of African women's sexuality, colonialists had presented a contradictory picture of African women's sexuality. On the one hand, they cast African women as the epitome of primitive sexuality—weird genitalia and uncontrolled sexual appetite. The "Hottentot apron," the mythical elongated labia of women in southern Africa, came to define the features of African women's sexual anatomy. Somehow, a nonexistent anatomical feature became the defining characteristic of African women's sexuality. Critiquing that presentation in European sources, Anne McClintock quoted one source that did not mince words on how Europeans perceived African women's sexuality: "In the nineteenth century the [African] black female was widely perceived as possessing not only a 'primitive' sexual appetite but also external signs of this temperament—primitive genitalia."[8] On the other hand, Europeans claimed that African women were sexually repressed because of traditions such as polygyny and female circumcision. The fact that colonialists did not care to correct the contradictions in their representation of African women's sexuality speaks to a level of carelessness that did not manifest in other aspects of their operations in Africa.

Of course, these were claims that had to be debunked or explained in their context, for, as Maria Lugones and Elizabeth Spelman observe,

> A(nother) reason for not divorcing life from the telling of it or talking about it is that as humans our experiences are deeply influenced by what is said about them, by ourselves or powerful (as opposed to significant) others. . . . We can't separate lives from the accounts given of them; the articulation of our experience is part of our experience.[9]

And so, in the same way, that African (feminist) scholars have analytically rescued gender from twisting representations by Western scholars, so also have they undertaken to present contextual analyses of sexuality to give validity to the experiences of African women from their standpoints. Scholars such as Babacar M'Baye, Signe Arnfred, Isaac Addai, Clifford Odimagwu, and others have used country-specific studies to illustrate the diversity of experiences that portray sexuality in a light that is different from what European colonialists portrayed of Africans. The beauty of these contextual analyses is that they are undertaken from diverse theoretical and empirical perspectives that yield a rich body of scholarship that accurately reflects local beliefs and practices without the kinds of generalizations and caricature that characterized earlier European accounts. The AIDS pandemic has also engendered another body of literature that links sexuality and pathology as educational resources to help stem the tide of the spread of the virus on the content and to point to gaps in its mitigation. These studies inspired us to write this book.

GHANA COUNTRY BACKGROUND

Ghana is a British colonial creation, known in colonial annals as the Gold Coast. While the British eventually colonized Ghana, they were not the first Europeans to set foot there. The Portuguese were the first to settle along the coast in modern-day Ghana where they built the first castle at Elmina in the second half of the fifteenth century. The Portuguese were followed by the Swedes who built their castle a few miles east of Elmina, in Cape Coast. These castles played pivotal roles in the infamous Atlantic slave trade. The mineral wealth of the region attracted other Europeans including the Dutch, such that the 350-mile coastline of what became Ghana had the highest concentration of European forts and castles in all of Africa. The arrival of Europeans signaled a long process of cultural diffusion in an area that was already ethnically diverse. Along the coast were groups like the Ewe, Fanti, and Ga; in the immediate hinterland were the Akan (who include the Akyem, Asante, Bono, and Kwahu); and to the north were the Dagomba, Frafra, and Tallensi, among others. By 1900, the British takeover of what comprises modern Ghana was complete. In 1957, the British portion of Germany's former colony of Togo joined Ghana.

The process of gradual colonization brought together people of different ethnicities with different histories, belief systems, and traditions. Superimposed on these groups were British cultural influences in religion, education, and commerce. Thus, cultures in Ghana have been hybridized to a degree due to the British presence; even so, some indigenous beliefs and practices have remained intact and continue to influence social interactions. Somehow, indigenous ways of knowing and doing things have been termed traditional, in contradistinction to the modern that is ascribed to foreign influences. The contrast suggests that tradition is primitive and not amenable to change, a view that is unfortunate because it denies indigenous Ghanaian societies the dynamism associated with cultures. We want to emphasize that the use of traditional in this book should not be construed as standing in opposition to modern; rather, it is used to reflect distinctive leitmotifs of Ghanaian cultures.

CONCEPTUALIZING FEMALE SEXUALITY IN GHANA

Sexuality is one of the principal markers of individual identity. People identify as heterosexual, gay, lesbian, bisexual, etc. Sexuality is thus the expression of behaviors, attitudes, ideas, and expectations associated with those social categories. As a core marker of identity, sexuality defines roles and power dynamics in society. That is, who defines sexually (in)appropriate behavior, as well as sanctions governing such behavior, depends on the political, religious, and social structure of the nation-state. In patriarchal and Judeo-Christian cultures, what is viewed as sexually (in)appropriate behavior is undergirded by beliefs about the nature and purpose of sex. And when such beliefs about sexuality are coupled with gender, sexual expression becomes intimately linked with the gender binary. That is, all relations of a sexual nature are permitted only between men and women, the underlying belief being the idea of the procreative quality of sex. Any other kinds of sexual expression, especially same-sex relations, are not only frowned upon but may be criminalized. The coupling of gender and sexuality is the underlying factor for the preeminence of heteronormativity in patriarchal societies.

Ghana is patriarchal and culturally diverse and presents a bit of difficulty identifying a theoretical perspective that can adequately capture the nature of sexuality within such diversity. The point is that each culture has its own belief and value systems governing sexual expression such that we may be dealing with unique situations more so than looking for similarities that link sexualities in the cultures. Even so, there are works that offer perspectives that can be utilized to analyze sexuality in Ghana. One of these perspectives is developed by Anima Agyepong in her concept of invading ethnography. Agyepong uses the concept of invading ethnography to capture the "reflexive practice [of] strategically interrupt[ing] the ethnographic narrative to illustrate how normative assumptions about gender, race, and sexuality not only shape the organization of social spaces but also inform ethnographic possibilities."[10] Agyepong's theory of invading ethnography provides a counterpoint to research conducted by scholars who did not have cultural and linguistic attachments to the cultures they studied. Invading ethnography encourages researchers to embed themselves in the community they are studying, to familiarize themselves with its traditions and values, and look within themselves to examine any latent biases that can bear on the outcome of the research. As we will see, some of the chapters in this collection are written by experts who live and work in the communities in which they conducted their research. They do not only know the traditions of the communities; they also participate in those traditions as members of the communities. As such, they write as insiders with vested interests in the subjects they researched. The product of their research reflects the experiences and views of the research subjects and not the ideas and interpretations of the researchers as they seek validation for their academic credentials and expertise.

The theory of social disorganization helps to explain nuances in sexual expression in Ghana. First developed by Clifford Shaw and Henry D. McKay and popularized by other social scientists, the theory of social disorganization does not focus on sexuality; it examines delinquent behavior and the social contexts and institutions that engender such behavior. The theory posits that strong (and positive) social bonds and institutions insulate the youth from deviant behavior. According to the theory, the reverse is also true: when familial and other social institutions "disorganize" (i.e. become weak), they are unable to control or insulate the youth.[11] The relevance of the theory to an understanding of gender and sexuality in Ghana lies in its focus on social institutions and their ability to shape behavior. Gender, a social construct, is a significant social institution and a strong pillar of patriarchy. As a construct, gender assigns roles, defines expectations, and maintains sex differences, among other characteristics. Importantly, rules that govern gender are not frozen in time; they are always in flux. Since gender and sexuality are intricately intertwined, changes in gender roles and expectations invariably affect sexual behavior. For instance, education and migration are phenomena that affect women's gender roles and sexual behavior. Educated women may decide to postpone marriage or not marry at all to pursue a career. In this case, traditions governing marriage are "weakened" in the sense that they lose their grip on such women. Similarly, when women migrate, they are no longer subject to the authority of their cultural leitmotifs, although they may continue to hold on to certain values in their areas of sojourn. A migrant woman can easily establish sexual relationships without the interference or sanction of family elders.

The theory of social disorganization can also help to explain sexuality in the realm of religion. Ghana stands at the crossroads of religious diversity, the result of the introduction of Christianity (and Islam) to already existing indigenous belief systems. Like gender, religion is an important bedrock of patriarchal society and dictates the moral foundation of society. Various communities in Ghana worshipped supreme deities indirectly through lesser gods. Local gods served as watchdogs over morality, among other functions. Crimes such as murder and theft, and lapses in daily human relationships such as sexual impropriety, could activate the fury of the gods toward individual culprits or an entire community depending on how egregious the crime was. People were generally afraid of the gods and thus guarded their behaviors. Then the British who had lived along the coast since the late seventeenth century started pushing into the interior as they embarked on the process of colonization and proselytization in the late nineteenth century. The infiltration of Christianity weakened the bonds between the communities and their gods as people began to accept the new faith. Ironically, Christianity's hold on sexuality has not been as strong when compared with the power the gods wielded over sexuality partly because of the idea of delayed punishment in Christianity. As we will read later, some pastors have disregarded their own Christian beliefs and teaching, and engaged in sexually inappropriate behaviors that undermine traditional values of sexual propriety.

CULTURAL DIVERSITY AND SEXUAL BEHAVIORS IN GHANA

Indigenous Ghanaian cultures have different rules governing gender and sexuality, but one can discern commonalities in the ways that gender and sexuality are defined. All the cultures in Ghana recognize the two-gender system and heterosexuality as the norm. A person is a girl/woman or boy/man; there is no room for any other kind of gender expression. Among the Akan, a man who exhibits female characteristics may be derided as *Kwadwo Besia* (*Kwadwo* is the name for a male born on Monday and *Besia* is another name for a woman.) and a woman who behaves like a man is called *obaa barima* (literally, woman-man). These names are only labels and may not lead to any sanctions because they do not deny or question the underlying gender identity of people so stereotyped.

In Ghana, sexuality and gender identity go hand in hand. Homosexuality was a crime during British colonial rule to control the sexual behavior of their colonial subjects. Post-independence constitutional reforms did not criminalize homosexuality in direct terms but criminalized "unnatural carnal knowledge," which was explained in its antithesis by a law professor thus:

> A natural carnal knowledge is understood to mean a natural sexual connection between male and female human beings. Homosexuality is no less unnatural than for a male human being to have carnal knowledge of an animal. The essence of unnatural carnal knowledge is that the sexual intercourse is done contrary to the norms of nature.[12]

Since sex can legally happen between only women and men, the law complicates sexuality for transgender people. The only known transgender woman in Ghana, Angela Coleman,[13] has become a celebrity in her neighborhood and curiosity to people in the media. A male TV presenter went as far as feeling her breasts on a live show to ascertain if they were "real." Another woman interviewing Ms. Coleman on a radio talk show asked very intimate questions that were not appropriate for a public audience.[14] The interviewer easily conflated Ms. Coleman's gender identity and sexuality by asking her time and again if she was sexually active. Another host of the radio talk show went to the extent of insinuating that a church where Ms. Coleman is a praise leader has lost its way for allowing a transgender person in its midst. Ms. Coleman's story is told here to reflect not just Ghanaian society's unease with breaking the gender binary but also how that perceived aberration can impact sexuality.

The conflation of gender and sexuality also means that any other forms of gender or sexual expression are aberrations. Until recently, homosexuality was not a phenomenon that was articulated either in traditions or practice. Some critics have charged that homosexuality is foreign to Ghana and its presence is the result of foreign influences. However, there is an Akan word that describes a sexual act that suggests that sex can happen in ways other than the nebulous "natural" description on the statute books. *Atu* is used to describe preadolescent (heterosexual) sex, but the root word *tu* (anus) is quite suggestive of the kind of sex implied. Also, in secondary school dorms in the 1970s girls engaged in relationships, often of a sexual nature, that they called *supi* that resembled the butch and femme relationships in the US. Although not widespread, *atu* and *supi* suggest that same-sex sexual relations are not new in Ghana. Indeed, before Covid-19 disrupted life and put most events on hold, Ghana was caught in a fierce public debate over a planned pan-African LGBTQ conference in the country. Politicians and religious leaders alike denounced the proposed conference (to have been held in July 2020) as antithetical to Ghanaian cultural values and demonic. The chief imam of Kumasi, Ghana's second-largest city, called on all religious groups—Christian, Islamic, and Traditional—to come together to stop the conference. Some civil rights organizations in turn denounced the public outcry and argued for the human rights of LGBTQ citizens of Ghana (and Africa in general) to be respected. The reaction to the proposed conference was not an isolated incident. In 2019, the Ministry of Education announced that it was going to introduce sex education to the basic education curriculum. Parents, religious bodies, and opposition political party operatives took to the airwaves and condemned the government for attempting to introduce sex to children. The initiative was dropped. The abortive LGBTQ conference and Ministry of Education initiative opened a window through which to view the complexities and nuances surrounding same-sex sex in Ghana.

Regarding heterosexual sex, the matrilineal Akan, the largest ethnic group in Ghana, provides examples that give insights into sexual behavior among that ethnic group. The Akan allowed, indeed encouraged, what might appear to an outsider as cousin marriage, which was that a woman could marry her father's nephew (father's sister's son). Also, a widow could marry the successor of her deceased husband if the successor was inclined to do so. The two practices, a man's daughter marrying his nephew and a widow marrying her husband's successor, were undergirded by inheritance and the distribution of property. Since nephews inherited maternal uncles, the marriage of a man's daughter to his nephew ensured that his daughter had access to his property through his nephew upon his death. These traditions are no longer attractive due to women's increasing education and migration that give them agency in the choice of a marriage partner. Also, in 1992, the government passed the Interstate Succession Law that requires husbands to bequeath part of their property to their children and spouses. Thus, the material basis that undergirded the kinds of marriage referred to above is no longer attractive among the Akan.

A cultural practice that reflected differences in sexual expression among the various ethnic groups was patterns of marital residence. Women in patrilineages generally practiced virilocal residence. Virilocality engendered family dynamics in which sexuality and gender roles blended into a woman's domestic culture of animosity, competition, and jealousy. Wives, unmarried sisters, and mothers-in-law jostled for the resources of families, including the affection of the men. Women put unnecessary pressure on themselves to cook the best meals, look their best, cultivate the best farms, or have children in quick succession. Among the matrilineal Akan, women generally lived in their natal homes after marriage. It was also common for pregnant Akan women living out of town to go back to their natal homes to give birth and be cared for. (That practice partly explained why some men would take second wives so that they would continue to enjoy the services of a woman when one wife was unavailable.) Although Akan women might not have experienced intense competition among women in close quarters, they could easily lose control over their sex lives when they lived away from their spouses. By the late 1960s, these residential patterns and their associated practices were dying out except in remote rural areas where traditions run deep. Education, increased migration, particularly to European and North American destinations, and wealth, altered residential patterns for many Ghanaians. Homeownership away from home towns and villages encouraged the nurturing of nuclear family residential patterns. Women's need to behave in certain ways to protect their turf and attract husbands' attention was greatly reduced when they lived in nuclear family units.

A feature of sexuality that was common in Ghana but that is waning now is polygyny. Polygyny made sense in the late nineteenth century and into the early twentieth century when the cash economy expanded, and men used women and children as extra labor on cocoa plantations and other cash-producing ventures. Multiple wives and children also enhanced the social status of men. With economic contraction in the late 1960s, increased female education, women's strong participation in the formal and informal economy, and new measures of wealth and social prestige, men's ability or desire to maintain large families including multiple wives was affected. Regardless of its status as attractive or undesirable, polygyny presented interesting dynamics in the ways that women experienced it. People engaged in polygyny established timetables to enable each wife to have her "cooking and sleeping time" with the husband. Women usually had a week that they expected to have exclusive sexual access to the husband. During a woman's week, she cooked for the man and slept in his room, often using bedding that she would take with her when her week was over.[15] The arrangement did not mean that the man did not interact with his other wives; it simply meant that for any particular time a particular woman had the right to sleep in the husband's room and to cook for him. If women in a polygynous marriage lived in their respective natal homes, it was difficult for them to claim exclusive sexual rights even during their week of such right. As the twentieth century drew to a close and economic problems became increasingly common, polygyny lost its allure. Besides, Christianity and formal education have changed the thinking about the value and desirability of polygyny. The irony is that men and women who will not enter polygynous marriages can feel comfortable having relationships in which one partner is formally married or has multiple lovers.

It is clear from the foregoing that sexual expression in Ghana is complex and nuanced, and that women's sexuality can be appreciated depending on context and circumstance. Whether in a matrilineal or patrilineal environment, women's sexual expression is foundational to social structure and organization.

A NOTE ON THE ORGANIZATION OF THIS BOOK

For an edited volume about sexualities in a multicultural country such as Ghana, one would have expected more chapters on diverse topics relating to sexuality. That, indeed, was the original plan as several experts had signed on to submit chapters, but by March 2020, when we expected all authors to submit their final entries, Covid-19 hit. A few authors submitted their chapters while others simply disappeared. We hope that those who could not honor their commitment are safe from the ravages of the coronavirus. Due to our inability to receive chapters as anticipated, there are glaring exclusions in the subject matter. For instance, there is no chapter on LGBTQ+ issues or chapters on femininity and masculinity. The epilogue, however, draws attention to disturbing trends characterizing the LGBTQ+ community in Ghana. Despite these limitations, it is interesting to note that research on three submissions was conducted in and around Cape Coast, one of the most diverse metropolitan areas in Ghana. Thus, while few, the chapters in this book offer a bird's-eye view of the nuances and dynamics of sexuality in Ghana. The various chapters reveal the agency of women as they negotiate their sexuality against the backdrop of traditional expectations and norms in societies that are undergoing changes in a rapidly globalized world.

The book opens with a discussion of women's interactions and reactions to sexual dynamics in the church and society. It also examines historical and contemporary social attitudes and expectations toward sex. Chapter one argues that women's need to fulfill certain social expectations and the presence of churches whose male leaders claim to have the spiritual gifts to help women fulfill those expectations create an atmosphere that is conducive to infidelity in the church. The chapter emphasizes that women's agentic recourse to personal and social capital often exposes male pastors' sexual advances on the one hand while enhancing women's sexual appeal and integrity on the other. Another point that the chapter makes is that traditional patriarchal surveillance of women's sexuality has responded to changes in society such that women's sexual behavior, in and out of the church, has been caught at the crossroads of changing social dynamics. Women are not afraid to flaunt their sexuality or seek means to enhance their sexual pleasure in the bedroom.

Chapter two builds on the theme of flaunting sexuality by examining the meaning of cleavage and breast exposure in Ghana. The authors explore perceptions, interpretations, and experiences associated with cleavage and breast exposure and argue that the different meanings associated with breast size and cleavage reflect the cultural intersection of femininity, beauty, and women's agency or lack thereof. The chapter reveals that cleavage and breast exposure have become an important part of the modern Ghanaian woman's sexual appeal and identity, even if society is slow in accepting that fact.

Ghanaians often pride themselves on their strong kinship and familial bonds. Families ground individuals as legitimate members of specific communities who can call on members of the community for collective assistance in times of need. While kinship and family structures have stayed relatively strong in the face of rapid social change, there are aspects of family life that have undergone shifts and have affected how members can or want to help other family members in need. A neoliberal, individualistic aspect has crept into families such that members are increasingly shying away from the communal consumption of individual resources. In chapter three, the authors examine the issue of divorce from the perspective of familial support. They demonstrate that communal support is not unidirectional. Family members who get the opportunity to improve their circumstances but fail to share their resources are likely to be paid back in kind when it is their turn to need help. This "asymbiotic" relationship among family members may cause initial financial hardship for divorced women, tension among family members, and temporary loss of social status of the divorcees.

Conceptions about the repressed sexuality of women in Africa are not new. While some locate it within the confines of patriarchal cultures, others emphasize new possibilities in terms of how culture empowers women sexually. In chapter four, the author investigates young adults' experiences of sex on a first date. The author highlights how young women draw on their cultural training—morality, sexuality and gender mistrust, and health beliefs and practices—for engaging in sex. The chapter demonstrates an inverse gender dynamic in dating that largely determined whether or not sex will occur on a first date. Young women are socialized to date older men, and men normally date younger women. The intersection of age and gender placed young women at a disadvantage, which led the women to fall back on family upbringing, religious beliefs, choice, emotions, and safety issues to decide to have sex on a first date or not. The conclusion echoes earlier works that show that men perceive sex as a declaration of "real" masculinity; the conclusion also calls for a rethinking of women's cultural "capital" as an agentic tool to combat masculinist perceptions of women's sexuality.

Divorce has been one area of nuptiality that has attracted little scholarly attention in Ghana. Chapter five adds to the emerging literature by examining the experiences of divorced women against the common belief among Ghanaians that divorce negatively impacts women's ability to be financially self-sustaining. The chapter thus reveals shifts in attitudes and norms that reflect the dynamism of cultures in Ghana. A significant contribution that the chapter makes to the literature on the experiences of women after they have gone through a divorce is that women's supposed poorer financial circumstances post-divorce are simplistic and require nuance in analysis. Women may have suffered from divorce and been frustrated with their natal families' refusal or inability to help, but their resilience largely determined their coping strategies. Women who faced the contradictions in their lives, having a positive attitude toward the future despite the anger and frustration, successfully adapted to single life while those who allowed emotions to overwhelm them continued to struggle financially and socially.

Positioning motherwork as a derivative of Patricia Hill Collins' Black Feminist Thought framework, chapter six explores the impact of imperialism and colonialism on the roles of mother and queen in Ghanaian societies, and how this has affected Black women, specifically those who may identify as descendants of those who survived the Maafa. The chapter conflates the five tenets of Black Feminist Thought with a sociopolitical recitation of what it means to identify as a US-born Black woman and then be enstooled as a Ghanaian queen mother. Chapter six concludes that through the reclamation of their indigenous pedigree, Black feminists must use both motherwork as pedagogy in conjunction with the identity of queen mother as an essential armament in the liberation of Black womxn, girls, and femmes.

The book ends with attention drawn to cultural perceptions about gays and lesbians and the danger that the LGBTQ community potentially faces as members attempt to announce their presence and carve a niche in society. Public reactions toward gays and lesbians reflect more than just patriarchal equilibrium; the reactions also point to attempts by Ghanaians to resist Western cultural influences that are perceived to be eroding the moral foundations upon which society was built.

The relatively low number of chapters in this collection notwithstanding, the book offers a robust read of the diversity of ideas and perspectives on gender and sexuality in Ghana. Covid-19 undoubtedly has affected every facet of human life. It remains to be seen how it reshapes sexuality in Ghana and indeed worldwide. This book suffered from the novel coronavirus in that several contributors pulled out at the last minute to attend to important issues when the lockdown began. While we wish them well, we hope that they get time to finish their chapters for another volume on sexuality in Ghana.

NOTES

1. Signe Arnfred, *Sexualities in Africa* (Upsala: Nordiska Afrikainstitutet, 2004), 7.

2. Hugh Clapperton, Jamie Bruce-Lockhart, and Paul E. Lovejoy, *Hugh Clapperton Into the Interior of Africa: Records of the Second Expedition, 1825–1827*, ebook, 2005, 89.

3. Ifi Amadiume, *Male Daughters, Female Husbands: Gender and Sex in an African Society*, 2nd ed. (London: Zed Books, 2015), 14.

4. Kirk Arden Hoppe, "Review of Ifi Amadiume, Male Daughters, Female Husbands: Gender and Sex in an African Society," *International Feminist Journal of Politics* 18, no. 3 (2016): 499.

5. Chandra Talpade Mohanty, "Under Western Eyes Revisited: Feminist Solidarity through Anticapitalist Struggles," in *Feminism without Borders: Decolonizing Theory, Practicing Solidarity* (Indianapolis: Duke University Press, 2003), 501.

6. Ester Boserup, Claire Robertson, Margaret Snyder, and Margaret Strobel, "Research on African Women since 1972: A Commentary," *Canadian Journal of African Studies / Revue Canadienne Des Études Africaines* 22, no. 3 (1988): 427.

7. Amadiume, *Male Daughters, Female* Husbands, 15–16.

8. Anne McClintock, *Imperial Leather: Race, Gender and Sexuality in the Colonial Contest* (New York & London: Routledge, 1996), 41–2.

9. Maria C. Lugones and Elizabeth V. Spelman, "Have We got a Theory for You! Feminist Theory, Cultural Imperialism and the Demand for the 'Woman's Voice,'" *Women's Studies International Forum* 6, no. 6 (1983): 573–4.

10. Anima Agyepong, "Invading Ethnography: A queer of color reflexive Practice," *Ethnography* 20, no. 1 (2019): 28–9.

11. Clifford Shaw and Henry D. McKay, *Juvenile Delinquency and Urban Areas* (Chicago, IL: University of Chicago Press, 1942).

12. Martha Donkor, *Child Rape in Ghana: Lifting the Veil* (Lanham, MD: Lexington Books, 2018), 52.

13. Ms. Coleman has been nicknamed Madina Broni—Madina is a suburb of Accra where she lives and Broni (also oburoni) is the Akan word for a white person. Ms. Coleman has used creams to lighten her complexion. Thus, Madina Broni means simply the white person in Madina.

14. Ghafricnews.com, "Ghana's First Transgender Madina Broni now Born again? Spotted singing at Church," April 4, 2019, https://www.youtube.com/watch?v=XE_7FQiq8Co.

15. Among the Akan, it's culturally frowned upon for a man to sleep in the room of a wife who lives in her natal home. While I don't know the cultural meaning behind the disapproval, I think there's a practical reason that undergirds the disapproval. A wife who has children sleeps with them in the same room. If a husband joins her, there would be no privacy. For more perspectives on parents sharing rooms with children, see Donkor, *Child Rape in Ghana*, 29.

BIBLIOGRAPHY

Agyepong, Anima. Agyepong, Anima. "Invading Ethnography: A queer of color reflexive practice." *Ethnography* 21, no. 1 (2019): 27–46.

Amadiume, Ifi. *Male Daughters, Female Husbands: Gender and Sex in an African Society*, 2nd ed., [Critique Influence Change]. London: Zed Books, 2015.

Arnfred, Signe "'African Sexuality'/Sexuality in Africa: Tales and Silences." In *Rethinking Sexualities in Africa*, edited by Signe Arnfred, 7–29. Upsala: Nordiska Afrikainstitutet, 2004.

Boserup, Ester, Claire Robertson, Margaret Snyder, and Margaret Strobel. "Research on African Women since 1972: A Commentary." *Canadian Journal of African Studies / Revue Canadienne Des Études Africaines* 22, no. 3 (1988): 427–430.

Clapperton, Hugh, Jamie Bruce-Lockhart, and Paul E. Lovejoy. *Hugh Clapperton Into the Interior of Africa: Records of the Second Expedition, 1825-1827*, ebook, 2005.

Donkor, Martha. *Child Rape in Ghana: Lifting the Veil*. Lanham, MD: Lexington Books, 2019.

Ghafricnews.com, "Ghana's First Transgender Madina Broni now Born again? Spotted singing at Church," April 4, 2019, https://www.youtube.com/watch?v=XE_7FQiq8Co.

Hoppe, Kirk Arden. "Review of Ifi Amadiume, Male Daughters, Female Husbands: Gender and Sex in an African Society," *International Feminist Journal of Politics* 18, no. 3 (2016): 498–512.

Lugones, Maria C., and Elizabeth V. Spelman. "Have We got a Theory for You! Feminist Theory, Cultural Imperialism and the Demand for the 'Woman's Voice.'" *Women's Studies International Forum* 6, no. 6 (1983): 573–581.

McClintock, Anne. *Imperial Leather: Race, Gender and Sexuality in the Colonial Contest*. New York & London: Routledge, 1996.

Mohanty, Chandra Talpade. "Under Western Eyes Revisited: Feminist Solidarity through Anticapitalist Struggles." In *Feminism without Borders: Decolonizing Theory, Practicing Solidarity, 221–252.* Durham, NC: Duke University Press, 2003.

Shaw, Clifford, and Henry D. McKay. *Juvenile Delinquency and Urban Areas.* Chicago, IL: University of Chicago Press, 1942.

Chapter 1

Women, Gender, Sex, and the Church

Martha Donkor

One of the enduring characteristics of a patriarchal culture is heteronorma-tivity and its differential application of sexuality to women and men.[1] For instance, both women and men are expected to marry individuals of the opposite sex, yet there is a lot more pressure on women to marry than on men. Similarly, marriage is expected to confer dignity and security on women regardless of class but there is no such expectation for men; men marry as a matter of course. Another aspect of patriarchal heteronormativity is that women and men are expected to be morally upright and remain faithful to their spouses in marriage, yet sanctions and censures that govern marital infidelity are differentially applied to women and men. Marital infidelity is considered more egregious when it is committed by women than when men engage in it. In short, patriarchal norms and expectations define sexual behavior in strictly binary terms, grounded on values of morality and fidelity. And when social institutions like gender and religion undergird definitions of morality and fidelity, women's sexuality becomes an important prop in the organization of social life in a patriarchal society.

From Africa to Asia, Europe to the Middle East, women's sexual purity has defined the dignity and respectability of families and entire communities. In monarchical Europe, men would rather have their wives become murder-ers and heretics than for the women to be less chaste than the husbands.[2] In India, Hindu wives were required to immolate themselves on their hus-band's funeral pyres before the practice was outlawed in the early nineteenth century.[3] There is continuity between these historical examples and what is happening in many places today. Patriarchy reinforces social institutions while the institutions in turn give legitimacy to patriarchal expectations. This symbiosis places undue pressure on women, not men, to guard their sexual behavior. But what happens when the church, a strong pillar of patriarchy, is the site of infidelity? How are women expected to guard their sexuality at this site? Equally important, how are the expectations for fidelity in the church different for women outside the church? These questions are examined in detail in the Ghanaian[4] context in this chapter. A point the chapter makes is that traditional patriarchal nurturing of women's sexuality has changed over time such that women's sexual behavior in society has been caught at the crossroads of changing social dynamics. The chapter emphasizes that women's agentic recourse to personal and social capital results from a definition of female fulfillment that is premised on sexuality. Regarding the church, it is argued that women's need to fulfill certain social expectations and the presence of churches whose male leaders claim to have the spiritual gifts to help women fulfill those expectations create an atmosphere that is conducive to infidelity in church leadership.

CONCEPTUAL FRAMEWORK

Research across disciplines in different locations and times has established a direct correlation between religiosity and women's sexual behavior.[5] And like much else with so much diversity and richness, the scholarship on the impact of Christianity on women's sexuality has proceeded from different perspectives to capture its complexity and nuances.[6] Most studies in the field have focused on adolescent and college students' sexual behavior. Some have emphasized the differential denominational impact on sexuality while others have stressed religious commitment rather than affiliation as a major determinant of sexuality.[7] With few exceptions, most studies conclude that Christianity has a direct effect on women's sexual behavior in that the more religiously committed women are, the less likely they will engage in premarital sex. While these studies provide baseline thinking about religion and sexuality, their perspectives cannot be adequately applied in Ghana because of cultural context. Most studies on Christianity and religion are produced in the United States and can be useful in understanding the correlation between religion and sexuality in Ghana only if we assume that Christianity has always been a part of Ghanaian society and culture. But that has not been the case. Besides, there is a growing body of scholarship on sexuality in Ghana[8] but few focus on religion as a bastion of patriarchal sexuality.[9] Thus, it is necessary to utilize other perspectives to think about how Christianity influences women's sexuality in Ghana. Consequently, I use the concept of change and continuity, popular in historical analyses, as a useful conceptual framework to analyze women's sexual behavior in and out of the church.

Change and continuity provide a backdrop to understanding the convergence of domestic (indigenous) and foreign (Christian) ideas and practices within a patriarchal context and their impact on women's sexual behavior. Christianity and other European cultural motifs were not introduced into a cultural vacuum; they were introduced into communities that were highly developed in conceptions of the divine. The communities had also established strong social institutions and traditions that supported religious observances and practices. The introduction of Christianity certainly influenced aspects of the social life of converts but it did not entirely supersede traditional culture, including sexuality. Thus, we cannot speak of sex in the church without discussing sex outside the church, for without that contextual discussion, it will seem like there were no traditions governing sexual behavior before Europeans arrived and introduced Christianity. Simply put, change and continuity allow us to juxtapose women's sexual behavior in and out of the church to reflect the complex dynamics embedded in the clash of cultures as well as debunk the notion that Africans did not have a history of their own until they met Europeans. Also, since the closing years of the twentieth century, urban, middle-class Ghanaian women have promoted a kind of sexuality that deviates from traditional social prescriptions of proper female sexual behavior and reflects social change and women's agency that is not a result of Christian influence. To understand this evolving sexuality and how it deviates from traditional prescriptions of female sexuality, it is necessary to describe traditional constructions of sexuality against the backdrop of femininity and masculinity and the role of traditional religion in that construction.

FEMININITY AND MASCULINITY IN TRADITIONAL CONTEXTS IN GHANA

Gender, the cultural interpretation of biological sex, prescribes characteristics and roles for women and men in society. Roles are taught or enforced through socialization to give individuals their gender identity. Thus, when we say that gender is a social construct, we imply that ideas and norms about gender are defined by society about biological sex and that these ideas and norms are then presented as natural aspects of our lives as females and males.[10] Femininity and masculinity thus proceed from the internalization of these ideas and norms. In patriarchal cultures, femininity and masculinity are defined as "complementary opposites," with the feminine often defined in subdued terms in relation to the masculine. Qualities such as submission, cooperation, nurturance, and emotionality are associated with femininity while their opposites—aggressiveness, independence, competitiveness, toughness, and rationality—are associated with masculinity. Although opposites, these qualities are desired for their respective genders and do not make room for the possibility that gender could be a continuum, that women and men can exhibit similar characteristics. Also of note is the fact that rules about gender characteristics are prescriptive and can be contravened, and so society devises sanctions that penalize individuals who do not adhere to their prescribed gender characteristics. It is also important to stress that contrary to the belief that female characteristics are not desired in a patriarchal society, the reality is that they are cherished to the degree that women adhere to them and internalize them, for it is by having a docile, submissive, quiet, and nurturing group of women that men's superior social position can be enhanced and maintained.

Like its characteristics, gender roles are institutionalized on a binary basis. As a social institution, it has its conventions, modes of transmission, rewards, and censures to ensure compliance. Gender is thus one of the main pillars of patriarchal society. Alan G. Johnson points out that one of the defining characteristics of a patriarchal society is that it is male-dominated, male-identified, and male-centered.[11] Male domination, identification, and centeredness do not preclude women from occupying important social positions; rather, women occupy high positions as tokens. The preponderance of men in positions of authority in government, defense, economy, religion, and the family, creates the impression that men have a natural ability to exercise authority in society. That impression, indeed belief, that men are naturally disposed to exercise authority, has implications for how both women and men exercise and experience sexuality.

Ghana is culturally diverse, but the patriarchal nature of the various cultures makes common analysis of traditional femininities and masculinities possible. Gender is defined as a binary; however, the binary has not always translated into subordination and inequality between women and men. In the economy, family, politics, but less so in religion, roles are assigned by gender and men occupy top positions. Even so, there is room for women to act on their own behalf in certain situations. Generally, men hold the title to land on behalf of the family among both the matrilineal Akan and the patrilineal groups. Yet Akan women, for example, can inherit land as sisters and nieces of the men in the matrilineage and can cultivate the land on their own account.[12] Women in the patrilineages work on the land on behalf of men in their lives. Much has been said about women in farming communities cultivating subsistence crops while men cultivate cash crops and thus making women depend on men financially. What is left out in the discussion is that women may not make large sums of money from the sale of subsistence crops but they sell year-round, as opposed to male cash crop farmers who make money within a short window of time. In the lean season, which is the period before the next harvest, some men depend on their wife's income. While that is not a widespread practice, it speaks to nuances in gender relations in farming communities in Ghana.

While farming has been the main economic activity for women in rural communities, women dominate the retail trade nationwide. And again, like women in subsistence farming, critics have pointed out that they mostly sell perishable goods as opposed to men's wares. While accurate in the past, the domination of women in retail trade is such that it is useful to emphasize the dynamics among female traders than to compare women's and men's retail goods. Whether in rural or urban areas, women buy and sell year-round. Some may not have capital and sell on a credit basis. That is, they "buy" items from wholesalers and pay back based on the arrangement of sale. Some operate small shops that do not require huge capital investment while others are well-established importers of consumer goods in the fashion and real estate industries. Trade has engendered a demographic of upper- and middle-class women whose sexual behavior is largely dictated by a definition of self-fulfillment that is centered on having a man in one's life.

In the realm of politics, women's participation has been mixed. Among the Akan, Ewe, and Krobo, queen mothers complement the roles of chiefs. Akan queen mothers nominate candidates for consideration as chiefs; they can also hold the position of a male chief until that position is legitimately filled. Among other patrilineal groups, traditional political power is reserved for men. Interacting with traditional society is the political economy of the modern state that opens avenues for women's participation in the formal sector in the professions, economy, and government, albeit at lower levels of representation compared with men. Thus, like women everywhere, Ghanaian women are not a monolithic category whose experiences can easily be pigeonholed.

TRADITIONAL NURTURING OF WOMEN'S SEXUALITY

Like women in patriarchal societies everywhere, Ghanaian women have historically been expected to be wives and mothers, an expectation that made spinsterhood and barrenness abhorrent.[13] The expectation that women become wives and mothers directly influenced their sexuality. Among the various ethnic groups, the Akan and some Krobo enclaves are the only groups that elaborately prepared girls for marriage. A few differences distinguish *dipo* from *bragoro*. The Krobo still perform *dipo*, however, Christian Krobo do not allow it in their families anymore. *Dipo* is a community affair, performed for a group of girls and it involves ritual cleansing by a traditional priest, thus emphasizing its social and religious dimensions and significance. The Akan *bragoro* is no longer performed, although until about seventy years ago, it was the main process of preparing girls for adulthood and marriage. *Bragoro* was done for individual girls and did not involve a traditional priest in any of its rituals, although it had spiritual significance. The Akan believed that a family could suffer misfortune if a pre- or pubescent girl got pregnant before she was known to have had her period. Such a girl became *kyiri bra*. Akan girls were thus presented to the queen mothers of their towns when they had their first period. Depending on local practice, girls were presented a second and third time to affirm that they were not pregnant.[14] Thereafter, families that had the means organized a second, public initiation rite to announce that a daughter had reached the age of maturity and was ready to marry.[15] Girls who got pregnant before the inspection had broken a taboo; they would be banished from their communities after sacrifices had been made to appease the gods.[16] They could return after the birth of the babies, but the humiliation of the banishment was enough to keep some women away for good. A child born in such a circumstance could be given a symbolic name, for example, *Nimo*, to permanently mark her or him as the product of illicit sex.[17] Incidents such as rape and incest were not supposed to happen, but if they occurred, then the culprit, not the victim, would be the one to be censured.

Among the Nankani, sex was not taken lightly. Life was a continuous cycle that involved the living and the dead. Thus, the Nankani viewed sex as an important act that produced children who completed the circle of life. Women's role in maintaining the circle was crucial and their fecundity was significant in ensuring that the community stayed connected with the ancestors. And so Nankani society had rules governing sexual behavior, especially that of women.[18] Society frowned upon premarital sex regardless of gender; however, married women's sexuality was especially guarded because, as Amenga-Etego explains, married women's sexuality stood at the crossroads of community survival and vitality, the dignity of families, and ancestral goodwill.[19]

Different ethnic groups had rules regarding when and where sex could occur. Among the Akan, a menstruating woman was not expected to have sex or cook for a man, a reason that was used to justify polygyny. Women could also not have sex in the bush unless there was a structure with a hearth and domestic animals present.[20] Among the Ewe, husbands had charms that they could use to threaten wives against adultery. The Ewe also attributed a difficult birth or death during childbirth to adultery.[21]

The examples above show that women's sexuality was nurtured and carefully guarded as preparation toward marriage, the perpetuation of families, and sustaining links between the living and dead. But there was another dimension to the policing of women's sexuality. There seemed to be an underlying fear of adultery on the women's part. The Akan expressed that fear in the saying that "only a woman knows her child's father." The reverse was that one could not contest a child's maternity, a view that is not always consistent with kin fostering and other social arrangements involving the care of children. Thus, among the Akan, an uncle could invest resources in his nieces and nephews (e.g., taking responsibility for their education) because he was directly related to them by blood through his sister. He might not have the same confidence that there was a blood connection between him and his children. Some Akan men ignored the education or general development of their children without considering that not every child had an uncle.

Another Akan idiom that expressed men's fear of women's sexuality states, *obaa, me suro wo gya mu fita,* to wit, "woman, I fear the way you fan your fire."[22] The implication was that women were secretive and dangerous; they could not be trusted to be faithful in intimate relationships. That mistrust could be attributed to the fact that women could and did control their sexuality to some extent. In polygynous marriages, for example, women had to deal with a complicated sexual arrangement. Sexual access to the husband was not always guaranteed. For instance, a man who had ten wives would arrange for the women to sleep in his room on a weekly rotational basis. If, say, wife A had her turn the first week of January, she would have to wait until the second week of March for another turn to sleep in her husband's bed unless the man finds some way to visit her room. Depending on wife A's inclination (or any other wife for that matter), the possibility of seeking sexual satisfaction elsewhere could not be ruled out.[23] Also, given that wives in polygynous marriages would be competing to have babies, "arranged sleep" could delay pregnancy for some. It might be expedient for some wives to clandestinely "seek help" elsewhere. Whether or not women actually sought that help was a matter of speculation, but it did not prevent men from entertaining the fear that their wives could cheat.

The guarding of women's sexuality extended to mores and norms that undergirded marriage. In all ethnic groups, the man's family bore the expenses of the marriage. Among the Akan, the man's family initiated the marriage process with the "knock" whereby they presented alcoholic beverages, usually schnapps, to the prospective wife's parents and maternal uncles. While the potential wife's family accepted the drink, it did not mean that the way was cleared for the formal rites to be performed. The woman's family would launch an investigation into the man's family to ascertain if the men in his family were hardworking, took good care of women, provided for their children, were not wife beaters, criminals, or carried a communicable disease. The man's family would have carried out a similar investigation before the "knocking." They would have investigated if there was barrenness in the woman's family, among other important considerations. If satisfied, the woman's family would invite the man's family to perform the marital rites. If not, the man lost the gifts he presented during the knocking. Drinks (*ti nsa;*

literally head drink) and money that the prospective husband provided were symbolic only, signifying the union of not just the couple, but of two families.[24] Once married, close relatives of the couple could not marry in either family; it was considered a mixing of blood, a taboo. If the man had his own house, then the woman moved in with him; otherwise, she continued to reside in her natal home.

Among patrilineal groups in the northern sections of the country (Gonja, Dagomba, Gurunsi, etc.), men might provide labor and/or livestock to the prospective wife's father prior to the performance of the marital rites, after which the woman moved into her husband's house. Often, the husband lived in a house that was part of houses enclosing a large compound where his parents, married brothers and their wives, and unmarried sisters lived. The new wife joined a larger family unit that hierarchized women based on their relationship to the men in the family. Mothers and sisters ranked higher than wives, and older wives ranked higher than new wives. This arrangement meant that newly married women performed more domestic chores than the others. In all cases, whether among the matrilineal Akan or patrilineal groups, women who married in culturally prescribed ways neither wore rings nor took their husbands' names. Marital norms in the various ethnic groups differed, but collectively they challenged European accounts of African women who were used as pawns in the marriage process at the hands of older men in their families.[25]

Women were expected to be prolific once married. A couple's inability to conceive was often blamed on the woman and that could be used as a reason for the man to have a second wife. Women who believed they were barren could attribute it to witchcraft or a curse.[26] They might consult the gods or seek treatment from herbalists. A married woman who suspected that her husband was the reason she was unable to conceive was careful not to be caught in an extramarital affair in hopes of getting pregnant. I have already noted that among the Ewe, husbands had charms that they could use to threaten women against infidelity. Among the Akan, the charge that *obi akyere awia* (literally someone has pointed to the sun) always meant that a married woman had been caught cheating. There was no such description when a married man was caught in an affair. And while there were not strict social sanctions when an Akan man cheated (except when he cheated with a married woman), a wife could take drastic measures against a cheating husband. She could refuse to cook for him and/or refuse him sex; she could stop working on his farm or give him the cold shoulder when they went to farm together. She could also publicize the affair by calling an arbitration with the elders. An arbitration often ended with the husband pacifying the wife with money and/or clothing; in some cases, the husband would then declare that he would like to marry the woman with whom he cheated. A strong wife might react to that announcement with a declaration of divorce. But a married woman who was caught cheating did not have the opportunity of attending an arbitration and asking to be pardoned; she was almost always divorced, after she had been publicly disgraced by her sisters-in-law. Even so, it is important to echo Judith Bennett that Akan women were not "passive victims of [patriarchal] power."[27]

It was also common for women to use aphrodisiacs to spice up the sex. They might eat certain special roots or insert special herbs ground into powder to tighten the vaginal walls to give themselves and the men maximum friction and pleasure during sex. Other ways that women prepared for sex included having a bath and alternatively using cold and hot water to wash the vagina or "heating" the vagina by sitting close to live embers after bathing. Some women ate roasted dry corn to freshen their breath before going to bed at night. Women did not engage in these elaborate preparations for sex for their own exclusive pleasure; they considered the sexual pleasure of the men in their lives to be equally important, especially when they were in polygynous marriages. Men's preparation for sex, if they did, was often quite simple; they drank "bitters," a concoction of roots and barks soaked in gin, which was believed to make them last longer during sex. Despite all the preparation women made toward sex, Ghanaians generally did not engage in public sex talk.[28] Indeed, women refrained from flaunting their sexuality to avoid being labeled as *tuutuu* (pronounced "two-two" and meaning prostitute in Twi). Sexually suggestive language was often in code or in dance in special eye, hand, and waist movements. Thus traditionally, Ghanaian women, regardless of ethnicity, were not overly sexually controlled or oversexualized as some European accounts initially claimed about African women generally.[29]

CULTURAL CHANGES IN SEXUALITY

Patriarchy has a way of reinventing itself because, like all social systems, it is continually in flux. Historian Judith Bennett gave expression to patriarchy's ability to adapt and then maintain the gender status quo when she coined the term patriarchal equilibrium. Bennett explains that patriarchal equilibrium occurs when women are held to the same age-old standards and traditions even when their experiences undergo considerable change.[30] Bonnie Anderson and Judith Zinsser exemplified Bennett's point by showing that during the industrial revolution, European societies created the cult of womanhood that defined a true woman—a lady—as a wife, mother, and homemaker who did not work for pay. As attractive as the label of the lady was, its real reflection was not on women but on the men who maintained those middle-class women. Middle-class European women's experience of the industrial revolution changed, but there was no transformation in their status as women.[31] American feminist icon Betty Friedan described the sub-urban housewife of the 1960s as "healthy, beautiful, educated, concerned only about her husband, her children, her home. She had found true feminine fulfillment."[32] In an ironic twist, the cult of womanhood created a dependency syndrome for middle-class women in Europe and America. The point is that in periods of economic expansion in those places, society found a way to keep middle-class women where they were expected to belong, in the home.

Patriarchy is taking a similar trajectory in Ghana. What has happened since the latter part of the twentieth century is a discourse on womanhood that does not have the potential to return women to their "rightful'" place in the home as it did with Euro-American women, but one that defines "true feminine fulfillment" in the context of marriage. Starting from about the mid-1990s, a segment of Ghanaian women, middle-class, relatively young, educated, and urbanite, developed the perspective that a successful woman is one who is married, preferably to a wealthy man in a church wedding, has children, lives in a modern house, and drives her own car. A woman who subscribes to this view may be gainfully employed, but she may not feel completely fulfilled if she is not married and/or have children. Of course, the expectation that a woman should be married and have children is not new or unique to Ghana; it has been a standard that women have been held to in patriarchal societies. Its iteration in Ghana in recent years has been championed by women who have broken through some patriarchal strictures and claimed a high level of autonomy for themselves.

The expectation that a certain class of women must live a certain kind of lifestyle has had an impact on women's sexual behavior by challenging old assumptions about cultural norms and fidelity. Gone are the days when women were expected to be the paragons of morality, staying chaste until they had gone through rites to prepare them for marriage. More and more women are receiving higher education or moving from rural and suburban areas into cities and large towns. Away from home, they are no longer subject to strict cultural expectations except the ones they choose to keep. Indeed, a new term, side chickism, has evolved to describe the phenomenon of younger women dating wealthy and older married men in hopes of acquiring the essentials befitting their status. In the 1970s, relationships of that nature emphasized the wealth and status of the sugar daddies; now the attention is on the side chicks and slay queens who openly embrace their status even if they receive public backlash for doing so.[33]

Sex talk is now commonplace. On the airwaves, on social media sites, and at open markets, people talk about sex in flamboyant language. There are live sex "education" shows[34] that are posted on Youtube for interested parties to access, and so-called counselors who give advice and organize workshops on relationships and sex. There are peddlers who claim to have medications for impotence and endurance for men, and fertility medicines for women. One of these peddlers, "Auntie Comfort," is a regular feature on Youtube and local tabloids. Another woman, Mama Gee, opened what one can call a sex store at Madina, a suburb of Accra, principally for women. These developments speak to changes in society and women's response to such changes in the aspect of sexuality.

The crew of SVTV Africa, a local television and internet-based network, went to Mama Gee's store to interview her after some women claimed that she sells a husband-snatching potion. Mama Gee explained what her business is about in language that reflects current liberties with sex talk. She said, "What I do is, we are aphrodisiac. Everything about . . . sex, sex life, your maintenance, how to have it clean, pussy, about a man; all of that; everything about sex life or bedroom life, that's what we do here." When asked what motivated her to start the business, she further explained:

> I had a personal issue, a personal problem and trying to solve my personal issues I realized it will help the general public, it will help family and friends and so when it worked for me I introduced a couple of friends who had the same issues and it worked out. Then it was like okay, so I can sell this to other ladies who are in the same or having the same problem . . .; every woman sometime hormonal changes make you get a loose pussy; you won't feel for sex even if a man caresses you, you are just not ready for it. So, in order to make my man happy, through research my grandma helped me out with some of their traditional tips and I was able to make my home like, it was fire, it was bomb, yes, and when we get on show the way my man will confess I'm like wow, I've not seen this before.[35]

Mama Gee indicated that her business boomed because of referrals from women who had used her products. Asked if she was competing with the pastors, she said an emphatic "no" and stressed that unlike pastors who use oil, she uses herbs that can correct irregular menstrual cycles, hormonal imbalances, and clear vaginal odor.[36] Mama Gee also said that women use her products because the products help them to get money from men. She explained:

> If you are having sex with a partner and you know he has money and he is not giving you money, you use it. It's just the sweetness and normal herb. It upgrades your vagina from every woman's own to a higher place. It's like you cooking and adding spices. It's like cooking fish; if you don't add ginger and onions it won't taste good so if a person eats once they won't eat again. That's a bad pussy for you. But a good pussy is spiced pussy with Mama Gee's product. He will eat, eat again, sign checks, buy you the car you want and set up businesses for you.[37]

Activities of vendors like Mama Gee and Auntie Comfort underscore the intensity and urgency for women to sexually satisfy men to maintain their relationships, and for some, as a first step toward a permanent relationship. Mama Gee in particular, appears to have a large client base, made up of a cross-section of women in her area of operation. To put these changes in sexual behavior in Ghana into perspective, there was only one television station in the country in 1990 and that was the state-owned Ghana Broadcasting Corporation. It started transmission on weekdays at 6 p.m. and ended at midnight (unless there were special events like the World Cup soccer). On weekends when transmission started early and foreign films were telecast, they were heavily redacted to remove sexual content that would not be appropriate to Ghanaian sensibilities. By 2020, there were scores of privately run television stations that showed locally produced and foreign movies and soap operas with explicit sexual content. Radio stations have proliferated in Ghana that do not appear to be censured in the kinds of stories they broadcast. Radio hosts and guests often engage in sex talk that would have shocked audiences a generation ago, and most of the people who bring matters of sexual nature to radio stations are women. Rapid social change has had an impact on women's sexuality; it is yet to be seen how society adapts to maintain patriarchal equilibrium in the sense of returning women to traditional norms that guarded their sexuality.

SEX IN THE CHURCH

The dynamics surrounding women and sexuality in society at large are quite different from what pertains to sex in churches in Ghana. Before Europeans introduced Christianity, religion and spirituality permeated all aspects of social life in Ghana. As described below, various ethnic groups believed in a supreme deity, had origin or creation stories as well as legends that told of their relationships with the divine. For example, the Ga had an androgynous supreme deity called Ataa Naa Nyonmo (Ataa is the male element and Naa female); the Akan had Nyankopon; the Ewe called theirs Mawu Lisa and the Nankani had Naba Awina. The peoples of Ghana did not have one name for the creator and did not have a single creation story, unlike the European borrowing of the Judaic story of creation. Regarding creation, the Akan, for example, have the legend that at some point in their existence, Nyame (another name for the supreme deity and represented by the sky), was so close to humans that people could touch it. According to Akan folklore, there was an old woman who always poked the sky whenever she pounded her food. When the sky could not take the poking any longer, it retreated beyond reach.[38] Thus, women were responsible for the strained relations between the creator and humanity. The creation story of the Ewe is more elaborate than that of the Akan. Their story of creation involved two deities in a godhead: Mawu the female element and the giver of life and everything that sustained life, and Lisa the male part and the protector, provider, and the giver of laws, among other attributes. Ewe legend has it that Mawu Lisa created lesser gods to govern components of the universe and assigned the children of the lesser gods to oversee the activities of humanity. Having created vegetation and animals, Mawu Lisa capped the creation process by forming humans from clay and water.[39] None of the ethnic groups worshipped their deities directly; they did so through lesser gods or the ancestors. The ancestors were believed to be part of the living, even if they were not seen physically, and formed the link between the living and the gods. Thus, like any organized group of people everywhere, Ghanaians were religious and spiritual. Indeed, for Ghanaians, the line between spiritual and secular was a fine one.[40] In greetings, eating, marriage, birth and death, preparing land for sowing and harvesting, going to sea to fish, traveling, etc. people perfunctorily invoked the divine for blessings and protection. Belief in a supreme being created a spirituality that governed all aspects of social life including sexual behavior. Whom one could marry, whether a couple was able to have children or not, or where a couple could have sex were all aspects of social life that were regulated with reference to the spiritual and divine.[41] People were careful not to break religious rules and taboos because of fear of swift spiritual reprisal.

The Europeans who spread Christianity in Africa, including Ghana, in the nineteenth century brought with them a cultural baggage that set up a dichotomy between their religion and traditions on the one hand and African religions and cultural traditions on the other. The Europeans considered Africans as morally depraved and their religious practices as superstition. They considered Africans' way of life as primitive, backward, and savage. Africans' dress, music, modes of entertainment, and general social interactions were viewed as inferior and backward.[42] Having thus designated Africans, Europeans used religion and Western education to "civilize" Africans.[43] The "white man's burden" became the trope of the civilizing mission, ergo, deculturation of Africa. Africans who converted to Christianity or received Western education or both, were put under pressure to deculturalize. It did not matter to the Europeans that there were parallels between African religions and their religion. For example, Catholics believed in and revered saints, but when Africans venerated ancestors, Europeans condemned them as superstitious. Christian relics and icons of worship were considered holy; similar items in African worship were called fetish. The Old Testament has numerous references to animal sacrifice, but when Africans engaged in the same practice, they were labeled as barbaric and satanic. Christians had pastors or priests; Africans had witch doctors. In these ways, Europeans denigrated and vilified

African religions and religious practices. To make sure that converts were weaned of their Africanisms, some Christian missionaries like Basel created settlements around their churches so that new converts would be removed from their cultural environments.

Apart from religion, Europeans denigrated African traditions such as polygyny. Both missionaries and colonial officials condemned polygyny as a reflection of Africans' unbridled sexuality. It did not matter to the proselytizers that the Bible was replete with examples of men who had multiple wives and concubines; nor were they eager to study the underlying sociocultural meanings attached to polygyny. As far as the Europeans were concerned, Africa was the antithesis of Europe and there was no point in looking for or justifying equivalencies in their cultures that would have given meaning to Africans' ways of life. African male converts were discouraged from marrying multiple wives and those who did were denied communion in their churches. Female converts were excluded from church leadership although in African religious practices women could be custodians of the gods. Missionaries constantly disparaged converts of their Africanisms which led some Africans to question their place in the churches. A philosophical schism occurred between educated Christian Africans who were proud of their "Africanness" and European church leaders who disdained African traditions.

An incident that occurred in the town of Akropong located in the eastern part of Ghana in 1933 exemplified that schism. An acclaimed teacher and composer, Ephraim Amu, was dismissed by the Presbyterian Synod because he dared to wear African attire to preach instead of wearing a suit and tie as the Europeans expected.[44] While Amu did not start his own church, others used such treatment to break away and founded churches that generally had no affiliation with the mainline (i.e., European) churches. The new churches were called African initiated churches (AICs). According to Allan Anderson, the AIC movement was the African reformation of Christianity.[45]

The AIC movement did not end with the end of colonialism. New churches sprang up and have continued to this day. Some of these churches can be differentiated from one another by name arrangement. There are churches like the Apostolic Church, Christ Apostolic Church, Christ Apostles, Apostles of Christ, Apostles Continuation Church, etc. Similarities in names notwithstanding, AICs are not homogenous. Some, like the Pentecostal charismatic churches (PCCs), act in some ways like the mainline European transplant churches. They have a hierarchy of authority with revolving leadership. They also generally do not ordain women as pastors. Some, like the Church of Pentecost, have diasporic presence and are firmly rooted. Then there are AICs founded and owned by one person (man or woman) that are often small in terms of membership and confined to their towns of origin. These are locally called "spiritual churches."[46] There are also "miracle-performing" churches, often founded and owned by men, that have a very large following and have several branches in the country. AICs have become increasingly popular and attractive because some (like the miracle and spiritual churches) construct a world that resonates with local belief in a spiritual world of good and evil forces that influence the lives of the living.[47] The spiritual and miracle churches purport to have the antidote to evil and to help members overcome personal and spiritual problems. The PCCs preach a gospel based on a neoliberal framework that undermines communal ownership of wealth, encourages individual accumulation and prosperity, and advances physical well-being.[48] The programming of some AICs creates conditions for sexual episodes between pastors and parishioners.

The issue of sex in the church is not unique to Ghana generally or AICs specifically. An African American radio talk show host, Lance Scurv, addressed sex in the Black church in the US and asked a question that is relevant to the analysis in this chapter. He asked pointedly: "How come the church has become the best place to get laid?"[49] Although Scurv did not provide an answer to his question, it is not difficult to see why the church can be the site for people to hook up in intimate relationships. The church is as much a social institution as it is a spiritual organization. It brings together people with shared cultural values and expectations in life. As such, it is not out of place for church members to seek partners among themselves. Unfortunately, that seemingly innocent process has reached a level, often championed by church leaders, that threatens to drag the name of the church into disrepute. AICs, in Ghana and elsewhere in Africa, are deeply enmeshed in the phenomenon of sex between leaders and parishioners, although it has not been a subject of serious academic discourse in Ghana. Nonetheless, there are media sources that show the extent to which sexuality has become an integral part of the programming of some AICs. For instance, there is a video of a pastor in Uganda who illustrated with a female parishioner in front of his congregation how a man should have sex with a woman doggy-style, to the applause and delight of the mostly female congregants.[50] Even if outrageous, at least that pastor and the woman were both dressed, compared with another pastor (background unknown) who demonstrated how to get a woman to reach orgasm in a live performance in front of a group of parishioners in a private setting. The pastor, fully clothed, had a naked female on a blanket on the floor while church members sat close and watched him put his fingers in the woman's vagina and caress her thighs until she began to moan and the spectators laughed and clapped.[51] Nigerian movies often show pastors duping female parishioners into believing that they are going to pray for the women only to turn around and demand sex. In Ghana, sex in the church is a dominant theme in the nascent film industry. Whether in movies or real-life situations, most pastors who are featured in sex scandals in Ghana and elsewhere in Africa are

AIC pastors. Thus, the focus on AICs in this chapter stems from the notoriety that sex has gained within their ranks in recent years.

AICs in Ghana differ in the ways that they integrate sexuality in their preaching. Indeed, PCCs and other large congregations are strict on sexuality and sexual purity of all members. Sexual purity is at the heart of their preaching. They emphasize virginity, especially for female parishioners, as a noble quality to take into marriage. PCCs have gone to the extent of assuming certain roles associated with sexuality that were traditionally reserved for families. While insisting on traditional marital rites before couples can be married in the church, PCCs influence the process by disallowing the exchange of alcoholic beverages during the rites. They instead offer money equivalents or soft drinks. PCCs are conservative in their sexual behavior, and sex scandals, particularly those involving pastors and parishioners, are not common, if at all. Sex in AICs occurs mostly in the miracle performing and spiritual churches that are not affiliated with the Christian Council of Ghana. Such churches are not subject to rigorous oversight other than occasional social outbursts from the public when something egregious happens in their ranks. The sections below use specific scripts from some of those churches to illustrate the dynamics of sex in their midst.

In early November 2018, a woman appeared on a radio show in Manfe in the Eastern Region to complain that her pastor sexually assaulted her. According to the woman, she had problems and sought help from the pastor. The pastor, in turn, advised that he must bathe her in a nearby stream to help solve the problems. The two went to the stream one night and while the pastor bathed her, he touched her inappropriately and warned that he would kill her if she resisted. He asked her to stoop and proceeded to sexually assault her. The chief of the town was outraged when he heard the story. He held the land and its resources in trust of the gods and ancestors; an event like that not only negatively reflected on his spiritual authority but it polluted the stream and could potentially anger the gods. We have already noted that sex in the bush under certain conditions was a taboo; now sex in a stream in the bush was doubly sacrilegious. The chief called a meeting of local chiefs and pastors including the alleged perpetrator and the assault victim to get to the bottom of the matter. During the meeting, the chief reminded the pastor that a traditional priest would not engage in such behavior. The comparison was remarkable given how Christian proselytizers have demeaned and denigrated indigenous African religious beliefs and practices.[52] In an ironic twist, the pastor was ordered to offer a sheep to be sacrificed as pacification to the river god. There was no mention of restitution to the woman. The woman could claim punitive damages from the pastor in a court of law if she could prove that the sex was nonconsensual, but it did not appear she pursued that course of action.

In a different incident in another small church, the pastor continually made sexual overtures to the wife of one of the elders of his church. The woman told her husband who, in turn, asked other churchmen to help him catch the pastor red-handed. The unsuspecting pastor visited the married parishioner in her house, and at the point where he began to undress, the elder and his men entered the room. The pastor explained that despite his position in the church, he was a human being.[53] That was a remarkable admission, considering that he was married and was making sexual overtures to a married woman.

Although different incidents, the two sex stories described above are significant in that they sit at the intersection of religious ethics, fidelity to faith, spouse, and culture. Regarding religious ethics, the Bible does not condemn sex; it is rather the misuse of sex that it considers a sin. The seventh commandment enjoins believers to not commit adultery, and in the New Testament several of Paul's letters emphasize moral uprightness by urging converts to refrain from adultery. For men who are supposed to be interpreters of the Bible to flagrantly flout one of its cardinal injunctions meant that they did not hold their faith to the highest ethical standards. Nor did the men show regard to the traditions governing sex in the communities in which the churches were situated. Christianity does not nullify one's allegiance to and observance of one's cultural traditions. Sex in the bush or with a married woman is culturally unacceptable regardless of the religious beliefs of the person committing that act. But what about the women at the center of the pastors' actions? Whether or not they fell victim to the pastors' sexual advances, the women made sure to expose the men. In these contexts, the women exhibited higher moral standards that the pastors obviously lacked. With particular reference to the woman who was sexually assaulted in a stream, it is clear that she showed poor judgment by believing the pastor and following him into the bush at night, yet it is remarkable that the woman acted on cultural and religious convictions to make her case public. She had been victimized, but she rejected the idea that she was a victim.

The pastors' behaviors also speak to the sexual objectification of women by men in social situations. Put in its social context, sex in those churches appears to be part of a larger phenomenon in Ghanaian society that is akin to a quasi-quid pro quo in which men in positions of authority demand sex from women as prerequisite for preferment or service for women. In October 2019, a BBC undercover stint exposed what it termed "sex for grades," a caption that belied the actual power dynamic embedded in the phenomenon. In the nation's premier university,[54] the investigation alleged that some male faculty members sexually harassed female students or demanded sex from female students in exchange for better grades. The investigator posed as a student and captured some professors asking her for sexual favors. Female students did not throw themselves at their professors in hopes of getting "free grades." The professors were the initiators and pursuers. Once the matter became public, several students complained that they too had been victims of professors' sexual predations. The fact that students kept quiet until the BBC investigators exposed the problem speaks to the element of control and domination that characterize female-male relations in patriarchal society. The pastors whose sexual behaviors have been described above seemed to be borrowing from a public playbook in which men expect women to give sex in return for something.[55]

Other sexual incidents in some of the churches defy simple analysis of sexual objectification or a quid pro quo involving a pastor and a female parishioner. Two egregious incidents happened at the End Time Church of Nations that deserve special mention. Neither of the incidents involved the pastor having sex with any female parishioners but his actions were loaded with sexual innuendo. In the first instance, the pastor sat in a barrel full of water during church service and served the water to his mostly female parishioners.[56] Once footage of the event appeared online and people started talking, the pastor rushed to a popular television show to explain what happened. He said that he received revelation from God to do what he did. He said that the week prior to serving the "holy" water, he did not bathe, and that the 'bathing" in church (during which he wore only boxers) purified the water. Interestingly, neither he nor his wife drank the water because he claimed that they did not have the same needs as the parishioners.[57] Although that incident did not have any sexual connotation, it reflected the ease with which female parishioners bent to the power of their pastors.

Another incident happened at a branch of the same church in September 2020 that was more egregious than the one described above. A video posted online showed the same pastor shaving the pubic hair of female parishioners with his associate pastor collecting the hairs. During the shaving session, the pastor railed against pastors of different churches who had criticized his method of ministration, blamed his church members who videotaped services and posted them online, and questioned the lifestyles of female parishioners that had led him to engage in the shaving. In fact, he commanded everybody in the sanctuary to put their phones in a designated place. They all complied, again reflecting the hold that these so-called men of God have over their parishioners.

Critics of the video ranged from those who suggested that it was not real but part of a television production series, to those who called for the arrest of the pastor. And as he did in the first instance, Pastor Atta went on KofiTV to explain the rationale for his actions. He appeared on the show with one of the women he had shaved who identified herself as Florence. She explained that she subjected herself to the ritual because she had marital problems. The host seized on the woman's admission and asked Pastor Atta why he felt it necessary to engage in a very private act in church in the full glare of his parishioners even if the women had marital problems. Pastor Atta explained:

> For some time, things were not going well in the lives of some of my church members. Because of that I embarked on a sixty-day fasting. On exactly day fifty-nine I saw the heavens open and saw angels and God standing there. And they explained to me that the reason some of the women were experiencing difficulties in their lives was that in their destiny their virginity was to be broken by men of God but the women did so with the wrong individuals . . . and as a result they are not [spiritually] clean.[58]

The pastor further explained that God and his angels showed him Leviticus 14:8 where it is written that individuals who were undergoing cleansing should bathe and shave their body. The cleansing was required for people who had skin diseases and were deemed unclean. Granted that Pastor Atta found the women unclean, there is no requirement in the verse that says another person must do the shaving, and that it should only be pubic hair. Nonetheless, the pastor claimed that he was guided by the verse to shave the women. He also claimed that he placed each woman's hair on the altar and fire from above consumed them all except the hair of five women that did not burn. That means he would have to shave those women again, and then bathe them and the others to make them fully clean spiritually. Asked how he would bathe the women, he indicated he would do so in wash basins.[59]

But why did the women subject themselves to the situation? Florence, the parishioner who followed Pastor Atta to the television interview, offered a window into the thinking of the women. The pastor promised them something they could not resist. The women wanted husbands or stable marital relationships and they would do whatever it took, even if it meant having their pubic hairs shaved in public, to achieve their goals. The oldest woman to be shaved was already in her sixties but went through the procedure so that her daughters could get the kinds of men she desired for them.

Pastor Atta and small AICs like his are not the only ones notorious for such actions. Pastors of a few very large AICs have also been known to have engaged in sexually explicit incidents involving female parishioners. At the forefront of these actions is one of the most popular pastors in Ghana, Pastor Obinim, founder and senior pastor of International God's Way Ministries. The church has a very large following with several branches in the country. An incident that engendered widespread discourse on sex in the church occurred at the Tema branch on Sunday, October 22, 2017. The famous pastor asked parishioners to bring their underwear to church for ritual cleansing. He requested for only old intimate wear: brassieres and pants from women and boxer shorts and singlets from men. He also encouraged other branches to turn in their intimate wear and those of their family members who did not attend his church. He promised to burn all collected items in two days so there was very little time for people to respond. Even so, he collected a huge pile of old, used underwear, organized a night prayer session with some associate pastors on October 24, 2017, and burned the heap to ashes.[60]

On another occasion Pastor Obinim used his foot to agitate the pubic area and stomach of a woman during church service. The woman said she could not get pregnant and had been advised by her doctor to undergo surgery; she was afraid and could also not afford the cost of the surgery. That was her reason for seeking divine intervention through Obinim. The way the pastor poked the woman with his foot left no imagination as to its sexual nature.[61] On yet another occasion, Obinim lay on a couch with a woman and mimicked making out with her during Sunday church services. The woman had stepped forward during service to plead with the prophet to help her get a husband. When he lay in "bed" with her, he was assuring her that it would not be long before she got the man with whom to share her bed.[62]

There are parallels between the actions of Atta and Obinim and the women in their respective churches. Both pastors collected intimate items and burned them, but they did not tell what they did with the ashes. Both claimed that their actions were based on revelations from God. The old underwear represented problems the members faced—poverty, barrenness, sickness, failed marriages, failed businesses, etc. The burning was symbolic; it represented the wiping away of the problems the people faced. An underwear or pubic hair is part of a person's intimate life. It must take a great act of faith for people to freely give such items to their pastor, knowing that in traditional belief, such intimate items can be used by people wishing to charm or hurt others. In these instances, there was a melding of traditional religious belief and Christianity, a syncretism that seems to make some of the AICs relevant in their cultural contexts. The women did not seem to interpret the pastors' actions in terms or charming or harming them. Rather, they might have believed what the pastors said and hence threw away all caution.

Pastors have allegedly had sex with women who wanted to become pregnant because the pastors claimed they had "holy" sperms; some are said to anoint women's breasts and stomachs by rubbing "holy oil" on those parts to stimulate pregnancy. While such stories are anecdotal and not easily verifiable, they cannot be discarded as mere gossip due to what happens in churches in the open. Some of these so-called men of God are now selling oils, creams, wrist bands, and holy water to parishioners. These items are supposed to protect users from harm and to grant them their wishes. Marriage counselors have sprung up to advise wives and other women looking to get married to adopt certain strategies so that their men would not have reason to engage in extramarital affairs. One of them, Counselor Lutterodt, told participants during a public talk that "when you meet your mistress you miss your stress."[63] The play on the words made his meaning clear: having a side chick is therapeutic for men. The implication for married church women is that they must do whatever it takes to sustain love in their marriages, a notion that puts full responsibility for the success or failure of marriages on women's sexual behavior.

Opanin Kyere, a preacher and renowned and respected marriage counselor, does not tolerate infidelity of any sort. He admonishes men who call other men fools for divorcing their wives to refrain from that practice. He states that if a man marries a divorced woman with children and thinks that his wife's previous husband is a fool, he should think again and ask himself who is the bigger fool. He admonishes women to have children only after they have married and not settle as second wives. He shared these perspectives in a public counseling session to parishioners of the International Central Gospel Church in Accra, where he warned that women without children are finding it difficult to find husbands these days, let alone those with one or two "trailers."[64] Then he said, "Don't embarrass yourself. Aren't you beautiful enough to be somebody's only wife? Why do you want to play second degree wife, grade two wife? It does not befit you."[65] Opanin Kyere is unlike neophyte counselors on the Christian marriage counseling scene right now; he does not appear on television and radio talk shows to give bombastic advice to married and unmarried women alike about sexual behavior and other marital issues.

CONCLUSION

It is important to ask why women would engage in these kinds of behavior. We need to understand that culture has something to do with this. Women belong in cultures that prioritize marriage and childbirth over other important aspects of social life. One has to ask whether or not women engage in these behaviors because they do not have any other avenues. But if we understand that the cultural expectation is for women to be married and have children then we can understand why women would go to such great lengths to get married. Having said that, it is also important to note that marriage and childbirth are social prescriptions only. In other words, women who choose to follow these prescriptions do so on their own volition, so, in this regard, they cannot be seen as victims.

It is not always that we get a woman to come forward with her story as the woman from Manfe did, nor do we get women who would set up predatory pastors as another woman did, but stories circulate of pastors using direct and indirect means to solicit sex from parishioners. Women's responses to such solicitations have been nuanced. Some have resisted the pastors' attempts and others have succumbed. Consensual or coerced, it is important to ask whether the women are victims of unscrupulous pastors or if they use the church as the means to an end. The answers lie in examining the cultural milieu in which these churches operate. Most women patronize these churches to have their breakthrough. Society expects them to be successful within the framework of marriage. Society expects them to be mothers and wives. AICs offer these women a milieu in which they believe they can fulfill those expectations. Also, unlike mainline churches that generally marginalize women in their programming, AICs offer women more responsibility that brings them in close contact with the pastors. Women can be associate pastors, deaconesses, praise leaders, and prayer warriors. They may also be church secretaries and treasurers. In these positions, they get the chance to exercise authority that may have been denied them in society at large while also interacting with the pastors daily. These are aspects of patriarchy that tend to portray women as active participants in society and thus mask their marginal positions and restricted behaviors.

Importantly, AICs operate in a patriarchal context in which women's ability to climb the social ladder occurs largely by their association with men. The churches provide the milieu in which women's agency and desire for self-fulfillment can occur. The pastors of the churches are relatively young, some are handsome and wealthy, and claim to possess spiritual gifts that can help parishioners in all manner of ways. Women who patronize these churches may be looking forward to eternal salvation, but there is also the social dimension to their membership that cannot be ignored. The possibility of having one's social expectations fulfilled—getting a husband (possibly even the pastor), curing barrenness, protecting oneself from evil forces—makes church membership transactional and sex in the church a quasi-quid pro quo in which the pastors demand sex for favors that they themselves cannot provide in most cases. This view accords with Trzebiatowska and Bruce's argument that women are more religious than men not because of an innate tendency that predisposes them to religiosity but rather the social differences in roles relating to pivotal life events like birth, death, and illness.[66] Women do not go to church "to get laid," to echo Lance Scurv's observation. They go to church seeking other things in life in addition to spiritual salvation. It is rather the male pastors who use their position as men of God and their cultural understanding of women as sex objects to solicit and, in some cases, succeed in having sex with female parishioners or subject women to other sexual practices. This is not suggesting that women are helpless victims at the hands of powerful pastors. If that were the case, we would not have some women coming forward with their stories of sexual harassment or rape. Women approach the sex issue in complex ways that reflect the challenges they must confront in a patriarchal setting. They must be morally upright citizens of their communities, and they must guard their sexual behavior and reputations. In short, women shoulder immense burdens in society. Seeking fulfillment in the church may be yet another layer of burden that women must deal with.

NOTES

1. Same sex relationships are illegal in Ghana and will not be part of the discussion in the chapter.

2. Bonnie S. Anderson and Judith P. Zinsser, *A History of their Own: Women in Europe from Prehistory to Present*, vol. 2 (New York: Oxford University Press, 1999), 28–29.

3. Monika Fludernik, "Suttee Revisited: From the Iconography of Martyrdom to the Burkean Sublime," *New Literary History* 30, no. 2, (Spring, 1999): 411–437.

4. Throughout the chapter, I use Ghana to refer to both the colonial state and country after independence.

5. Isaac Addai, "Religious Affiliation and Sexual Initiation among Ghanaian Women," *Review of Religious Research* 41, no. 3 (March 2000): 328–343; Caroline Rigo, Vassalis Saroglou, and Philip Uzarevic, "Make Love and Lose Your Religion and Virtue: Recalling Sexual Experiences Undermines Spiritual Intentions and Moral Behavior," *Journal for the Scientific Study of Religion* 55, no. 1 (2016): 23–39; Mark D. Regnerus, "Religion and Adolescent Sexual Behavior," in Christopher G. Ellison and Robert A. Hummer, eds. *Religion, Families, and Health: Population-Based Research in the United States* (New Brunswick, NJ: Rutgers University Press, 2010), 61–85; Valérie K. Orlando, "Women, Religion, and Sexuality in Contemporary Moroccan Film: Unveiling the Veiled in *Hijab al-Hob* (*Veils of Love*, 2009)," *Palimpsest: A Journal on Women, Gender, and the Black International* 2, no. 1, (2013): 106–123; Dena M. Abbot, Jeff E. Harris, and Debra Mollen, "The Impact of Religious Commitment on Women's Sexual Self-Esteem," *Sexuality & Culture* 20 (2016): 1063–1082; Jeremy E. Uecker, "Religion, Pledging, and the Premarital Sexual Behavior of Married Young Adults," *Journal of Marriage and Family* 70, no. 3 (August 2008): 728–744.

6. Dena M. Abbott, Jeff E. Harris, and Debra Mollen, "The Impact of Religious Commitment on Women's Sexual Self-Esteem," *Sexuality & Culture* 20 (2016): 1063–1082.

7. Ellen H. Zaleski and Kathleen M. Schiaffino, "Religiosity and Sexual risk-taking behavior during transition to College," *Journal of Adolescence* 23, no. 2 (2000): 223–227; Eva S. Lefkowitz, Meghan M. Gillen, Cindy L. Shearer, and Tanya L. Boone, "Religiosity, sexual behaviors, and sexual attitudes during emerging adulthood," *The Journal of Sex Research*, 41, no. 2 (2004): 150–159.

8. Kofi Awusabo-Asare, John K. Anarfi, and D. K. Agyeman, "Women's control over their sexuality and the spread of STDs and HIV/AIDS in Ghana," *Health Transition Review* 3, Supplement, Sexual Networking and HIV/AIDS in West Africa (1993): 69–84; Daniel Y. Fiaveh, Michael P. K. Okyerefo, and Clara K. Fayorsey, "Women's Experiences of Sexual Pleasure in Ghana," *Sexuality and Culture* 19

(2015): 697–714; Eric Yeboah Tenkorang and Yaa A. Owusu, "Coerced First Sexual Intercourse Among Women in Ghana: Evidence from the Demographic and Health Survey," *Sexuality and Culture* 17 (2013): 167–184; Alimata Abdul Karimu, "Exploring the sexual and reproductive health issues of visually impaired women in Ghana," *Reproductive Health Matters: An international journal on sexual and reproductive health and rights* 25, no, 50 (June 2017): 128–133; Jane E. Soothill, *Gender, Social Change and Spiritual Power: Charismatic Christianity in Ghana*, Brill ebook titles, 2007.

9. Addai 2000; Anarfi and Owusu 2011; Awusabo-Asare et al., 2006; Bochow 2012.

10. Judith Lorber, "Night to his Day: The Social Construction of Gender," in *Paradoxes of Gender* (Boston: Yale University Press, 1994), 13–14.

11. Alan G. Johnson, *The Gender Knot: Unravelling our Patriarchal Legacy,* 3rd ed. (Philadelphia: Temple University Press, 2014), 37.

12. Gwendolyn Mikell, "Ghanaian Females, Rural Economy and National Stability," *African Studies Review* 29, no. 3 (September 1986), 74.

13. Awusabo, Anarfi, and Agyemang, "Women's control over their sexuality," 70.

14. It is not clear whether pubescent girls' visit to queen mothers' houses was for the latter to check for intact hymen or simply to verify that girls were in their periods. The elderly women who talked about their own visit as young women refused to answer questions regarding insertion. They explained, though, that their breasts and menstrual lints were inspected as a way for the queen mothers to be satisfied that they were not pregnant.

15. *Bragoro is a* kind of outdooring of a girl who has come of age.

16. The Akan believed that failure to go through the proper initiation rites could pollute the land and affect agricultural output; female members of the affected family might also suffer from barrenness or infant mortality. Hence the need to avert misfortunes through propitiation.

17. Martha Donkor, *Child Rape in Ghana: Lifting the Veil* (Lanham: Lexington Books, 2019), 28.

18. See, Rose Mary Amenga-Etego, "Sex and Sexuality in an African Worldview: A Challenge to the Contemporary Realities," in Dwight N. Hopkins and Marjorie Lewis, eds., *Another World Possible: Spiritualities and Religions of Global Darker Peoples*. Cross Cultural Theologies (London: Equinox Pub., 2009), 238–240.

19. Amenga-Etego, "Sex and Sexuality in an African Worldview," 238–239.

20. Donkor, *Child Rape in Ghana,* 29.

21. Awusabo, Anarfi, and Agyemang, "Women's control over their sexuality," 71.

22. The story behind the saying was that a woman connived with a boyfriend to kill her husband so she and the boyfriend could marry. The sign for the boyfriend to strike was the way she fanned the fire. Having achieved their goal, the new husband became suspicious when another man visited their home and the wife started fanning the fire in a certain way.

23. For other conditions that could lead a woman to cheat in a polygynous marriage, see Awusabo, Anarfi, and Agyemang, "Women's control over their sexuality," 70.

24. Peter Sarpong, *Ghana in Retrospect: Some Aspects of Ghanaian Culture* (Accra: Ghana Publishing, 1974).

25. See Mark Epprecht, "Religion and same-sex relations in Africa," 517.

26. Mensah Adinkrah, *Witchcraft, Witches and Violence in Ghana* (New York: Berghahn, 2015), 170.

27. Judith Bennett, *History Matters: Patriarchy and the Challenge of Feminism* (Philadelphia: University of Pennsylvania Press, 2007), 59.

28. Donkor, *Child Rape in Ghana,*

29. For a critique of the European view, see Signe Arnfred, "'African Sexuality'/ Sexuality in Africa: Tales and Silences," in *Rethinking Sexualities in Africa*, Signe Arnfred, ed., (Uppsala: Almqvist and Wiksell Tryckeri AB, 2005), 67–69.

30. Bennett, *History Matters*, 73–75.

31. Anderson and Zinsser, 131–134.

32. Betty Friedan, *The Feminine Mystique* (New York: W. W. Norton, 1963), 18.

33. An example of this is Christine Amanpour's interview of Moesha Buduong and the fallout in the news. See Ghanaweb, General News of Tuesday, April 24, 2018, https://www.ghanaweb.com/GhanaHomePage/NewsArchive/ Moesha-Buduong-s-full-interview-with-CNN-s-Amanpour-645971.

34. In the episodes, participants are fully dressed while they demonstrate different sex acts. The host and male participant give a commentary as the show goes on.

35. SVTV Africa, "Meet Mama Gee, the woman who sells aphrodisiac to attract men for money," June 3, 2019, https://www.youtube.com/watch?v=bkVMRtDfBXY&t=462s.

36. Mama Gee was arrested on July 10, 2019, by the Food and Drugs Authority and the police because she had neither registered nor sought approval to market her products. She was later released and is back running her store. See "Mama Gee who sells 'Juju' ladies use to charm men arrested," July 11, 2019, https://www.youtube .com/watch?v=ktorXiP3_y4.

37. SVTV Africa, "Meet Mama Gee, the woman who sells aphrodisiac to attract men for money."

38. Samuel Kwesi Nkansah, "The Quest for Climatic Sanity: Re-reading of Akan Creation Myth," *Language in India* 12, no. 8 (2012): 370.

39. Thomas Houessou-Adin, "Mawu-Lisa," *Encyclopedia of African Religion,* 2009, 411–412.

40. Addai, "Religious Affiliation and Sexual Initiation," 330; Peter Sarpong, *Ghana in Retrospect: Some Aspects of Ghanaian Culture* (Accra: Ghana Publishing, 1974).

41. Addai, "Religious Affiliation and Sexual Initiation," 330.

42. See Sanford J. Ungar, *Africa: The People and Politics of an Emerging Continent* (New York: Simon and Shuster, 1989), 19–25.

43. The so-called religious civilizing mission went hand in hand with the political process of colonization that began in the seventeenth century and formally recognized in 1884.

44. Kofi Agawu, "The Amu Legacy: Ephraim Amu 1899–1995," *Africa: Journal of the International African Institute* 66, no. 2 (1996): 275.

45. Alan Anderson, "Types and Butterflies: African Initiated Churches and European Typologies," *International Bulletin of Missionary Research* (July 2001): 107.

46. Allan H. Anderson, "Types and Butterflies: African Initiated Churches and European Typologies," *International Bulletin of Missionary Research* (July 2001):

107–112; Jane E. Soothill, *Gender, Social Change and Spiritual Power: Charismatic Christianity in Ghana*, Brill ebook titles, 2007; Birgit Mayer, "Christianity in Africa: From African Independent to Pentecostal-Charismatic Churches," *The Wiley-Blackwell Companion to African Religions*, First Edition, edited by Elias Kifon Bongmba, Blackwell Publishing Ltd, © 2012.

47. Amoah, "Poverty is Madness: Some insights from traditional African spirituality and mental health," in Dwight N. Hopkins and Marjorie Lewis, eds. *Another world is possible: spiritualities and religions of global darker peoples* (London: Routledge, 2014), 208.

48. Matthews A. Ojo, "Pentecostal and Charismatic Movements in Modern Africa," in *African Religions*, 1st ed., edited by Elias Kifon Bongmba (Blackwell Publishing Ltd., 2012), 297.

49. The LanceScurve Show, "Saved, Sanctified and Promiscuous: Secret Anointed Lust," June 22, 2012, https://www.youtube.com/watch?v=fTr0_il2Q-g&t=242s.

50. "Uganda Pastor Teaching Sex Position in Church," Oct 11, 2019, https://www.youtube.com/watch?v=RnrnoW8PkoE&has_verified=1

51. "Pastors at their best," Apr 11, 2019, https://www.youtube.com/watch?v=GRDUQerrKVE.

52. "Ghanaian Pastor sleeps with a member of his Church in a Stream," Nov 8, 2018, https://www.youtube.com/watch?v=V-TSRf34YTs.

53. "Pastor caught in bed trying to have sex with his elder's wife," January 10, 2020, https://www.youtube.com/watch?v=79rB_zxLp9k.

54. The operation was carried on in two prestigious West African universities: University of Lagos and University of Ghana, Legon.

55. Sara Sam, "Sexual Harassment against Women in the Security Forces; The Case of Women in Ghana," paper presented at the 9th annual conference of Women in International Security, June 2015, Halifax, Canada; see also Ishmael Norman, M. Aikins and F. N. Binta, "Sexual Harassment in Public Medical Schools in Ghana," *Ghana Medical Journal* 47, no. 3 (Sept 2013): 128–136.

56. Andreas Kamasa, "Ghanaian pastor bathes in church and members line up to drink his bathwater for anointing," December 17, 2019, https://www.pulse.com.gh/filla/ghanaian-pastor-bathes-in-church-and-members-line-up-to-drink-his-bathwater-for/3zm7680.

57. KofiTV, "PASTOR WHO F£D HIS CHURCH MEMBERS HE B@THED WATER IS LIVE ON KOFI TV," https://www.youtube.com/watch?v=wgJ0EpgsCCs&t=137s.

58. KofiTV, "THE PASTOR WHO SHAVED HIS CHURCH MEMBERS TOTO SPEAKS FINALLY," October 12, 2020, https://www.youtube.com/watch?v=kExt09_DioA&t=395s.

59. KofiTV, "Pastor shaves church members."

60. Obinim burns parishioners' underwear,"

61. "Pastor Obinim steps on woman's stomach to deliver her," December 8, 2014, https://www.youtube.com/watch?v=Zv0ySJhxLuM.

62. "Again, Angel Obinim Sleeps with a Lady in Church live again," May 30, 2019, https://www.youtube.com/watch?v=EZ3P1dR30Vo.

63. "Communication before, during and after sexual intercourse," Counselor Lutterodt's orgasm conference, December 27, 2017, https://www.youtube.com/watch?v=7nWbyB5SoCU&t=309s.

64. A "trailer" in this context refers to a child born to a single woman out of wedlock whose father is not in the picture.

65. "Opanin Kwadwo Kyere at a Marriage Seminar," November 27, 2018, https://www.youtube.com/watch?v=7GwZKdP152w.

66. Marta Trzebretowska and Steve Bruce, "Why are women more religious than men?" *Oxford Scholarship Online,* January 2012.

BIBLIOGRAPHY

Abbott, Dena M., Jeff E. Harris, and Debra Mollen. "The Impact of Religious Commitment on Women's Sexual Self-Esteem." *Sexuality and Culture* 20 (2016):1063–1082.

Addai, Isaac. "Religious Affiliation and Sexual Initiation among Ghanaian Women." *Review of Religious Research* 41, no. 3 (March 2000): 328–343.

Adinkrah, Mensah. *Witchcraft, Witches and Violence in Ghana.* New York: Berghahn, 2015.

Adomako Ampofo, Akosua, and John Boateng. "Multiple meanings of manhood among boys in Ghana." In *African sexualities: A reader*, ed. Sylvia Tamale, 420-436. Pambazuka Press: Kindle Edition, 2011.

Adomako Ampofo, Akosua. "When Men Speak Women Listen: Gender Socialisation and Young Adolescents' Attitudes to Sexual and Reproductive Issues." *Journal of Reproductive Health/La Revue Africaine de la Santé Reproductive* 5, no. 3 (Dec 2001): 196–212.

Agawu, Kofi. "The Amu Legacy: Ephraim Amu,1899–1995." *Africa: Journal of the International African Institute* 66, no. 2 (1996): 274–279.

Amenga-Etego, Rose Mary. "Sex and Sexuality in an African Worldview: A Challenge to Contemporary Realities." In *Another World Possible: Spiritualities and Religions of Global Darker Peoples*, edited by Dwight N. Hopkins and Marjorie Lewis, 234–249. London: Routledge, 2014.

Amoah, Elizabeth. "Poverty is Madness: Some insights from traditional African spirituality and mental health." In *Another world is possible: spiritualities and religions of global darker peoples,* edited by Dwight N. Hopkins and Marjorie Lewis, 207–218. London: Routledge, 2014.

Anderson, Allan H. "Types and Butterflies: African Initiated Churches and European Typologies." *International Bulletin of Missionary Research* (July 2001): 107–112.

Arnfred, Signe. "'African Sexuality'/Sexuality in Africa: Tales and Silences." In *Rethinking Sexualities in Africa*, edited by Signe Arnfred, 7–29. Uppsala: Almqvist and Wiksell Tryckeri AB, 2005.

Awusabo-Asare, Kofi, John K. Anarfi, and D. K. Agyeman. "Women's control over their sexuality and the spread of STDs and HIV/AIDS in Ghana." *Health*

Transition Review 3, Supplement. Sexual Networking and HIV/AIDS in West Africa (1993): 69–84.

Bennett, Judith. *History Matters: Patriarchy and the Challenge of Feminism.* Philadelphia: University of Pennsylvania Press, 2007.

Butler, Judith. *Gender Trouble: Feminism and the Subversion of Identity.* New York: Routledge, 2011.

Donkor, Martha. *Child Rape in Ghana: Lifting the Veil.* Lanham: Lexington Books, 2019.

Epprecht, Mark. "Religion and same-sex relations in Africa." In *African Religions,* 1st ed., edited by Elias Kifon Bongmba, 515–528. Hoboken, NJ: Blackwell Publishing Ltd., 2012.

Falola, Toyin, and Nana Akua Amponsah. *Women, Gender, and Sexualities in Africa.* Carolina Academic Press African World Series. Carolina Academic Press, 2013.

Fiaveh, Daniel Yaw, and Michael P. K Okyerefo. "Femininity, Sexual Positions and Choice." *Sexualities* 22 nos. 1–2 (2019): 131–147.

Fiaveh, Daniel Yaw, Michael P. K Okyerefo, and Clara K. Fayorsey. "Women's Experiences of Sexual Pleasure in Ghana." *Sexuality & Culture* 19 no. 4 (2015): 697–714.

Fludernik, Monika. "Suttee Revisited: From the Iconography of Martyrdom to the Burkean Sublime." *New Literary History* 30, no. 2, (Spring, 1999): 411–437.

Friedan, Betty. *The Feminine Mystique.* New York: W. W. Norton, 1963.

Ghafricnews.com. "Ghana's First Transgender Madina Broni now Born again? Spotted singing at Church," April 4, 2019, https://www.youtube.com/watch?v=XE_7FQiq8Co.

Ghanaweb. "22 arrested by Mpraeso police over alleged lesbian wedding," March 29, 2021.

Ghanaweb. "Moesha Buduong's full interview with CNN's Amanpour." General News of Tuesday, April 24, 2018. https://www.ghanaweb.com/GhanaHomePage/NewsArchive/Moesha-Buduong-s-full-interview-with-CNN-s-Amanpour-645971.

Gyeke, Kwame. *African Cultural Values: An Introduction.* Accra: Sankofa Publishing Company, 1996.

Hendriks, Thomas, and Rachel Spronk. "Introduction: Reading "Sexualities" from "Africa." In *Readings in Sexualities from Africa,* edited by Hendriks Thomas and Spronk Rachel, 1-18. Bloomington: Indiana University Press, 2020.

Houessou-Adin, Thomas. "Mawu-Lisa." *Encyclopedia of African Religion,* 2009, 411–412.

Johnson, Alan G. *The Gender Knot: Unravelling our Patriarchal Legacy,* 3rd ed. Philadelphia: Temple University Press, 2014.

Kamasa, Andreas. "Ghanaian pastor bathes in church and members line up to drink his bathwater for anointing." December 17, 2019. https://www.pulse.com.gh/filla/ghanaian-pastor-bathes-in-church-and-members-line-up-to-drink-his-bathwater-for/3zm7680.

Karimu, Alimata Abdul. "Exploring the sexual and reproductive health issues of visually impaired women in Ghana." *Reproductive Health Matters: An international journal on sexual and reproductive health and rights* 25, no, 50 (June 2017): 128–133.

KofiTV. "Pastor who fed his church members his bath water is live on KofiTV." https://www.youtube.com/watch?v=wgJ0EpgsCCs&t=137s.

KofiTV. "The Pastor who shaved his church members toto speaks finally." October 12, 2020. https://www.youtube.com/watch?v=kExt09_DioA&t=395s.

Lefkowitz, Eva S., Meghan M. Gillen, Cindy L. Shearer, and Tanya L. Boone. "Religiosity, sexual behaviors, and sexual attitudes during emerging adulthood. *The Journal of Sex Research*, 41, no. 2 (2004): 150–159.

Lorber, Judith. "Night to his day: The Social Construction of Gender." In *Paradoxes of Gender,* 13–36. Boston: Yale University Press, 1994.

M'Baye, Babacar. "The Origins of Senegalese Homophobia: Discourses on Homosexuals and Transgender People in Colonial and Postcolonial Senegal." *African Studies Review* 56, no. 2 (September 2013): 109–128.

Mayer, Birgit. "Christianity in Africa: From African Independent to Pentecostal-Charismatic Churches." In *The Wiley-Blackwell Companion to African Religions,* 1st ed., edited by Elias Kifon Bongmba, 154–170. Hoboken, NJ: Blackwell Publishing Ltd., 2012.

Mikell, Gwendolyn. "Ghanaian Females, Rural Economy and National Stability." *African Studies Review* 29, no. 3 (September 1986): 67–88.

Nkansah, Samuel Kwesi. "The Quest for Climatic Sanity: Re-reading of Akan Creation Myth." *Language in India* 12, no. 8 (2012): 370.

Norman, Ishmael, M. Aikins, and F.N Binta. "Sexual Harassment in Public Medical Schools in Ghana." *Ghana Medical Journal* 47, no. 3 (Sept 2013): 128–136.

Odimegwu, Clifford. "Attitudes and Behaviour among Nigerian University Students: Affiliation or Commitment?" *African Journal of Reproductive Health* 9, no. 2 (2005): 125–140.

Ojo, Matthews A. "Pentecostal and Charismatic Movements in Modern Africa." In *African Religions*, 1st ed., edited by Elias Kifon Bongmba, 295–309. Hoboken, NJ: Blackwell Publishing Ltd., 2012.

Orlando, Valérie K. "Women, Religion, and Sexuality in Contemporary Moroccan Film: Unveiling the Veiled in *Hijab al-Hob* (*Veils of Love*, 2009)." *Palimpsest: A Journal on Women, Gender, and the Black International* 2, no. 1, (2013): 106–123.

Regi, Tamas. "The concept of the primitive in texts and images: from colonial travelogues to tourist blogs in Southwestern Ethiopia." *Journeys* 14, no. 1 (June 2013): 40–67.

Regnerus, Mark D. "Religion and Adolescent Sexual Behavior." In Christopher G. Ellison and Robert A. Hummer, eds, 61–85. *Religion, Families, and Health: Population-Based Research in the United States.* New Brunswick, NJ: Rutgers University Press, 2010.

Rigo, Caroline, Vassalis Saroglou, and Philip Uzarevic. "Make Love and Lose Your Religion and Virtue: Recalling Sexual Experiences Undermines Spiritual Intentions and Moral Behavior." *Journal for the Scientific Study of Religion* 55, no. 1 (2016): 23–39.

Sam, Sara. "Sexual Harassment against Women in the Security Forces; The Case of Women in Ghana," paper presented at the 9th annual conference of Women in International Security, Halifax, Canada, June 2015.

Sarpong, Peter. *Ghana in Retrospect: Some Aspects of Ghanaian Culture.* Accra: Ghana Publishing, 1974.

Shaw, Clifford R. and Henry McKay. *Juvenile Delinquency and Urban Areas.* Chicago: University of Chicago Press, 1969 [1942].

Soothill, Jane E. Gender, Social Change, and Spiritual Power: Charismatic Christianity in Ghana. Brill ebook titles, 2007.

SVTV Africa. "Meet Mama Gee, the woman who sells aphrodisiac to attract men for money." June3, 2019. https://www.youtube.com/watch?v=bkVMRtDfBXY&t=462s.

Tenkorang, Eric Yeboah, and Yaa A. Owusu. "Coerced First Sexual Intercourse Among Women in Ghana: Evidence from the Demographic and Health Survey." *Sexuality and Culture* 17 (2013):167–184.

The LanceScurve Show, "Saved, Sanctified and Promiscuous: Secret Anointed Lust." June 22, 2012. https://www.youtube.com/watch?v=fTr0_il2Q-g&t=242s.

Trzebretowska, Marta, and Steve Bruce. "Why are women more religious than men?" *Oxford Scholarship Online,* January 2012.

Uecker, Jeremy E. "Religion, Pledging, and the Premarital Sexual Behavior of Married Young Adults." *Journal of Marriage and Family* 70, no. 3 (August 2008): 728–744.

Ungar, Sanford J. *Africa: The People and Politics of an Emerging Continent.* New York: Simon and Shuster, 1989.

Youtube. "Again, Angel Obinim Sleeps with a Lady in Church live again." May 30, 2019. https://www.youtube.com/watch?v=EZ3P1dR30Vo.

Youtube. "Ghanaian Pastor sleeps with a member of his Church in a Stream," November 8, 2018. https://www.youtube.com/watch?v=V-TSRf34YTs.

Youtube. "Mama Gee who sells 'Juju' ladies use to charm men arrested." July 11, 2019. https://www.youtube.com/watch?v=ktorXiP3_y4.

Youtube. "Opanin Kwadwo Kyere at a Marriage Seminar." November 27, 2018. https://www.youtube.com/watch?v=7GwZKdP152w.

Youtube. "Pastor caught in bed trying to have sex with his elder's wife," January 10, 2020, https://www.youtube.com/watch?v=79rB_zxLp9k.

Youtube. "Pastor Obinim steps on woman's stomach to deliver her," December 8, 2014, https://www.youtube.com/watch?v=Zv0ySJhxLuM.

Youtube. "Pastors at their best," Apr 11, 2019. https://www.youtube.com/watch?v=GRDUQerrKVE.

Youtube. "Uganda Pastor Teaching Sex Position in Church." Oct 11, 2019. https://www.youtube.com/watch?v=RnrnoW8PkoE&has_verified=1.

Youtube. "Communication before, during and after sexual intercourse." Counselor Lutterodt's orgasm conference, December 26, 2017. https://www.youtube.com/watch?v=7nWbyB5SoCU&t=309s.

Chapter 2

Identity, Agency, and Subjugation: Cleavage and Breast Exposure among University Students in Ghana

Georgina Yaa Oduro and Nana Afia Karikari

Human anatomy explicitly shows that the breast is a common feature of both men and women. In public discourse on the breast, however, it is often skewed towards women. Indeed, the breast is one of women's precious possessions. While some people equate the female breast with sexual attractiveness and eroticism, others perceive this feminine feature with negativity. Gabrielle Palmer, for example, minced no words when she described the breast as both a "life-giver and life-destroyer"; *Life-giver* because of the milk it produces to sustain newly born babies and because of the possibility of infection with cancer and resultant death in women. Marilyn Yalom points out that when it comes to the breast, "babies see food, men see sex, doctors see disease, and businesspeople see a dollar sign."[1] Thus, the female breast is often pitched against itself within the context of goodness and life, or a whore and life-destroyer image. In effect, there are different meanings, attributes, and per-ceptions associated with the female breast depending on one's background, encounters, and experiences. Media discourses linked to the female breast are, for example, replete with headlines such as "everything boobs," the "boob show," "celebrity boobs," "tits," "sexy cleavage," etc. Central to these discourses is the inability of many people to distinguish between breast and cleavage exposure. The two are often used interchangeably, but in the strictest sense, breast and cleavage are not the same, though they are related. Whereas breast refers to the two-organ body part containing mammary glands on the chest of women and men (the attention is on the female breast in this chapter), cleavage refers to the cleft, hollow, or gap between a woman's breast revealed by a low neckline dress or an outfit. Unsurprisingly, globally, both cleavage and the female breast evoke different meanings, interpretations, and feelings. As Samantha Brett observed in her article, "The Great Cleavage Conundrum: should men look if it is on display?" "Cleavage . . . The very word (let alone the image) goes right to the jugular, sending shivers straight to the minds and loins of men the world over, conjuring up all sorts of conflicting thoughts and scintillating fantasies."[2]

In most Western cultures, exposure of the breast, and the area surrounding it, is considered beautiful, erotic, a form of femininity, physically attractive, flirtatious, and seductive.[3] Sarah Reynolds added that what often pertains in modern-day Western societies is either a huge or little display of breast and cleavage as seen with the wearing of ball and evening gowns as well as revealing lingerie and swimwear among others. Frederick et al. observed that the breast is one of the most eye-catching organs of the female body, thus, most men in Western cultures tend to derive erotic pleasure from seeing a woman's cleavage, with a few enjoying seeing their female partners expose cleavage and/or breast.[4] Within the context of Africa, however, Patricia Stuart-Macadam and Katherine Dettwyler provide a contrasting perspective. Drawing on examples from traditional African societies and anthropological literature largely from Mali, Sierra Leone, and Ghana, Stuart-Macadam and Dettwyler report that breasts traditionally had no sexual connotations or meanings such that elderly women at home could remain naked from the waist upward without any reservations or inciting eroticism.[5] They argued comparatively, the naked breasts of elderly women do not arouse any sexual feelings in men like that of young ladies.

In Mali, as in most cultures in Africa, breasts hold no sexual connotations for either men or women. Sexual behavior does not involve the breasts, which are perceived as existing for the sole purpose of feeding children. "When I told my friends and informants in Mali about Americans' attitudes toward women's breasts, especially sexual foreplay involving 'mouth to breast contact' by adult men, they were either bemused or horrified or both. In any case, they regarded it as unnatural, perverted behavior, and found it difficult to believe that men would become sexually aroused by women's breasts, or that women would find such activities pleasurable."[6]

This is why, as Stuart-Macadam and Dettwyler suggest, it is still common in Ghana to find elderly women unreservedly exposing their breasts in the domestic sphere without any inhibitions. However, cultural norms and mores frown on the exposure of sensitive body parts including the breast and the display of cleavage by young ladies in public. Cleavage and breast exposure in public and in some contexts are culturally tabooed and socially disapproved in Ghana.[7] Although breast exposure is not culturally encouraged in Ghana, there are some contexts such as puberty rites, for example, the dipo[3] rite of the Krobos of Ghana where the breasts of teenage girls are exposed.

Also, breastfeeding babies in public is acceptable without sexualizing the breast.[8] Georgina Oduro observed that contexts define where and when breast exposure and cleavage are appropriate and permitted. Ghanaian tradition generally abhors exposure of sensitive body parts such as breasts, thighs, and buttocks by females, especially unmarried women in the public sphere. This is reflected in the Akan concept of "*akatasia*" literally meaning "cover yourself up/ decently dressed lady."[9] Drawing from historical and critical perspectives, Deborah Boadu observed that during the 19th and 20th centuries, Ghanaian ladies were not in the habit of exposing their private body parts, especially the breast. It is for this reason that the Akans, the largest ethnic group in Ghana, call ladies "*akatasia*." The story is, however, different in present-day Ghana. According to Bernard E. Dzramedo, the impact of social change and the global media, as well as fashion demands and related activities, have encouraged the showing of cleavages and other parts of the breasts by Ghanaian young ladies—a sign of agentic development. As Carl Ratner espoused, people are not passive recipients of norms but play active roles in the making and remaking of such norms. In other words, innovations are introduced by people to challenge the status quo daily, with such innovations exhibited through the behaviors of people. Thus, Dzramedo explains, it is now common to see Ghanaian ladies dressed provocatively, exposing their cleavages and breasts. This is evident in a fashion trend known as "*mahye-dwa,*" which means "I am advertising my goods for sale." Although some women exercise agency by this *mahye-dwa* fashion sense, there are some elements of subjugation reflected in the insults and disdain heralded at such ladies. This development has led to Boadu's claim that Ghanaian young ladies have adopted the Western mode of dressing, the kind that is often considered immoral, indecent, and nonconforming to Ghanaian morals, cultural ethics, and the concept of "*akatasia*." Women who practice breast and cleavage exposure are often labeled as immoral, regardless of their statuses or real nature. For example, a former minister of state received public backlash when she went to parliament in an attire that showed part of her breasts. It was seen as provocative and indecent and some people described her as a desperate woman seeking attention, a minister selling her boobs and other defaming tags.[10] Also, Zynnel Zuh, a popular actress, was criticized for meeting the president in a dress that showed her breasts excessively. Several people criticized the look and termed it as gross and disgraceful.[11] A popular counselor in Ghana has categorically branded women who expose their breasts and cleavage as prostitutes.

From the discussion so far, it appears that some believe that Ghanaian decency is being tainted daily, and morality has plunged into a state of confusion with the "*mahye-dwa*" fashion of Ghanaian young ladies. The clothing pattern of most youth in today's Ghana tends to relegate modesty to the background. Clothes that triggered moral outcry some years back in various cultural settings in Ghana are now being worn openly.

THE RESEARCH GAP AND CONTEXT OF GHANAIAN UNIVERSITY STUDENTS

It is very common to see female university students and other young ladies dressed to "show some skin" including breasts and cleavage. Within the context of cultural disapproval of cleavage and breast exposure vis-à-vis modern permissiveness, this chapter explores the perception and meanings associated with breast exposure and cleavage display among some university students in Ghana. Views and experiences of participants are informed by discourses on identity, agency or power, and subjugation. Thus, the chapter examines how breast exposure and cleavage are interpreted within the context of identity, agency, and subjugation. The exploration is underpinned by Ghanaian cultural constructions and acknowledges the impact of social change. The chapter is relevant because, though cleavage and breast exposure are common in present-day Ghana, little or no known academic investigation has been conducted on the subject matter.[12] Most studies on breasts in Ghana are often related to breastfeeding and breast cancer and aesthetic use of breasts has not been the subject of any serious academic inquiry.[13] It is this gap that the study seeks to bridge in the current chapter. The chapter begins by contextualizing cleavage and breast exposure. This is followed by a theoretical framework. Next is an examination of how the study was conducted, data presentation, analysis, and discussion. The chapter concludes with some relevant policy recommendations and academic implications.

THEORETICAL FRAMEWORK

This chapter is underpinned by Rational Choice and Dramaturgy theories. Rational choice theory is attributed to George Homans and Peter Blau. The theory stipulates that individuals have preferences among available choices at their disposal.[14] The theory hinges on motivation and decision-making. It has been used extensively in economics and psychological research projects as well as sociological works. Rational choice theory argues that rational beings consider available information, probabilities of events, and weigh the potential costs and benefits in determining preferences, and act accordingly in choosing the self-determined best choice of action.[15] It is assumed that individuals always make prudent and logical choices that provide them with the greatest benefit or satisfaction which are in their highest self-interest. The theory helps explain social outcomes by constructing models of individual action and social context. In selecting this theory, we are mindful of Hechter and Kanazawa's caution that rational choice can be problematic in examining social norms, obligations, and ensuring group interest over self-interest.[16]

Relating the rational choice theory to breast and cleavage exposure brings to the fore those sociological processes which inform a woman's decision to display cleavage or expose breasts, especially in a culture that frowns on such practices. Do university students and youth in Ghana, for example, engage in a cost-benefit analysis in their decision to expose breasts and cleavage in relation to Ghanaian traditional and cultural norms? Would it be in the interest of such individuals to engage in the practice of breast and cleavage exposure or would it be to their disadvantage? This chapter draws on the rational choice theory to explore why some ladies, particularly university students, wear breast and cleavage-exposing dresses while others do not.

The next theory adopted to explain perceptions about women who expose their breasts and cleavage is dramaturgy. Dramaturgy is attributed to Erving Goffman who drew on the metaphor of the theater to describe life. He related the concept to life as a never-ending play with people as actors.[17] The theory, which evolved from symbolic interactionism is commonly used in microsociological accounts in everyday social interaction. Goffman believed that when we are born, we are zoomed onto a stage called everyday life, and through socialization, we learn how to play our assigned roles from others. We learn both acceptable and offensive behavior from others, who are in turn enacting their roles while interacting with us. Goffman believes that whatever we do, we are playing out some role on the stage of life. He opines that people engage in front-stage behavior when they are conscious of the fact that others are viewing their projected behavior. The front-stage behavior usually is the internalized norms, purposeful and learned social scripts, whereas the backstage is more relaxed but the performance is often prepared. People rehearse behaviors in preparation for future front-stage performance. He argues that even backstage, people are conscious of the norms and expectations that influence what they think about and do. This acting of roles is what Goffman calls dramaturgical analysis, or the study of social interaction in terms of theatrical performance. Goffman also intimates that as social actors, our visible actions are what we intend to portray.[18] Therefore, taking the female body as a stage, a woman's decision to expose her cleavage and breasts could be an intended act with an imagined expected reaction from other individuals and audiences.

THE SOCIOCULTURAL AND
METHODOLOGICAL CONTEXT

Ghana, formerly known as the Gold Coast, is a West African country located on the Gulf of Guinea. Ghana is bordered by three French-speaking countries: Burkina Faso to the north, Côte d'Ivoire to the west, and Togo to the east. The country is the first sub-Saharan African country to gain independence from the British, becoming an independent Commonwealth nation in 1957. Ghana has a population of approximately 28 million, with 42 percent being youth below 15 years of age and 51 percent being women.[19] The country has about 10 public universities and several private universities.[20]

The University of Cape Coast was selected for this study. The University is one of the leading public universities in Ghana. The University of Cape Coast was established in October 1962 as a University College. In October 1971, the university attained the status of a fully independent university. The university is located in Cape Coast, a coastal city in Ghana. Currently, the university operates a collegiate system with five colleges which are the College of Education Studies, the College of Distance Education, the College of Humanities and Legal Studies, the College of Health and Allied Sciences and the College of Agriculture and Natural Resources. The university has over 70,000 students pursuing programs at undergraduate and graduate levels; this includes sandwich and distance and continuing education students. The university is a liberal institution that accommodates students from different backgrounds and so does not have stringent rules on the mode of dressing or prescribed dress code.[21]

Qualitative research was adopted for this study, specifically the researcher's phenomenological research design. This approach was adopted basically to explore the meanings and perceptions associated with cleavage and breast exposure among students at the University of Cape Coast and to solicit experiential accounts from students who practice breast and cleavage exposure. A combination of purposive, convenience and snowball sampling techniques were employed to recruit research participants. The duration of data collection was 6 weeks, from February 8 to March 21, 2018. Before conducting the interviews, a feasibility assessment was done by visiting the cafeteria, lecture theaters and some halls of residence of the University to recruit participants. In recruiting participants, students were approached, informed about the study and volunteers requested. Participants for the focus group discussion were selected conveniently. For the one-on-one interviews, however, we purposely looked for ladies who had exposed their breasts and cleavage and informed them about the study. They voluntarily agreed to participate in the study. Some of the participants from the one-on-one interviews as well as focus group discussion referred us to friends whom they deemed as fitting our selection criteria and were likely to be interested in the study. A few participants withdrew after initially agreeing to participate in the study. A total of 40 full-time undergraduate students were voluntarily recruited for the study. The students were selected because of their availability as well as meeting the criteria for the study. As a purely qualitative study, five sets of 6-member focus group discussions were held making up a total of 30 students. Specifically, we had two sets of six all-male group discussions. Then we had two sets of all-female focus group discussion, also of six members each. Finally, we sampled a mixed group of 3 males and 3 females. Thus, fifteen males and fifteen females were engaged in the focus group discussions which centered on the perception of students about breast and cleavage exposure. For the one-on-one interviews, 10 interviews were conducted with students, specifically ladies who dressed to expose their breasts and cleavage. The interviews were, therefore, phenomenological or experiential.

On average, focus group discussions and interviews lasted between 45 and 90 minutes depending on the intensity of the discussion. The questions touched on views, perceptions, meanings and functions or uses of the female breast; breast and cleavage exposure; Ghanaian culture and breast size; preferred breast size; types of ladies who expose their breasts and cleavages; places and occasions for breast and cleavage display; reasons for breast and cleavage exposure; and effects of wearing breast and cleavage-exposing dresses among others.

As a highly sensitive study, ethical issues were observed from start to finish. To ensure anonymity, pseudonyms were used for participants. Participants were also voluntarily recruited without any coercion while their consents were secured. Debriefing sessions were held with them after each activity. The different sets of data were audio-recorded, transcribed and categorized thematically drawing on Miles, Huberman and Saldana's analysis framework.[22] The data were analyzed manually. Coffey and Atkinson describe analysis as the systematic procedures of identifying essential features and relationships in data. It is also described as a way of transforming data into interpretations.[23] The analysis was therefore done guided by the research objectives and questions as well as the themes of identity, agency and subjugation.

RESULTS AND DISCUSSION

Participants were between ages 19 and 24 years. In all, there were 40 participants; the participants were comprised of 16 final year students, 10 in the second year, 11 in the first year and 3 in the third year. They were drawn from both Christian and Islamic religious backgrounds and different ethnic groups.

Three key concepts, identity, agency and subjugation, emerged strongly in response to how students at the University of Cape Coast construed ideals about those who dress to expose breast and cleavage. Meyers, Weinreich and Saunderson in different writings define identity as how a person views or construes himself or herself in relation to others.[24] Identity is mapped and defined by the self and significant others and relates to what makes one different and/or unique. It is, therefore, common to come across expressions such as self-identity, personal identity, social identity, ethnic identity, religious identity, and gender identity among others.

Identity: The Breast is an Attractive Part of Womanhood; it Differentiates Males from Females

The quotes below were elicited from both the individual interviews and the focus group discussions of the study. The quotations reflect the following themes: identity, femininity and the role of the breast in the construction of feminine beauty.

The female breast shows femininity, it is an attractive part of a woman's body.[25]

My breast is very important to me. It is my powerful asset so I don't joke with it. It is who I am. Even my friends recognize me by the size of my breast so eiii I don't joke with it at all.[26]

The female breast gives a woman an identity. It makes a woman beautiful so to me I think it is an important part of womanhood.[27]

Ooooh, the breast is very important to me. It shows how feminine a woman is. So to me, it is important. I accord it the same importance I give to the other parts of my body.[28]

The breast is a gift from above. It is nature's gift to women. Aside, its evidence of femininity and attractiveness, it is a perfect medium of showing love intimately.[29]

Ten interviewees alluded to the role of the breast in giving women identity. While it made some people pretty and attractive, it was also a sign of femininity. According to 22-year-old Faye, the breast is an important part of her self-identity and she gains recognition and agency from it, mainly because she has big breasts. Breast as a sign of identity also emerged in all five focus group discussions which confirm findings from the individual interviews. This is evidenced in one of the male group discussions as represented below:

Tetteh: Breast differentiates females from males.

Asante: It is an attractive part of the female. It is the first thing you see about a female.

Smart: I support him. It is a catchy aspect of a lady.

Baba: It makes you whole. When it is not there it is like something is missing.

Eddie: It gives an identity.

From the group discussion, both female and male participants acknowledged that breasts make a woman whole, and their absence affects the female identity. This finding resonates with studies that show that breasts give women identity, cultural femininity, and beauty.[30]

The influence of socialization and media in identity acquisition was also explored in this study. Dzramedo argued that traditional fashion is being greatly influenced by socialization and globalization. He observed that there is adulteration in our way of dressing in recent times which to him is unfortunate. According to him, ladies of today have grossly adopted the fashion sense of Westerners reflected in indecent exposure.[31] The adoption of Western ways of dressing portrays Ghanaian youth as Westerners which makes them lose their Ghanaian identity. Buttressing Dzramedo's argument, Boadu intimated that Ghanaian ladies were used to covering up the sensitive parts of their body (including the breasts) which gave them the identity/tag of "*akatasia*" (which means a decently dressed lady). However, the concept of *akatasia* is tainted in recent times with the adaptation of Western ways of dressing by most Ghanaian youth.[32] The relationship between the female breast and female identity was succinctly captured by one participant:

> Right from the word go, we form our identity as women through socialization. We are taught the sociocultural demands of our gender—who a woman is, what makes a woman and how to behave as such. As we progress our identity is further molded and shaped by one powerful agent of socialization, which is the media. We are informed by what we read, see and hear. The constructions attached to the breasts are more highlighted by the media. As we watch movies and music videos, we see celebrities in their provocative dresses showing their breasts and we mimic them and gradually we pick up those practices.[33]

PLACES FOR CLEAVAGE AND BREAST EXPOSURE
VERSUS FUNCTIONS OF BREAST AND CLEAVAGE

The extent to which a woman may expose the breasts depends on social and cultural contexts. Showing cleavage or any part of a female breast may be considered inappropriate or even prohibited depending on the dress code and the setting of the exposure. For instance, displaying much cleavage and exposure of the breast is possible and permitted in settings like parties, clubs, pubs, and beaches but not at church. Interestingly, the exposure of breasts and cleavage has become pervasive. Where such practice was once frowned upon, now the practice has gradually crept in, here and there. An example is the church and funeral grounds. Participants mentioned some of the places where cleavage and breast exposure are trending in modern-day Ghana. Including the places identified above, we can now see cleavage and breast exposure at schools, and social gatherings such as dinners and awards events and even the solemn contexts of the church and at funerals. Thus, argued 22-year-old Lucky, "Initially ladies wore provocative dresses to parties and clubs. Now the practice of breast and cleavage exposure has infiltrated everywhere. You will find them on the streets, social gatherings, and even churches and so on." It is thus suggestive that cleavage and exposure of the breast have become a popular practice among Ghanaian women.

The study further investigated the roles or functions of the breasts in the modern Ghanaian context. Participants identified many functions. The first and foremost function, according to them, is breastfeeding of babies. They also identified the female breast as a secondary sex organ that functions as a sexual stimulant for erotic and sexual pleasure. It is also used to enhance beauty and attractiveness, and for fashion and/or dressing as reflected in one of the focus group discussions:

> Asantewaa: Men love the breast. They normally use it as a pillow and lie on it for relaxation and pleasure.

> Jane: They suck it.

> Lily: It is a playing tool for men. They like to fondle it. Interestingly, children also love it. See how the baby holds the breast firmly when he or she is breastfed by the mother. It is not only men who get aroused when they come into contact with the breast, some women also do.

> Rehana: The breast is a gift from God. It is nature's gift to women. Apart from its evidence of femininity and attractiveness, it is a perfect medium of showing love intimately.

Aishetu: In times of stress the breast serves as a comforting abode. Men and children find solace in the breast. The men use it as a pillow to de-stress, children love to be in the bosom of their mothers.

From the voices of the participants, we can see that the female breast is viewed as a sexual stimulant (SS) or an important female secondary sex organ (FSSO), mainly for the pleasure of men and for the nurturing of babies. The participants' SS and FSSO view corroborate the arguments advanced by the authoritative writer on breast, Marilyn Yalom, who maintained three decades ago that "for most of us and especially for men, breasts are sexual ornaments—the crown jewels of femininity . . . it is an agent of enticement and even aggression."[34] Our data revealed that most men derive erotic pleasure from seeing a woman's breasts. Thus, the breast does not just attract but aids in sexual intimacy. These assertions were also confirmed by the fifteen men involved in the study through group discussions. According to most of them, the breast is used for "breastfeeding and for sexual stimulation." Though anthropological literature reveals that the female breast in traditional African societies was not associated with sexual connotations,[35] the same cannot be said of contemporary times as reflected in the voices of the participants in this study.

PERCEPTIONS ABOUT WOMEN WHO EXPOSE THEIR BREAST AND CLEAVAGE

Leary and Tangney view identity as a label that is best construed relationally and contextually. Identification, therefore, derives from a process and is based on both self and group perceptions. Identity could be positive, negative, or destructive. Similarly, in this study, perceptions about women who expose their cleavage and parts of their breasts were explored. Most of the perceptions were negative with a few positive ones. Response to the question on perceptions about women who dress to expose their breast or cleavage revealed the following from Faye who often dressed to expose her breast:

> To me it is beautiful seeing a woman's breast, it is sooo nice, especially when the lady is fair or light in complexion and smears the exposed breast with a little oil, oooh my God it is nice and attractive. They look hot and sexy. For me, I admire it and that is why I dress like that.[36]

Faye did not only admire dressing that exposes breasts or cleavage but also wore them herself. She added that her boyfriend admired her for her style of dressing and display of cleavage. This assertion by Faye brings to the fore the dramaturgical perspective. Whatever the setting of the front stage behavior is, actors are mindful of how audiences perceive them and what they expect. This knowledge, therefore, tells the actors how to behave. Now, Faye feels comfortable in dresses that expose her breast and cleavage partly because there is some form of favorable sanction from the boyfriend. Faye's position further reflects the global lens and admiration of the breast as a sexual and feminine tool.[37]

Another female participant, Dela, also wore cleavage-exposing dresses even though she was aware of the societal disapproval of such dressing and its associated negative labeling. She said, "Hmm, people say we are immoral but that is not true. The fact that I wear such dresses does not make me immoral. It will shock you that some who don't dress like that are worse off when it comes to morality."[38] Twenty-two years old Sweetie supported Dela's view by remarking, "Well I would say people see us be of weak morals. They call us prostitutes, uncultured, and all sorts of bad names. Ghanaians are hypocrites. They take delight in insulting people so for me, I don't care." Another participant, Naadu, brought a very interesting dimension to the discussion when she labeled women who wear clothes that expose cleavage or breasts as frustrated women in search of partners or husbands. She observed that "the first thing that comes to my mind is that they are frustrated ladies. They are looking for men. What they forget is that the men are not interested in women who expose their breasts. They sleep with them and they don't marry them. So me I pity such women."[39]

The labels "hot and sexy," "immoral," "prostitutes," and "uncultured" emerged in the group discussions as well. The majority of the participants including those who dress to reveal cleavage and breast observed that Ghanaians look down upon such women and perceive them negatively. From both group and individual discussions, such ladies were labeled prostitute, cheap and available girls, sluts, easy to get, immoral, indecent, and uncouth, as evidenced by a female group discussion:

Asantewaa: I see such women as illiterates.

Peggy: I see them as prostitutes.

Barbie: To me they are uncultured, how can properly groomed ladies dress like that?

The foregoing demonstrates the extent to which most Ghanaians are unreceptive to the emerging culture of breast and cleavage exposure among young ladies.

CATEGORY OF WOMEN WHO EXPOSE THEIR BREASTS

Participants categorized women who expose their breasts and cleavage into single ladies, fair or light-skinned women, youth, celebrities, and few mature women. Generally, participants were of the view that all categories of women are associated with the practice of breast and cleavage exposure. They were, however, of the view that the practice is more prevalent among single or unmarried ladies who are desirous of getting male partners and marriage. It was also viewed as a common practice among fair or light-skinned women, youth including students and celebrities. They identified old or elderly women as the last category of women involved in the practice. Thus argued 21 year old Fatima, "I think single ladies, fair ladies and uneducated ladies are often involved in this practice . . . if you are light-skinned and you expose it, especially, when it is smeared with oil, the breasts become beautiful and attractive and people will know that yes you are endowed." There was however a lone dissenting voice. Abimarley, who articulated strongly that all categories of women wear cleavage or expose parts of their breasts said, "All women, whether educated, single, noneducated, young, old, all categories of women do it."

Cleavage exposure has implications for female appearance. As intimated by Karbani et al., women, especially singles, invest more in their appearance because there is a strong affective sexual market, where women are in competition with one another for the attention of men.[40] Regardless of that assertion, the general impression about women who wear cleavage or expose their breasts is not positive. Nevertheless, 19 year old Pinky argues against judging women who use cleavage exposure to enhance their appearance: "I don't judge. I don't know the reason why someone will wear a particular dress so I don't judge. However, people usually insult them as immoral and indecent."

Boadu's argument presented earlier in the chapter coupled with the concept of "*akatasia*," which prevails among Ghanaians, show the traditional abhorrence of breast and cleavage exposure as well as the exposure of other sensitive body parts in the country. On the contrary, cultural practices such as the "dipo" puberty rites among the Krobos permits young women during such rites to expose their breasts to signify womanhood and the fulfillment of custom.[41] Also, it is a common and acceptable practice to see women who breastfeed, exposing their breasts to feed their babies in both public and private spaces. It is also common in most rural areas to see elderly women moving about with their flabby and sagging breasts exposed even though their lower body parts are covered with cloth. Such exposure is acceptable and not associated with any eroticism or sexualization. This presupposes that context is key in the meanings and interpretations of breast and cleavage exposure.

As reflected in the voices of the participants, women who wear cleavage are often perceived negatively. So why would some women opt for such a dress code when society disapproves of it? This question takes us to the rational choice theory which argues that people are aware of the consequences of the choices they make but choose one option over the other. This implies that decisions made by a person on a particular option are informed by a conscious cost and benefit analysis of available options. For many of the women in our study, the anticipated benefits and satisfaction with exposing their breasts and cleavage far outweigh the cost. As 20-year-old Peggy argued, "I don't see anything wrong in exposing the breast or cleavage. It is a matter of comfortability and choice. We all have motives for doing what we do."

AGENCY VERSUS SUBJUGATION

Agency and subjugation are sometimes viewed paradoxically. While *agency* reflects a form of power, autonomy, will, choice, determination, and intentionality,[42] *subjugation* represents a picture of submission, repression, disempowerment, and dispossession.[43] Both concepts are examined in the exploration of cleavage and breast exposure as well as breast size and their relationship with power and humiliation among university students. A common view that participants expressed is that the size of a woman's breasts can either empower (give her self-esteem) or suppress her (feels quite humiliated/ uncomfortable). On the surface, the participants' views about the size of a woman's breasts may create an impression of standard breast size for women. But as Spiegel and Sebesta explain, there is nothing like one size fits all when it comes to breasts:

> On real women, I've seen breasts that are as varied as faces: breasts shaped like tubes, breasts shaped like tears, breasts that flop down, breasts that point up, breasts that are dominated by thick, dark nipples and areolae, breasts with nipples so small and pale they looked airbrushed.[44]

Breast sizes differ among women. Generally, participants showed a preference for big breasts and disliked small or flat breasts. Few participants admired medium-sized breasts. A common reason assigned by the majority who preferred big size breasts is that sizable breasts are a mark of beauty and a sign of femininity. There was also a preference for firm and pointed breasts (ones that have not sagged), popularly known as *bobi stand*. The participants felt that *bobi stand* tend to attract men and make such women more preferable. Women endowed with big to medium breasts are regarded as feminine by both men and women. In contrast, participants were of the view that women with small breasts usually suffer from an inferiority complex and humiliation. A participant from one of the focus groups lamented as follows:

> I am beautiful and I know I am beautiful, but one thing that makes my beauty incomplete is the size of my breasts. I have small breasts and my peers tease me. Sometimes I feel awkward when my partner keeps staring at ladies with big boobs and those who have exposed their breasts. . . . My observation and interaction with him suggest he fancy (sic) sizeable breasts. Well, I don't have money to go for surgery, but at least I can afford push-up bras to elevate and exaggerate my breast size. Wearing the push-up bras and low-necked dresses which reveal my cleavage and a bit of my breast, I would say is icing on the cake. It feels good since now I get attention not only from my partner but from other people.[45]

Another interviewee who has big sized breasts and feels empowered by her assets argued that "large breasts are beautiful. . . . for me, my partner always tells me he gets aroused by the size of my breasts. He says I 'kill' him especially when I show some skin, I guess you know what I mean. It is a good feeling as a woman [laughs in excitement]. So, having big breasts is good."[46]

From the voices of participants, as exemplified by Javanee and Samantha, it is obvious that breast size can either give a lady agency or subjugation. It is perhaps in this context that Fredrick et al. argue that the generality of the medium- to large-size breasts as preferred choices has led to women's concerns about their breast size and shape, thereby affecting their self-esteem, feelings of attractiveness, and sense of femininity. There are social recognition and general linkage between a woman's breasts and her self-confidence, personal well-being and social worth. In addition to concerns about the size of their breasts, women may also worry about the shape of their breasts. Furthermore, the preference of their romantic partner influences women's attitudes about their breasts. A woman's breast size can also be an asset in the field of sales and marketing. It can gain her advertising opportunities and the like—which is agentic. Typical examples of some Ghanaian women who have gained agency from the size of their breasts are Pamela Odame and Queen Patricia.[47] Endowed with large breasts, these ladies have branded themselves as Instagram models, flaunting their assets on Ghanaian social media. They have become internet sensations with a large following. Due to their large following on social media, they are often featured in advertisements, movies, and social events. They are often interviewed to find out about their lifestyles and how they manage all the positive and negative sensationalism that come with having large breasts. Due to the popularity they are enjoying, there is seemingly a rivalry between the two as to who is the most endowed and who has a larger fan base.

Cleavage display and breast exposure connote both choice and a kind of stage performance or drama where the exposure of the breast could be intended, as a woman flaunts her breasts, as an asset that has intrinsic and extrinsic value. The few participants who showed a preference for small and medium-size breasts thought that gravity acts on large breasts and facilitates breast sagging which is not attractive.

> I like medium breasts. Medium breasts are beautiful. I think those with medium breasts feel comfortable when they wear a dress. Sometimes big breasted women are teased. Although I am busty, I like medium size breasts. They are cute and attractive.[48]

During the focus group discussion, one male also argued in favor of small and medium-size breasts: "I prefer small and medium-sized breasts. They are cute and easy to handle. They do not sag. They are attractive and look good. Big breasts sag easily and look chubby."[49] The reasons assigned by the participants for their preference for small and medium-size breasts concurs with Oduro's study on beauty constructs among young people in Ghana. Her study revealed that ladies with very large boobs were often teased and given names such as "chesty balls," "*kosoro kobo*" (heavy top over down), "seeing chest before face," among others. The dynamics of agency and subjugation concerning breast size is quite interesting. This is because what is perceived as desirable is relative and context driven.

On the question of cultural preferences in terms of breast size, participants were divided in their views. Many were unsure if there was a traditional/cultural preference while a few thought that Ghanaian culture has a preference for medium-sized breasts against extremely large breasts. Indeed, this finding corroborates Oduro's doctoral research on embodiment among Ghanaian youth in which she articulated the preference for medium-size breasts in Ghanaian society.[50] Oduro, however, states that the preference for medium-sized breasts in traditional Ghanaian society is gradually giving way to preference for bigger breasts because of social change, Western influence, and growing celebrity culture. In Oduro's view, whereas Ghanaian women with larger breasts were traditionally teased and some carried negative self-images, many now have positive self-images and are thankful for their God-given assets which some flaunt in cleavage-enhancing clothes locally known as *mahye dwa*.[51] It is now common to see local stars and influential women in boob-exposing clothes on television and at public gatherings in Ghana.

The change from medium-sized to bigger breasts, according to some participants, has a relationship with the wearing of cleavage and breast exposing clothes. To them, it is a sign of social change and Western influence acquired from the media, especially from telenovelas and other TV series.

This development, they argue, has contributed to cases of moral degeneration which is a challenge to Ghanaian norms and culture. As Dzramedo succinctly argues, the clothing pattern of the youth of today relegates modesty in Ghanaian culture to the background. For example, a few years ago, wearing clothes that exposed sensitive parts of a lady's body like breasts triggered a moral outcry in the country's various cultural settings. However, it is now being adopted. Dzramedo further argues that these changes are signs of deep cultural and moral degradation in Ghanaian society because the concept of *akatasia* is being replaced by nakedness which is disappointing to the adult population.

The practice of cleavage and breast exposure may be associated with both positive and negative outcomes. As articulated by Swami and Tovee, the female breast is the strongest cultural symbol of beauty. It is often equated with physical attractiveness.[52] It is also a well-established fact that being beautiful or physically attractive confers many advantages on a person. Physical attractiveness has important social outcomes, especially for women. Attractive women are more likely to attract attention from others, have higher chances of getting suitors, receiving favors, being picked in interviews, among others. Thus, there is some agency in showing cleavage and exposing breasts in some situations. These notwithstanding, Berberick and Fredrick et al. contend that showing cleavage and breast exposure has contributed to the objectification and sexualization of the female body, especially in the media.[53] The depiction of women in the media has been manipulative and reflects sexual exploitation. This has created some form of humiliation and devaluation of women when they are measured by just their assets instead of their abilities and potentials. It is therefore not surprising when Ofori et al. cited an unfortunate incident in 2005, in which one of Ghana's top female artists who was known to be fond of exposing parts of her body or showing some skin was stripped naked by some male students after her performance in one of Ghana's male-dominated universities—the Kwame Nkrumah University of Science and Technology in Kumasi.[54]

Despite public outcry, few Ghanaians sympathized with the artist, claiming she deserved the treatment meted out to her because of her indecent way of dressing. Her cleavage exposure was considered an affront to the Ghanaian cultural value of decent dressing which is characterized by the concept of *akatasia*. While the attack from the students and some members of the public on the artist was uncalled for, it reflects Ghanaian society's abhorrence for indecent dressing and the possible risks associated with such public presentation of the self. Thus, in conforming to fashion trends, some women risk suffering from abuse, even though such abuse is unwarranted. Generally, cleavage and breast exposure as well as exposure of other sensitive parts of the female body tend to attract much backlash in Ghanaian society. It is common to come across media headlines such as "a boob gone too far," "of very low-cut necklines," "exposed cleavages," "bare backs and thighs," "women's bodies not for sale," and "Chief warns against the indecent dressing and breast exposure at festival," and "*apuskeleke*" phenomenon of breast exposure must stop."[55] Such media headlines support the social disapproval of exposure and cleavage.

Finally, the study elicited views from participants on whether breast exposure and cleavage should be continued or stopped. The following were the responses:

> I think cleavage and breast exposure should be encouraged. We have the freedom to do what we like. It is fashion and if you like it, you wear it. Why must our society curtail our freedom of putting on what we want?[56]

> People should learn to mind their own business and stop naming and labeling women who wear cleavage or display a bit of breasts.[57]

> I don't support cleavage or exposure of any sensitive body part. I think we copied such things from the televisions that we watch. The movies, telenovelas, etc. Ladies who dress like that should be shamed and labeled.[58]

From the above, whereas some held neoliberal views of freedom of expression reflected in dressing, others called for the eradication or control of such dressing.

CONCLUSION

As we saw from the data, the female breast and the showing of cleavage and parts of the breast have different meanings and interpretations for different people. As Frederick et al. articulate, women's breasts are imbued with social, cultural, and political meanings. The female breast is perceived as a marker of womanhood, a visual signifier of female sexualization, synonymous with femininity, and a sign of age, sexual maturity, and fertility. Thus, the meanings and interpretations associated with breast and cleavage exposure, particularly the size of one's breasts, gave some of the participants' agency and identity while disempowering and subjugating others. Further exploration of this area of study is encouraged as it will provide a sociological understanding of the behavior and lifestyle of young women in Ghana. This would aid educators, counselors, parents and youth workers by providing valuable information about young women's lifestyles, values and influences especially in this era of globalization, social change and extreme media influence. Additional research in this area would also help researchers to recognize the transitional and dualistic cultural context within which Ghana is positioned where tradition lives side by side with modernity. Those who stick to the traditional mode of living/dressing live side by side with those who have been acculturated into the Western lifestyle by way of globalization.

Based on the conclusion above, one key question arises: What are the implications or lessons for wearing cleavage and breast exposure for young ladies, society at large, policy and further research? While we acknowledge that the small size of our participants may not warrant a generalized conclusion, our conclusions are relevant to policy decisions. The in-depth nature of our study and the combination of two methods (interviews and group discussions) have given us very revealing and insightful data. The voices touched on identities, agency and subjugation from the perspective and voices of university students. The study is timely and relevant because whereas the practice of breast exposure and cleavage is popular among young women in Ghana, no known scientific study has been conducted on the subject. It contributes to the literature and discourse on popular culture and embodiment. Additionally, an elicitation into the sociocultural meanings and perceptions about breast exposure and cleavage is important for purposes of counseling, beauty constructs and self-image, education and community sensitization.

NOTES

1. Marilyn Yalom, *History of the breast* (Hoboken, NJ: Ballantine Books, 1997), 275.

2. Samantha Brett, The Great Cleavage Conundrum: should men look if it's on display? http://www.smh.com.au/lifestyle/life/blogs/ask-sam/the-great-cleavage-conundrum-should-men-look-if-its-on-display-20120215-1t5cx.html.

3. Sarah E. Reynolds, "Boobs out! A perspective on fashion, sexuality and equality," *Art and Design Review* 5, (2017): 115–128. doi.org/10.4236/adr.2017.52009.

4. Frederick, David A., Peplau, Anne, and Lever, Janet. 2008. "The barbie mystique: Satisfaction with breast size and shape across the lifespan." *International Journal of Sexual Health* 20 no. 3.

5. Patricia Stuart-Macadam and Katherine Dettwyler, *Breast feeding: biocultural perspectives* (New York: Aldine De Gruyter, 1995).

6. Stuart-Macadam and Dettwyler, *Breast feeding,* 171.

7. Yehoda Matei, "Effect of socio-cultural beliefs on late stage presentation of breast cancer among Ghanaian women," Digital library, Yale School of Medicine, 2011.

8. Priscilla Akua Boakye, "A rite of passage among the Krobos of Eastern Region of Ghana," MA thesis, University of Tromso, Norway, 2010.

9. Deborah Boadu, "Indecent dressing and its effects on the morals and cultural ethics of Ghana. In the case of ladies evening wear," PhD thesis, Takoradi Polytechnic, 2011.

10. Peacefmonline, "Otiko's cleavage causes stir in parliament," November 16, 2017, https://www.peacefmonline.com.

11. Ghanaweb, "Actress displays her breasts in front of Nana Addo," July 3, 2017, https://www.ghanaweb.com.

12. See Maura Spiegel and Lithe Sebesta, *The breast book: Attitude, perceptions, envy, and etiquette* (New York: Workmen, 2000); Yalom, *History of the Breast*, 1997.

13. Nana Afia Karikari, "Exploring the socio-cultural interpretations of breast cancer and the coping strategies of patients at the Cape Coast Teaching Hospital," MA thesis, University of Cape Coast, 2018; Alice Asobayire and Ruth Barley, "Women's cultural perceptions and attitudes towards breast cancer: Northern Ghana," *Oxford Journals* (2014): 8–20; Solomon Sika-Bright and Georgina Yaa Oduro, "Exclusive breastfeeding practices of mothers in Duakor, a traditional migrant community in Cape Coast, Ghana," *Journal of Global Initiatives: Policy, Pedagogy, Perspective* 8, no.1 (2013): 87–102.

14. Michael Hechter and Satoshi Kanazawa, "Sociological rational choice theory," *Annual Reviews of Sociology* 23, no. 1 (1997): 191–214.

15. Michael Hechter and Satoshi Kanazawa, "Sociological rational choice theory," *Annual Reviews of Sociology* 23, no. 1 (1997): 191–214.

16. Hechter and Kanazawa, "Sociological rational choice theory," (1997), 191–214.

17. Erving Goffman, *The presentation of self in everyday life* (New York: Doubleday, 1956).

18. See also George Ritzer, *Contemporary sociological theory and its classical roots: The basics* (New York: McGraw-Hill, 2007).

19. Population and Housing Census, 2010 (Ghana Statistical Service, Accra).

20. National Council for Tertiary Education, 2018.

21. University of Cape Coast, Home Page, 2019, https://www.ucc.edu.gh/homepage.

22. Matthew B. Miles, Michael A. Huberman, and Johnny Saldana, *Qualitative data analysis: A methods handbook and the coding manual for qualitative researchers* (Thousand Oaks, CA: SAGE, 2014), 381.

23. Amanda Coffey and Paul Atkinson, *Making sense of qualitative data: Complementary research strategies* (London: Sage, 1996).

24. Diana Tietjens Meyers, *Being yourself: essays on identity, action, and social life. Feminist constructions* (Lanham, MD: Rowman & Littlefield, 2004); Peter Weinreich and Saunderson Weinreich, *Analysing Identity: Cross-Cultural, societal and clinical contexts* (London: Routledge, 2003).

25. Pinky, 19 years, female, in a relationship.

26. Faye, 22 years, female, in a relationship.

27. Abimarley, 21 years, female, single.

28. Naadu, 23 years, single.

29. Sweetie, 22 years, female, in a relationship.

30. Samuel Mantey Ofori Dei, "Contextual and individual level determinants of breast cancer screening intention among women in Ghana." MA thesis, University of Lethbridge, Canada, 2013; Asobayire and Barley, "Women's cultural perceptions and attitudes towards breast cancer," 2014.

31. Bernard Edem Dzramedo, "Clothing and Fashion in Ghanaian Culture: A case study among the Akans," PhD thesis, Kwame Nkrumah University of Science and Technology, Ghana, 2009.

32. Deborah Boadu, "Indecent dressing and its effects on the morals and cultural ethics of Ghana. In the case of ladies evening wear," PhD diss., Takoradi Polytechnic, 2011.

33. Dela, 19 years, single.

34. Yalom, *History of the Breast*, 3.

35. Stuart-Macadam and Dettwyler, *Breast feeding*, 1997.

36. Mark R. Leary and June Price Tangney, *Handbook of self and identity* (New York: Guilford Press, 2003); Faye, 22, in a relationship.

37. Yalom, *History of the Breast*, 1997.

38. Dela, 19 years, single.

39. Naadu, 23 years, single.

40. Karbani et al., "Culture, attitude and knowledge about breast cancer and preventive measures: A qualitative study of South Asian breast cancer patients in the UK," *Asian Pacific Journal Cancer Prevention* 12, no. 6 (2011): 1619–1626.

41. Ankomah, Augustine, "Ghana," *The International Encyclopedia of Sexuality, 1 Argentina to Greece* (New York: Continuum, 1997).

42. Mustafa Emirbayer and Ann Mische, "What is Agency?" *American journal of Sociology* 103 (1998): 962–1023.

43. Christina N. Baker, "Images of women's sexuality in advertisements: A content analysis of black and white oriented women's and men's magazines." *Sex Roles* 52 no.1 (2005): 13–27.

44. Natalie Angier in Spiegel and Sebesta,10.

45. Javanne, 21 years, in a relationship.

46. Samantha, 20 years, in a relationship.

47. See https://www.ghanaweb.com-entertainment.news.

48. Naadu, 23 years, single.

49. Solo, male, 23 years, focus group discussion.

50. Georgina Yaa Oduro, PhD diss., "Gender Relations, Sexuality and HIV/AIDS Education: A study of Ghanaian Youth cultures," submitted to University of Cambridge, UK, 2010.

51. It means I am marketing or have put my wares on sale.

52. Viren Swami and Martin J. Tove′e, "Resource security impacts men's female breast size preferences," PLoS ONE 8 no. 3, 2013: e57623. doi:10.1371/journal.pone.0057623.

53. Stephanie Nicholl Berberick, "The objectification of women in mass media: Female self-image in misogynist culture," *The New York Sociologist* (2010): 5.

54. Ida Ofori, Albie Mensah, Franics Amenakpor, and Paul Goddey Gablah, "Perceptions of University of Ghana students towards campus female fashion," *Arts and Design Studies* 25 (2014), www.iiste.org.

55. *The Ghanaian Weekly Spectator*, 2012; *Daily Graphic*, 2013.

56. Pinky, 19 years, in a relationship.

57. Rehana, 24 years, in a relationship.

58. Baaba, 21 years, focus group discussion data.

BIBLIOGRAPHY

Ankomah, Augustine. "Ghana." In *The International Encyclopedia of Sexuality. Vol. 1 Argentina to Greece,* edited by Robert. T. Francoeur. New York: Continuum, 1997.

Asobayire, Alice, and Ruth Barley. "Women's cultural perceptions and attitudes towards breast cancer: Northern Ghana." *Oxford Journals* (2014): 8–20.

Baker, Christina, N. "Images of women's sexuality in advertisements: A content analysis of black and white oriented women's and men's magazines." *Sex Roles* 52, no.1 (2005):13–27.

Berberick, Stephanie Nicholl. "The objectification of women in mass media: Female self-image in misogynist culture." *The New York Sociologist* no. 5 (2010): 1–15.

Boadu, Deborah. "Indecent dressing and its effects on the morals and cultural ethics of Ghana. In the case of ladies evening wear." PhD diss., Takoradi Polytechnic, 2011.

Boakye, Priscilla Akua. "A rite of passage among the Krobos of Eastern Region of Ghana." MA thesis, University of Tromso, Norway, 2010.Brett, Samantha. The Great Cleavage Conundrum: should men look if it's on display? 2012. http://www.smh.com.au/lifestyle/life/blogs/ask-sam/the-great-cleavage-conundrum-should-men-look-if-its-on-display-20120215-1t5cx.html.

Coffey, Amanda, and Atkinson, Paul. *Making sense of qualitative data: Complementary research strategies.* London: Sage, 1996.

Dei, Samuel Mantey Ofori. "Contextual and individual level determinants of breast cancer screening intention among women in Ghana." MA thesis, University of Lethbridge, Canada, 2013.

Dzramedo, Bernard Edem. "Clothing and Fashion in Ghanaian Culture: A case study among the Akans." PhD diss., 2009. Kwame Nkrumah University of Science and Technology, Ghana.

Emirbayer, Mustafa, and Ann Mische. "What is Agency?" *American journal of Sociology* 103 (1998): 962–1023.

Frederick, David A., Anne Peplau, and Janet Lever. "The barbie mystique: Satisfaction with breast size and shape across the lifespan." *International Journal of Sexual Health* 20, no. 3. (2008): 200–211.

Ghanaweb. "Actress displays her breasts in front of Nana Addo." July 3, 2017. https://www.ghanaweb.com.

Goffman, Erving. *Frame analysis: An essay on the organization of experience.* Cambridge, MA: Harvard University Press, 1974.

Goffman, Erving. *The presentation of self in everyday life.* New York: Doubleday, 1956.

Hechter, Michael, and Kanazawa, Satoshi. "Sociological rational choice theory." *Annual Reviews of Sociology* 23 no. 1 (1997): 191–214.

Karbani, Gulshan, Lim, Jennifer N., Hewison, Jenny, Atkin, Karl, Horgan, Kieran, Lansdown, Mark, and Chu, Carol E. "Culture, attitude and knowledge about breast cancer and preventive measures: A qualitative study of South Asian breast cancer patients in the UK." *Asian Pacific Journal Cancer Prevention* 12, no. 6 (2011): 1619–1626.

Karikari, Nana Afia. "Exploring the socio-cultural interpretations of breast cancer and the coping strategies of patients at the Cape Coast Teaching Hospital." MA thesis, 2018. University of Cape Coast.

Leary, Mark R., and June Price Tangney. *Handbook of self and identity.* New York: Guilford Press, 2003.

Martei, Yehoda M. "Effect of socio-cultural beliefs on late-stage presentation of breast cancer among Ghanaian women." Yale Medicine Thesis Digital Library, 1576.

Meyers, Diana Tietjens. *Being yourself: essays on identity, action, and social life. Feminist constructions.* Lanham, MD: Rowman & Littlefield, 2004.

Miles, Matthew B. and Huberman, Michael A. *Qualitative data analysis: An expanded sourcebook,* 2nd ed. London: Sage, 1994.

Modernghana. "Popular Counsellor in Ghana brands women who expose their breast and cleavages as prostitutes. January 14, 2018. https://www.modernghana.com.

Oduro, Georgina Yaa. "Beauty in space and time: The changing construction of beauty among Ghanaian youth." In *Cosmetic, Aesthetic, Prophetic: Beyond the Boundaries of Beauty*, edited by Alberto Ferreira and Lucy Moyse, 71–84. Leiden: Inter-Disciplinary Press, 2016.

Oduro, Georgina Yaa. "Gender relations, sexuality and HIV/AIDS education: A study of Ghanaian youth voices." PhD thesis, University of Cambridge-UK, 2010.

Ofori, Ida, Albie Mensah, Francis Amenakpor, and Paul Goddey Gablah. "Perceptions of University of Ghana students towards campus female fashion." *Arts and Design Studies* 25 (2014): 19–25.

Peacefmonline. "Otiko's cleavage causes stir in parliament." November 16, 2017. https://www.peacefmonline.com.

Ratner, Carl. "Agency and Culture." *Journal for The Theory of Social Behavior* 30 (2000): 413–434.

Reynolds, Sarah E. "Boobs out! A perspective on fashion, sexuality and equality." *Art and Design Review* 5 (2017): 115–128.

Ritzer, George. *Contemporary sociological theory and its classical roots: The basics.* New York: McGraw-Hill, 2007.

Sika-Bright, Solomon, and Georgina Yaa Oduro. "Exclusive breastfeeding practices of mothers in Duakor, a traditional migrant community in Cape Coast, Ghana." *Journal of Global Initiatives: Policy, Pedagogy, Perspective* 8, no.1 (2013): 87–102.

Spiegel, Maura, and Lithe Sebesta. *The breast book: Attitude, perceptions, envy and etiquette.* New York: Workman Publishing Co., 2002.

Stuart-Macadam, Patricia, and Katherine A. Dettwyler. *Breast feeding: biocultural perspectives.* New York: Aldine De Gruyter, 1995.

Swami, Viren, and Martin Tove´e J. "Resource security impacts men's female breast size preferences." *PLoS ONE* 8 no. 3 (2013): e57623. DOI:10.1371/journal.pone.0057623.

UCC. "Home page." March 11, 2019. https://www.ucc.edu.gh/homepage.

Weinreich, Peter, and Wendy Saunderson, eds. *Analysing Identity: Cross-Cultural, societal and clinical contexts.* London: Routledge, 2003.

Yalom, Marilyn. *History of the breast.* New York: Ballantine Books, 1998.

Chapter 3

Reflections of Women: Post-Divorce Experiences

Naa Adjeley Suta Alakija-Sekyi and Alex Somuah Obeng

One of the key social issues trending in family studies in recent years is rising divorce rates. Much of the research focuses on one or two aspects of divorce, namely its causes and impact on children. According to research on marriages, the instability in marriages is caused by factors such as kinship and family structure, family size and infertility, social disorder arising from urbanization and modernization, rising women's autonomy, religion, and individual characteristics.[1] Some researchers such as Anarfi and Awusabo-Asare have argued that the undue influence of the extended family, which sometimes leads to weaker bonds and subordinate relationships between couples, could be the major cause of marital instabilities in Ghana.[2]

Other scholars have looked at the impact of divorce on parents, children and society at large. Most of the work done in the West indicates that women and children are the most affected during and after the breakup because of their susceptibility to multiple situations in society. Women and children are, therefore, considered the main victims of divorce.[3] Nevertheless, the extent of the impact on women and children would be dependent on diverse conditional factors such as gender, age at the time of divorce, the socioeconomic status of the custodial household, religion, remarriage, environmental changes, and support system, among others.[4] The impact of divorce on divorcees, especially as it relates to supporting systems and divorcee survival strategies, has not received as much scholarly attention.[5] Some researchers have highlighted the significance of family post-divorce. Froma Walsh, for example, indicated that the supportive roles played by family members go a long way to help in their recovery post-divorce.[6] Others found that emotional support toward divorcees, which comes in the form of empathy and understanding from family members, made divorcees feel loved and cared for.[7]

In Ghana, researchers have indicated that there is an uptick in the divorce rate, but there is little research and analysis on divorcees.[8] This chapter is based on a study that attempts to bridge the gap by examining the availability of support for divorced women against the backdrop of their post-divorce experiences within families.[9]

THEORETICAL FRAMEWORK

This study used the family systems theory and its eight interlocking concepts, propounded by Murray Bowen, to explore the experiences of divorced women in Ghana.[10] The theory suggests that we cannot fully understand people if we separate them from one another. Rather, the theory suggests that individuals within a family must be understood as part of a group since the family is a group of people with an emotional attachment. These groups of people are interconnected and thus depend on each other for survival. In view of this, a member cannot be understood when separated from the group or the system. The emotional connectedness helps ensure strong bonding and cooperation between members of the system to provide such things as security, accommodation, and food for survival. However, there is also the likelihood of misunderstandings or problems which can come up among members and can lead to complications within the system. This can result in anxiety among members which may eventually lead to stressful situations leading to isolation and disunity. Bowen posited that individual members of the system have roles to play and rules to follow. Thus, all members are answerable to each other by virtue of their roles as agreed to by the group. Bowen further mentioned that a change in the conduct of one person is normally in response to a change in the behavior of another and so to ensure stability and equilibrium, there is the need for members to maintain a similar pattern of conduct within the family. When members are not able to or refuse to maintain the same behavioral pattern over a given period, the system becomes dysfunctional.[11]

Relating the family systems theory to this study gives the reader a deeper understanding of why families may not support divorced members. The divorced women in this study, as members of a system, were not supported by their families for seven reasons. These include: 1) refusing to try and work it out with a spouse, 2) bringing shame to the family, 3) viewing the marriage as beneficial to family and so the family felt there was no need for a breakup, 4) refusing to share the marital wealth with family, 5) coming back to the family as a poor person, 6) being disapproved by the family and finally, 7) the issue of nuclearization or individualism. From the above reasons, it was obvious that women were expected to help maintain the system by not going against the agreements of the system. Women were supposed to maintain the connection in the family by obeying parents, calling family members on the phone, visiting, or even financially supporting members of the family. Their refusal to do these things created disequilibrium. In other words, they disconnected themselves from the system. These actions led to a dysfunctional family system because of the disequilibrium created. Divorcees shared that family members distanced themselves from them during the time the women needed family members most. As the family systems theory posits, a change in behavior of a member of the system comes about as a response to a change in the attitude of a member. This change may bring about complications and eventually disunity and separation. The family systems theory, therefore, helped to explain the actions of family members of divorced women.

DYNAMICS OF MARRIAGE AND DIVORCE IN GHANA

Marriage is seen as a very significant institution in traditional societies in Africa. However, the process of marriage varies among ethnic groups. Marriage is contracted based on a host of factors including the religious and ethnic background of spouses. Marriages contracted under Islamic laws and the ordinances are legally recognized. Since marriage is a rite of passage, a ceremony is performed so that the couple is accepted by society, as husband and wife. In Ghanaian cultures, before this ceremony, there is an agreement by the parties to live together as husband and wife; consent to marry is sought from both families before the ceremony can take place. At the end of this process, members of both sides of the union are ready to come together as two families who will acknowledge and recognize each other as in-laws. In Ghana, the ceremony varies from one ethnic group to the other based on the requirements and the process; however, there are similarities such as the provision of head drink, a dowry and the bride-to-be acceptance of items brought for the ceremony by the man's family. The most important thing is that there is acceptance by both families and a legal agreement of the union. If anything goes wrong after tying the knot, a few key people on both sides of the family are supposed to come together to either ensure that peace prevails or dissolve the marriage if need be.

DIVORCE AND FAMILY SUPPORT

Divorce is one of life's events that can negatively or positively influence divorcees, their children and their families and friends. In other words, divorce brings about changes in the lives of individuals as well as their social networks.[12] Most divorcees lose their friends and family during and after divorce. However, some manage to get the support of family members to withstand post-divorce experiences. In her study of post-divorce experiences of women in Turkey, Kavas observed that women found it hard to adjust to their new status as single women. They had to juggle work and childcare that previously had been one or the other. Instead of turning to nannies to care for children when they were at work, the women reached out to their mothers.[13] One can say that Kavas's subjects were lucky because their mothers were willing to help them adjust to their status as divorcees with childcare responsibilities. Kavas indicated that women had to find ways to manage economic problems, which are intensified with childcare expenses. Listening to women's narratives in Kavas's study, it is possible to see that even though women mention some disadvantages, they emphasized how family aid supported them, particularly with childcare.[14] Due to the issue of trust, women prefer their mothers or close relatives to care for their children, rather than nannies. This allowed them to stay at the office late, if needed, because of the trust they have in their mothers.[15] The mothers then took over the childcare responsibilities at night and on weekends, which gave them more time and energy to spend on their work and career. Family help, therefore, turned out to be better help than they could have from nannies.

Kavas's research is supported by Hongyu Wang and Paul Amato who described the contributions of close family members to divorce adjustment and well-being.[16] Parents and siblings have been found to provide a reliable alliance, sense of companionship, comfort, reassurance of worth, and opportunity for nurturance. However, not all close relations avail themselves of post-divorce support. Because research consistently indicates that close relationships help people make positive post-divorce adjustments, an examination of how the divorce experience connects with these relationships may enhance our understanding of post-divorce adjustment processes. Anecdotal evidence from Ghana shows that in most cases when people marry and relocate from their hometowns to the city or other places, they are expected to support the family financially when things are going well, especially the less fortunate members by way of occasional remittance, contributions toward repairs and funerals as well as sending items from the city to the village. In other cases, they may also support nieces or nephews by helping with school fees.

METHODOLOGY

This discussion comes from a study that sought to explore the experiences of nineteen divorced women in the Cape Coast metropolis to determine why they were not supported by family members following their divorce. The study adopted the nonprobability sampling technique to select participants. Specifically, purposive and snowball sampling styles were used in the selection process. These techniques were used because of the special characteristics of participants such as a female divorcee who is still single and not remarried. The snowball technique was used because it helped in building trust between the researcher and participants, mainly because the researchers did not just show up without the consent of participants but were introduced by friends of participants who were also divorced. Thus, the snowball technique helped in recruiting women with similar backgrounds. Participants came from a combination of lower-class, middle-class and upper-class divorced women; however, the majority of the participants were middle-class divorcees. Their ages ranged from thirty-nine to sixty-eight. The participants had been married for a maximum of twenty-eight years and a minimum of five years and had been divorced for a maximum of fourteen years and a minimum of seven years. Two of these women had no children during the marriage; however, the remaining seventeen had children. The ages of their children ranged from nine years to forty-one years. While twelve were still living together with their children, seven were living alone because their children were either married or working elsewhere in a different region. All nineteen had moved on after the divorce and were doing very well, both financially and socially.

Semi-structured in-depth interviews were conducted either in the homes or other locations and the time of the interview was decided on by the participants. The researchers, therefore, make no claim of occupying a privileged and neutral space of an objective interviewer. The researchers sought permission from participants to tape-record the interviews. The tape-recorded interviews were transcribed verbatim. This is because the process of transcription puts the researcher in intimate contact with the words of the informants and allows for continual thematic speculation.[17] The researchers made use of this process by doing all the transcription and taking analytical notes. The data were collected within three months. Participants were asked questions pertaining to their socioeconomic background and post-divorce experiences regarding familial support.

With regard to ethnicity, twelve women were Fante from the Central Region where Cape Coast is the capital city; two were Ewe from the Volta Region, three were Ashanti from the Ashanti Region and two were Nzema from the Western Region. The two Nzema women were previously married to men who were also Nzema while the Ewe, the twelve Fante and three Ashanti were all previously married to Fante men. The educational backgrounds of the women were as varied as their ethnic backgrounds. Several women had attained university degrees in graduate and undergraduate study, with the highest achievement being a doctorate. There were also women with professional graduate degrees in human resources and business administration while others had junior and senior high school certifications. Some worked in the formal sector as professors, high school teachers and secretaries and others in the informal sector as petty traders, hairdressers, fashion designers, and high-class businesswomen. Their salaries ranged from 800 cedis a month ($140) to 6,500 cedis a month ($1,160). Out of the nineteen divorcees interviewed, only four of the cases were filed by ex-husbands; fifteen were filed by the women themselves. Apart from four participants who were not religious, the remaining fifteen were all Christians.

The diversity of the sample is significant. Ghana is multiethnic and multicultural, with matrilineal and patrilineal groups operating within an overarching patriarchal context. The Ashanti and Fante belong to the matrilineal group; Akan and Ewe and Nzema are patrilineal. These differences in descent will reflect differences in the ways that familial relationships and support are carried out.

The researchers are both qualitative Ghanaian researchers and our experiences as Ghanaians guide our methodology and approach to this study. We center the experiences of Ghanaian women, and we not only explore their experiences, but we also acknowledge that our lived experiences as Ghanaians give us a particular lens into the culture.

REASONS FOR NONSUPPORT

Even though social support is expected to be a network of family and friends who are supposed to assist an individual's adaptation to stress, crises, transitions, mental health among others, not all of them perform these functions.[18] There are times when an individual going through a crisis or a stressful situation may not get any support from family or friends. Some researchers have proved that individuals offering social support to divorcees are likely to change following the divorce because they may feel that divorcees were reluctant to heed the advice they gave before, during, or after the divorce.[19] Other studies have shown that support from family may be determined by whether the family members are in favor of the decision to divorce and how they see that decision influencing their own lives. If not in favor of divorce, then the divorcee will not receive any support from family members.[20] That is exactly what happened to the fourteen women in this study who initiated divorce proceedings against their husbands. Even though most of the family members were aware of the divorce, they were not enthused about the decision to divorce. They did not call to check on the divorcees or visit to find out how life was treating them. The family members never showed any form of love to their divorced female relatives. A few of the women, especially the business people and others with less substantial salaries or wages, started having financial challenges after the divorce. They were looking forward to having some sort of financial support from family members whom they had supported previously when they were married and in good standing, but they did not receive such support. Details of the reasons for nonsupport by family members are discussed below under various headings.

REFUSAL TO WORK IT OUT

Refusal to work on improving the marriage is one of the main reasons why some family members did not offer any form of support to the divorced members. Key among them was the idea that participants should have known that marriage would have challenges and so no matter the challenges, they were not supposed to divorce husbands but to ensure their marriages worked. Almost all participants had relatives asking them if they thought marriage was going to be simple and easy. The participants in this category were advised against going ahead with the dissolution because family heads and those involved believed that the women could work it out in various ways without necessarily divorcing; however, the women did not agree to work it out and the families were not impressed with their decisions. In view of this, most family members were reluctant to offer help to their divorced relatives, including parents and siblings in specific cases. One participant, Sewa explained:

> My big sister was one of the people who surprised me. I couldn't believe it when she asked if I thought marriage was all fun and I never expected to have challenges? She told my mother and other siblings to leave me to find solutions to my own problems because no one forced the marriage on me. They all neglected me because I did not agree to stay in the marriage as they advised.

Similarly, Anita reported that,

> I am very disappointed in my family members because of the kind of comments they are making regarding my divorce. Can you believe that my biological mother told me that if I can't make my marriage work then I should not come anywhere near her? And my siblings are all in agreement with her and so they are all saying what they like. . . . I really can't believe what is going on because

they are all very much aware of the challenges I was having in my marriage. . . .
I suspect they don't want me to come and burden them with any of my needs
which I am not thinking of doing. I am ready to fend for myself and my children.

Adjoa and Mansah were equally unhappy with their aunties because
they expected the aunties to know better. Adjoa sounded bitter when she
explained that,

> My mother's sister who has been my mum since my mother died is also a divor-
> cee who has lived for fifteen years without remarrying. Based on the stories she
> shared with me on different occasions when I went to tell her the sad stories
> of my marriage, I know she has a better experience than me and yet she kept
> telling me to endure whatever challenges I was going through in my marriage.
> She warned me not to agree to any divorce if my husband suggests. Because
> I disobeyed her, she has been pretending not to be aware of my divorce and I
> have also decided not to mind her. After all, my life has not come to a standstill.
> I know she is behaving this way because she will no longer have access to the
> land my husband promised her . . . hmmm.

On her part, Mansah indicated that,

> I have been silent on whatever is going on in my family after my divorce
> because I want God to judge my auntie for me because of her hypocrisy. This is
> my auntie who came to take care of me when I had a baby and she saw every-
> thing that went on even during the time I had just delivered. She is the one who
> consoled and encouraged me most of the time when my husband misbehaved
> towards me. Today she tells my uncles and cousins that she doesn't see why I
> should leave my marital home because there is nothing wrong with my husband
> and whatever it is, they should not mind me but tell me to go back and work
> things out myself. I just can't imagine what is happening, but I know God will
> speak. Maybe she thinks I will come back home to take over my room which
> is being occupied by her daughter. . . . I really can't understand her reactions
> towards me.

DIVORCE BRINGS DISGRACE TO THE FAMILY

The notion that divorce brings shame to families is undergirded by gender
expectations in Ghanaian societies. A divorced man may be applauded for
getting rid of a bad wife or may get sympathy when his wife divorces him.
However, a divorced woman doesn't necessarily get similar treatment. Instead,
she may be subjected to endless questioning by family and friends, advised,
judged, and/or ostracized by her religion. Women, in Ghana and elsewhere,

are expected to be submissive, quiet, respectful, etc., and nowhere are these characteristics expected more than in the family. This is particularly true for women who have taken on a role as a wife. Traditionally in Ghana, a good wife brings honor to her husband and natal family; a bad wife reflects poorly on the woman's natal family and could potentially jeopardize the chances of other women in the family getting married. Thus, when some of the divorced women in our study were blamed for bringing shame to their families, the accusers were invoking old ideas about family honor. Four participants, Aseye, Betty, Ekua and Abena fell into this category. Aseye narrated:

Hmmm . . . I am not very happy. I did not inform my parents and other family members about my divorce when the whole problem started but I am certain I did the right thing. I say this because my family believes any female member who divorces is a disgrace to the family and it will have nothing to do with her again because none of their ancestors ever divorced but always advised their daughters to do the best they can to keep their marriages regardless of the challenges they face in marriage. Up until now can you believe they are still not concerned about my divorce. Hmmm. Eiiii . . . my parents still told me to go and undo the divorce if I want to continue to be a member of the family.

Recent news stories in the Ghanaian press have highlighted the plight of women whose families either wanted them to stay in their marriages or did not try to find out what was happening to them until it was too late. The wife of a former member of Parliament revealed her anguish during the period of her divorce. In a lengthy social media post she wrote,

Leave leave leave (sic) but when I left and told my story . . . no one was willing to help in any way because they were "afraid people will say they're encouraging me to divorce." . . . My sister gave me her apartment and collected the rent in full and even harassed me for the money. Never mind that I was struggling with two kids on my own. Everyone called me a drama queen. I was leaving a whole MP because of a few slaps? . . . [But] It wasn't a few slaps; it was full scale beatings for years.[21]

Our research data also provides evidence of the violence that women face in marriages. One of the participants, Aseye, shared that her family takes the marital vow "until death do us part" literally. She recalled the case of her cousin who died in her matrimonial home due to marital violence which her kinsmen refused to help resolve. The family insisted that she stay to work things out. Things did not work out and she died under suspicious circumstances. Betty's family, like Aseye's, believed in staying in a marriage without any support from the family to help with conflicts. Betty states:

As for my family, I never involved them in my dissolution because immediately you get married they consider you a minor member of the family because you have left to form a new association. The only time you will see them around or hear from them is when you give birth or have any happy celebration. You are not permitted to come home and tell them your marriage is not working. They will tell you to go back and make it work because marriage is not rosy but full of ups and downs and you must make it work without bringing shame to the family. In fact, unlike other families where parents will either invite the man over or plan meeting the man in his house for discussions which will either help save the situation or end the marriage, my family will do contrary and so knowing this, I went through it with my church elders and friends because of their insensitive nature to marital issues.

Ekua and Abena have superstitious relatives, especially their grandparents, who believe that since none of their forebears divorced, dissolution of marriage is a shameful act that will bring ancestral curses to the rest of the family members, particularly if Ekua and Abena were accepted back as divorced members. In Ekua's words:

Hmm . . . sometimes I wonder if my grandparents are true Christians like they portray . . . yes ooo . . . because if they are, they won't continue to be so superstitious to the extent of rejecting their own daughter who went through such a distressful situation and needed their support. They really amaze me.

Abena lamented:

Sob . . . sob . . . I feel very sad not because of my divorce but because of my traditional family. I wish I was not a member of such a group . . . I wish I could redirect my children to another group of people whom they can call grandparents, aunties, and uncles. My children are always yearning to go and visit their grandparents, but I can't send them because they are not ready to accept us and unfortunately, I can't tell my children the whole truth because it is not healthy for them. . . . Why? Why? Why? *Sob sob.*

MARRIAGE WAS BENEFICIAL TO FAMILY

The third reason for nonsupport was that, for some participants, family members expected them to stay in a marriage because of the benefits it brought to the extended family. A case in point is that of Afia. In her opinion, the reason for the negative attitudes from her parents was because she divorced a rich man who supported them. The man was completing their house for them with his resources as well as helping with their medical bills every time they visited the hospital for their regular checkups. This was in addition to the money he sent them every month. He encouraged her sister's enrollment in a tertiary education and financially supported it. Her ex-husband, then, was responsible for academic fees as well as supporting the financial needs of the family; for these reasons, her parents have turned a blind eye to her challenges because of the financial support they are receiving from her abusive husband. In her words,

> My parents told me not to expect them in my house because I decided to divorce the man who has been giving them food and putting money in their pockets all these years, and so if I am a fool, they are not because they cannot cut a relationship with the person who puts smiles on their faces. And so, if I want to be on my own, I can go, however, they will not stop me from coming home to visit them though they will not come to my house to visit me until I decide to remarry my husband, this is because they don't want my ex-husband to think that they are in favor of my decision to quit the marriage. . . . Hmmm.

Afia shares that because she has not changed her mind, her relatives have also not changed theirs. Afia's parents' declaration that they could not ignore her husband despite the divorce confirms the assertion by Amato and Keith that divorce causes relational problems within the family that may also lead to other challenges.[22] As for Martha and Gloria, their parents do not even talk to them because they divorced men who were considered breadwinners. Martha thinks of herself as an orphan although her parents are alive. She believes her parents are selfish but then wonders if her husband might have done something to them spiritually.[23] Martha is the only daughter who is expected to have babies to carry on the bloodline. She was thus confused that her parents are on very good terms with her ex-husband and refuse to talk to her. Her comment at the end of her interview summed it up: "Who will understand this situation? What kind of money at all are they looking for?" For her part, Gloria said that,

> If not for my children, I think I would have died of depression and frustration from my parents. I thank God that I have mature children who have stood by me all these years. I am still praying that God will minister to my parents so that they will see everything wrong with their attitude towards their daughter because of a stranger. My parents have never picked my calls since I divorced and when I call with a different number and they realize it is me, they just end the call. Hmm. . . . I am so disappointed in the mother and father who raised me because I won't behave towards my children the way they are towards me. I will never side with an abusive husband at the expense of my child because of his wealth.

REFUSAL TO SHARE MARITAL WEALTH WITH FAMILY

Some family members decided not to support their divorced relatives because the women did not share their material wealth with the family members during the time when the marriage was happy. Family members would typically expect that a happily married family member will support them financially, if not regularly, then at least occasionally. One expectation, for example, is that the married relative would provide groceries every time the relative came to visit. Some even expected that relatives with well-to-do husbands would adopt some of their own children, provide for them financially and pay for their education. Some expected that these husbands would set up unemployed relatives in business or help find them a job. When these expectations were not met during the marriage, these relative are less likely to aid a divorcee when she needs assistance. Occasionally, a more reasonable relative will choose to assist a divorcee when she faces difficulties. For these women, the lack of support for relatives during the marriage caused a lack of support for the divorcee after the marriage dissolved. In Mensima's words:

> I can't just understand my family members for this action. Even if I never sent them anything during my happy times in marriage, is this the best way to handle my case as a relative? I still don't think it's right to neglect me after my divorce. At a time when I need them most.

Esther, one of the Fante participants, was convinced that her relatives had been waiting for her downfall or for a misfortune to come her way because of the things they said to her. She narrated:

> They are all saying the same thing, even my young cousins who I presume should not know anything about divorce, meet me and ask me why I neglected their parents when I was enjoying my good time in marriage . . . immediately they present their case, they will not give you a listening ear and then they end by saying, "Once you enjoyed it all alone, go and endure it all alone; we are not interested in your good or bad marital stories."

It amazed Esi that her relatives are not supporting her post-divorce. They claimed she did not share her marital wealth with them when everything was going well for her. In her words:

> I have always thought that our family should be happy for us when we are enjoying marital life because a good marriage is worth enjoying. I don't expect them to be looking forward to us bringing them things from our marriage every day. They should rather pray for us that we never come back home with any bad news, but if there is bad news they should not send us away because we didn't

bring them gifts when we were married. Once we are family, we remain family forever, no matter the situation. . . . I have just decided to relax and allow life to take its course because I really can't understand their arguments. It is a big shock to me.

These women have been neglected because they neglected family when everything was working out well for them. They were very much aware of their responsibilities to the extended family but chose to ignore them. They were surprised, therefore, when the family members were not sympathetic to their post-divorce needs. They feel that no matter what they have done wrong, they should still be considered as family members who have just faltered. What the divorced women in this category did not take into consideration was that marriage did not annul communal dynamics in the natal family. After all, the Akans, the largest ethnic group in Ghana, have a saying that "when a trap unhinges from its mooring, it goes back upright." This saying suggests that there are no guarantees in marriage and women should not break ties with or traditions of the natal family simply because they are married. When a marriage collapses, the natal family will be there to serve as a buffer as the divorcee rebuilds her life.

POVERTY

Some families not only neglected members who had refused to share their material wealth with them, but they also neglected individuals who had nothing to share post-divorce. This is a contradiction that can make life difficult for family members who may need help. Help can take the form of a room to sleep in, a parcel of land to farm on, or seed money to start a trade. However, when a divorcee is struggling financially, nobody wants to step up for fear that they will be burdened for a long time. Ama and Adadzewa were in that category. They were neglected because they were poor. Ama states:

Family members are only interested in coming to milk you and leave. They are not interested in taking in or accepting a member who has gone to marriage and has decided to end and come back home with nothing. I have nothing to say to them because they are all hypocrites.

Ama's experience demonstrates that divorcees who have no material wealth will not be accepted by relatives following a divorce. Adadzewa experienced a similar situation; because she no longer has material wealth following her divorce, the family has rejected her. She notes:

My family members have taught me a great lesson. This confirms the proverb which says that *ebusua kyir ka* [family hates poverty or debts]. When I was a rich businesswoman, a lot of them even came to the market when they had nothing to purchase. They will come straight to me knowing that I will shop for them and top it up with money for transportation. Now none of them wants to know where I reside or what I eat because my business is not as big as it used to be. In fact, nobody comes close to me anymore. Maybe I should take that in good faith because it may be for my good.

DISAPPROVAL

The sixth reason for families' lack of support had to do with the disapproval of the marriage to begin with. Emefa received no support from her dad because she had ignored his disapproval of her choice of partner. In her words:

I could not involve my parents because they were never in support of the union right from the onset. My father was not very comfortable because he believed men from the ethnic group of my ex-husband do not treat women with dignity and so for him I should look for another partner from an ethnic group he approves of, but I promised him my ex-husband was a God-fearing man and will take good care of me. My dad refused to be persuaded and thus never gave me his blessing but told me not to come back to him if my marriage failed because I will not love the experience if I should come back to him. Truly, he is not interested in my divorce.

Emefa did not get any support from her father before her marriage; in fact, he warned her not to come back to him if her marriage started to falter. Emefa's dad never offered support before or during her marriage and categorically stated that if she should return to her father because of problems in her marriage he would make the experience very unpleasant for her. In Ekua's case, apart from her grandparents being superstitious, her parents were also not supportive of the marriage. They 'washed their hands of her' because she disobeyed them. She never went back to her parents during her crisis; her grandparents finally told her she had brought shame to the family so there was no way they would support the divorce. In Ekua's words:

I regretted going back to my parents to inform them about my divorce. Madam, if you were there you would have asked if they were my biological parents. Hm . . . they sat there quietly, listened to me, and when I was done they asked me if I have any more information to give and when I said no, my mum and dad spoke together saying if you have nothing more to say then the door is ahead of you. This is how far your disobedience has brought you, go and suffer alone. . . .

I wept that day but they were too heartless to even say a word to me, but I have survived. I am just okay.

PROBLEM WITH NUCLEARIZATION

A seventh and final factor had to do with the increasing nuclearization of families in Ghana. Contrary to the prevailing notion that Africans have strong extended family networks, the case of the majority of participants in this study points to the increasing shift in Ghanaian families from extended to nuclear units, a shift that has implications for post-divorce support. In Mensima's case, the demise of her parents and remaining siblings left her with just extended family members to rely on and consult in times of trouble. Yet despite having extended family members, she was neglected because she forgot the communal lifestyle they shared as a family and chose individualism coupled with the refusal to contribute to family projects. Close family contact deteriorated since Mensima and the other participants rarely visited family or attended family gatherings. Nevertheless, their kinsmen asked them on several occasions to send financial contributions toward some familial projects. They were never able to fulfill these requests but they provided no specific reasons. They explained that they started paying attention to these expectations when they realized their marriages were on the verge of breaking and would therefore need their family's assistance. By this point, it was too late to repair the damage to the family relationship. She explains:

> I was not expecting my family members to turn their backs on me in my post-divorce. I thought I had no problem with them until I started hearing from the grapevine that my family says I never visited when I was married and was enjoying all my wealth with my husband but never gave them anything from my wealth. Not even contributions towards family projects. They said I behaved as though I had no extended family elsewhere.

Esi, like Mensima, had lost her parents in an accident a few years before her divorce. She found out quickly that her extended family was not willing to offer the kind of support she could have received from her nuclear family because she lived an individualistic life during marriage. She narrates,

> I was very surprised about the neglect because this same family stood by me as an only child to bury my parents and yet they expressed nothing which will even give me a hint that in the few years to come if I should come back to them, they will reject me. I still cannot understand the whole issue because when I go home, they tell me we will come and visit but when I leave nobody picks a

phone to even call to check up on me. They say a lot of bad things behind my back . . . most of them are complaining to neighbors that I lived my life like a white woman and so I should continue as a white woman. Hmmm.

Finally, in the case of Clara, she was abandoned by her relatives because she had ignored her family due to the nature of her work as a banker. She says that:

> I know I have not been regular with visits and calls to my family members, but I don't think that should call for this hostile attitude. Nobody even calls to ask about my children or my mental or physical state. Even when I attend family gatherings, it's like I'm a guest from somewhere. Hm . . . It's serious ooo . . . no one will come to you or even when you decide to get closer, it's as if they are running away from you. . . . I have gone through hell before, but now I don't even bother. I am just okay without them. I know when they are satisfied, they will draw closer.

Irrespective of the nonsupport by family, these women were determined to work harder to be able to survive all forms of pressures post-divorce. They did this to avoid depression and other health-related issues associated with divorce. Though few of them were not very happy about what they were going through, most of them claim they have moved on and thus, are not looking back. They are determined to survive their post-divorce experiences with or without family.

CONCLUSION

As the examples in this chapter demonstrate, some family members are willing to offer their support to divorcees in the family while others have clear reasons for not offering that support. This is often due to the reasons discussed above. Researchers, therefore, need to rethink, reconstruct, and do further interrogations on the issues facing the Ghanaian family. Modernization, urbanization, and social change have altered a lot of practices and beliefs to the extent that individuals will have to reorient themselves on certain issues, such as divorce. The Ghanaian family we grew up in has changed and as such, there is a need to adapt to the changes taking place for members to have peace and never feel disappointed when the unexpected happens. It is obvious from this research that most of the women in the study were impacted by the negative attitudes of their family members during the time they needed them most. Nevertheless, they had to accept the reality and adjust to survive the post-divorce experience. Even though the women never expected to be neglect by family post-divorce, they all managed to develop coping strategies which made them stronger. However, some are still looking forward to a positive attitude from family members regardless of how long they must endure the neglect.

As researchers, we reflected on our own families as we listened to the women's stories. The fact that some families not only neglected members who refused to share their material wealth with them during the marriage but also neglected those who had nothing to share and were living in poverty confirms for us that the way of life of Ghanaians is changing; therefore, the need for further research in this area remains.

NOTES

1. Baffour K. Takyi, "Marital instability in an African society: Exploring the factors that influence divorce processes in Ghana," *Sociological focus* 34, no. 1 (2001): 81.

2. John K. Anarfi and Kofi Awusabo-Asare, "Experimental research on sexual networking in some selected areas of Ghana," *Health transition review* (1993): 29–43.

3. Maureen R. Waller and Elizabeth H. Peters, "The risk of divorce as a barrier to marriage among parents of young children," *Social Science Research* 37, no. 4 (2008): 1188–1199; Patrick F. Fagan and Aaron Churchill, "The effects of divorce on children," *Marri Research*, no. 1 (2012): 1–48.

4. David A. Sbarra, "Divorce and health: Current trends and future directions," *Psychosomatic medicine* 77, no. 3 (2015): 329.

5. Jane Anderson, "The impact of family structure on the health of children: Effects of divorce," *The Linacre Quarterly* 81, no. 4 (2014): 379.

6. Froma Walsh, "The new normal: Diversity and complexity in 21st-century families," in Froma Walsh, ed., *Normal family processes: Growing diversity and complexity,* 4th ed. (New York: The Guilford Press, 2012).

7. Sidney Cobb, "Social support as a moderator of life stress," *Psychosomatic medicine* 38, no.5 (September/October 1976): 300–314.

8. Takyi, Marital instability in an African society, 81.

9. As used in the chapter, family refers to divorced women's matrikin or patrikin.

10. Murray Bowen, "Theory in the practice of psychotherapy," *Family therapy: Theory and practice* 4, no. 1 (1976): 2–90.

11. Bowen, "Theory in the practice of psychotherapy," 1976; Florence W. Kaslow, and Lita Linzer Schwartz, *The dynamics of divorce: A life cycle perspective,* Philadelphia, PA: Brunner/Mazel, 1987.

12. Monica McGoldrick and Betty Carter, "Advances in coaching: Family therapy with one person," *Journal of Marital and Family Therapy* 27, no. 3 (2001): 281–300.

13. S. E. R. A. P. Kavas, "Post-divorce experience of highly educated and professional women," Unpublished doctoral dissertation, Middle East Technical University Turkey (2010); David A. Sbarra, "Divorce and health: Current trends and future directions," *Psychosomatic medicine* 77, no. 3 (2015): 227–236.

14. Kavas, "Post-divorce experience of highly educated and professional women."

15. Kavas, "Post-divorce experience of highly educated and professional women."

16. Hongyu Wang and Paul R. Amato, "Predictors of divorce adjustment: stressors, resources, and definitions," *Journal of Marriage and the family* 62, no. 3 (2004): 655–668.

17. Nicholas Loubere, "Questioning transcription: The case for the systematic and reflexive interviewing and reporting (SRIR) method," in *Forum Qualitative Sozialforschung/Forum: Qualitative Social Research* 18, no. 2 (2017).

18. Catherine Haslam, et al., "The importance of social groups for retirement adjustment: Evidence, application, and policy implications of the social identity model of identity change." *Social issues and policy review* 13, no. 1 (2019): 93–124.

19. Fatih Ozbay, et al., "Social support and resilience to stress: from neurobiology to clinical practice," *Psychiatry (Edgmont)* 4, no. 5 (2007): 35.

20. Gay C. Kitson, "Divorce and Relationship Dissolution Research: Then and Now," in Mark A. Fine and John H. Harvey, eds., *Handbook of divorce and relationship dissolution* (Mahwah, NJ: Lawrence Erlbaum Associates Publishers, 2006), 27.

21. Ghanaweb, Ras Mubarak's ex-wife reveals how society, family worked against her over domestic abuse stance," March 12, 2021, https://www.ghanaweb.com/GhanaHomePage/NewsArchive/Ras-Mubarak-s-ex-wife-reveals-how-society-family-worked-against-her-over-domestic-abuse-stance-1202455l; see also Ghanaweb, "Deputy YEA boss allegedly beats girlfriend to death at Akatsi North," March 11, 2021, https://www.ghanaweb.com/GhanaHomePage/NewsArchive/Deputy-YEA-boss-allegedly-beats-girlfriend-to-death-at-Akatsi-North-1201624; Ghanaweb, "Husband caged over wife's death," March 10, 2021, https://www.ghanaweb.com/GhanaHomePage/NewsArchive/Husband-caged-over-wife-s-death-1200535.

22. Paul R. Amato and Bruce Keith, "Parental Divorce and Adult Well-Being: A Meta-Analysis," *Journal of Marriage and Family* 53, no. 1 (February 1, 1991): 49.

23. Ghanaians generally believe in spiritual forces and their influence on people.

BIBLIOGRAPHY

Amato, Paul R. "Research on divorce: Continuing trends and new developments." *Journal of marriage and family* 72, no. 3 (2010): 650–666.

Amato, Paul R. and James, S. "Divorce in Europe and the United States: Commonalities and differences across nations," *Family Science* 1, no.1 (2010): 2–13.

Amato, Paul R., and Bruce Keith. "Parental Divorce and Adult Well-Being: A Meta-Analysis." *Journal of Marriage and Family* 53, no. 1 (February 1, 1991): 43–58. doi:10.2307/353132.

Anarfi, John K., and Kofi Awusabo-Asare. "Experimental research on sexual networking in some selected areas of Ghana." *Health* transition review (1993): 29–43.

Anderson, Jane. "The impact of family structure on the health of children: Effects of divorce." *The* Linacre Quarterly 81, no. 4 (2014): 378–387.

Areen, Judith. "Uncovering the Reformation roots of American marriage and divorce law." *Yale JL & Feminism* 26 (2014): 29.

Bowen, Murray. "Theory in the practice of psychotherapy." *Family* therapy*:* Theory and practice 4, no. 1 (1976): 2–90.

Cobb, Sidney. "Social support as a moderator of life stress." *Psychosomatic medicine* 38, no. 5 (September/October 1976): 300–314.

Fagan, Patrick F., and Aaron Churchill. "The effects of divorce on children." *Marri Research* 1 (2012): 1–48.

Ghanaweb, "Deputy YEA boss allegedly beats girlfriend to death at Akatsi North." March 11, 2020. https://www.ghanaweb.com/GhanaHomePage/NewsArchive/ Deputy-YEA-boss-allegedly-beats-girlfriend-to-death-at-Akatsi-North-1201624.

Ghanaweb. "Husband caged over wife's death." March 10, 2021. https://www.ghanaweb. com/GhanaHomePage/NewsArchive/Husband-caged-over-wife-s-death-1200535.

Ghanaweb. "Ras Mubarak's ex-wife reveals how society, family worked against her over domestic abuse stance." March 12, 2021. https://www.ghanaweb.com/ GhanaHomePage/NewsArchive/Ras-Mubarak-s-ex-wife-reveals-how-society-family-worked-against-her-over-domestic-abuse-stance-1202455.

Goldsmith, Daena J. *Communicating social support.* Cambridge University Press, 2004.

Haslam, Catherine, Niklas K. Steffens, Nyla R. Branscombe, S. Alexander Haslam, Tegan Cruwys, Ben C. P. Lam, Nancy A. Pachana, and Jie Yang. "The importance of social groups for retirement adjustment: Evidence, application, and policy implications of the social identity model of identity change." *Social* issues and policy review 13, no. 1 (2019): 93–124.

Kaslow, Florence W., and Lita Linzer Schwartz. *The dynamics of divorce: A life cycle perspective.* Philadelphia, PA: Brunner/Mazel, 1987.

Kavas, S. E. R. A. P. "Post divorce experience of highly educated and professional women." Unpublished PhD diss. Middle East Technical University Turkey (2010).

Kitson, Gay. C. "Divorce and Relationship Dissolution Research: Then and Now." In *Handbook of divorce and relationship dissolution,* edited by Mark A. Fine and John H. Harvey. 15–40. Mahwah, NJ: Lawrence Erlbaum Associates Publishers, 2006.

Loubere, Nicholas. "Questioning transcription: The case for the systematic and reflexive interviewing and reporting (SRIR) method." In *Forum Qualitative Sozialforschung/Forum: Qualitative Social Research* 18, no. 2 (2017).

McGoldrick, Monica, and Betty Carter. "Advances in coaching: Family therapy with one person." *Journal of Marital and Family Therapy* 27, no. 3 (2001): 281–300.

Ozbay, Fatih, Douglas C. Johnson, Eleni Dimoulas, C. A. Morgan III, Dennis Charney, and Steven Southwick. "Social support and resilience to stress: from neurobiology to clinical practice." *Psychiatry (*Edgmont*)* 4, no. 5 (2007): 35.

Sbarra, David A. "Divorce and health: Current trends and future directions." *Psychosomatic* medicine 77, no. 3 (2015): 227–236.

Takyi, Baffour K. "Marital instability in an African society: Exploring the factors that influence divorce processes in Ghana." *Sociological* focus 34, no. 1 (2001): 77–96.

Waller, Maureen R., and Elizabeth H. Peters. "The risk of divorce as a barrier to marriage among parents of young children." *Social* Science Research 37, no. 4 (2008): 1188–1199.

Walsh, Froma. "The new normal: Diversity and complexity in 21st-century families." In *Normal family processes: Growing diversity and complexity,* 4th ed., edited by Froma Walsh, 3–27. New York: The Guilford Press, 2012.

Wang, H., and Paul R. Amato. Predictors of divorce adjustment: stressors, resources, and definitions. *Journal* of Marriage and the family 62, no. 3 (2004): 655–668.

Chapter 4

Gendered Scripts and Young Adults' Sexual Practices on a First Date in Urban Ghana

Daniel Yaw Fiaveh

Conceptions about the repressed sexuality of women in Africa are not new. While some locate it within the confines of patriarchal cultures, others emphasize new possibilities in terms of how culture empowers women's sexuality. Anthropologists, for example, provide a glimpse into the world of repressed sexuality in early cultures. Scholars such as Norman Haire, Hans Licht, Claude Lévi-Strauss, Steven Marcus, Margaret Mead, Bronislaw Malinowski, and Edward Evans-Pritchard, were concerned with customs and practices that regulated the sex drive of women in society. In the second half of the nineteenth century, for example, female sexuality was subjected to different forms of interpretations and the extent to which women's sexuality was licentious in a particular society.[1] Society expected higher moral behavior of women than men based on the patriarchal treatment of women as property. Indeed, as observed by Michel Foucault in his *History of Sexuality*, female sexuality was generally seen as a troubling condition best contained within the domain of marriage.[2] The rise of feminist activism in the mid-1960s to the mid-1970s influenced sexual cultures to be more liberal. This has afforded women and men spaces to make their own sexual decisions.[3] This chapter investigates young adults' narratives of sex on a first date and highlights how young women draw on their cultural training (morality, sexuality, and gender mistrusts) in Ghana as an agentic tool.

CONTEXTUALIZING THE CULTURAL
CONSTRUCTION OF WOMEN'S SEXUALITY

Cultures exert influences on human sexuality that can be empowering for women.[4] Thus, women across the world make choices about their sexuality by drawing on aspects of their cultural training and upbringing which are empowering to them;[5] yet very few studies have emphasized this phenomenon among young African women south of the Sahara. Some scholars have made the clarion call to rethink familiar concepts to open new perspectives and new questions about social relations. Pierre Bourdieu and colleagues, for example, see culture as a form of capital (i.e., knowledge). Cultural capital embodies the practices and behaviors shared and transmitted to young adults through family socialization or habitus—an important form of a culture geared to the perpetuation of structures of dominance.[6] While cultural capital reproduces social inequalities and education does not assume knowledge of self, the role that family plays in the production of self is important for understanding Bourdieu's framework.

From a feminist viewpoint, we can also draw from Bourdieu's analysis. In *Black Feminist Thought*, for example, Patricia Hill Collins argues that knowledge can be power, and oppressed people possess power.[7] She identifies various ways people come to know and suggests that knowledge is built upon lived experience, not upon an objectified position. Collins suggests that knowledge is based on individual subjective construction in a dialogical relationship with another actor. Because knowledge is built upon lived experiences, the assessment of knowledge influences the actor's beliefs (e.g., fear of STIs), values (e.g., sex before marriage is "bad"), and agency (sexual right and informed consent). Knowledge from these perspectives is a creative power, which results from negotiation. Similarly, in *Black Sexual Politics*, Collins demonstrates that power goes beyond documenting gender inequality. Collins suggests that sexual stereotyping is central to dominant gender discourses. She argues that stereotypical beliefs about the dominant man and submissive woman exert power by appearing to be "normal."[8] Collins's argument thus addresses ongoing epistemological debates in feminist theory and the sociology of knowledge by revealing new ways of thinking that allow individuals to define their reality.

Both Bourdieu's and Collins's frameworks have similar viewpoints about individual agency, which is the central idea in this chapter. Both perspectives fall within the broad paradigm of constructionism. The premise of constructionism is that there is no objective reality, and that reality is socially constructed, which enables humans to form shared meanings and behaviors. I want to premise my argument in this chapter on a similar note. For example, how do cultural reproduction and choice work together to influence how young women and men perceive sex and dialogue about it? This chapter contributes to the literature on how young women and men in sub-Saharan Africa draw on social and cultural reproduction in matters of sex, to negotiate their sexuality.

GENDERED SOCIALIZATION AND YOUTH SEXUALITY IN GHANA

Growing up in Ghana is marked by gendered socialization in both the nuclear and extended family. Boys play with boys and girls play with girls although these forms of socialization do not produce antagonistic behaviors or rivalries among the genders like in other cultures as found by some early/classical anthropologists such as Margret Mead and colleagues. While there is gendered socialization and sexual education across cultural groups in Ghana,[9] young adults of both genders are not expected to engage in sexual activities when they are unmarried. In sexual relationships, men tend to exert more power than women and, in most cases, initiate sexual intercourse although, in some cases, women initiate sex indirectly.[10] Society also expects women to be cautious and to take less risk because they are perceived as "cowards" as depicted in the Akan-Twi expression *εmmaa suro adeε* (women are cowards). Men are seen as risk-takers and adventurous, emphasized in proverbs such as *ne bo yε duru* or *ne koko yε duru* (he is brave, or he is courageous).[11]

In Ghanaian society in general, regardless of the liberal attitudes toward sex in recent times, there are social restrictions on sexual behavior. Blunt talk about sexual matters such as discussing one's romantic affair or naming sensual parts especially with a stranger is taboo and considered irresponsible and indecent. Individuals are frequently instructed to exercise self-control by abstaining from sex until marriage and to engage in background checks of possible suitors. Although young adults learn about their sexuality from their parents, it is sometimes taken for granted that every member of society, whether young or old, would learn about sex and abide by cultural moral codes. The Akan saying *obi nkyerε akwadaa nyame*, which translates to mean knowledge of God is inherent but euphemistically implies "no one teaches sex to a child," captures the moral codes that govern sexuality in Ghana. These codes are enforced through the teachings and practices of the major religious traditions in Ghana such as Christianity, Islam, and African/Ghanaian Traditional Religions/Beliefs.[12]

Cultural scripts dictate when, where and with whom one may or may not have sex, and violations of its mandates are also regarded as sacrilege. These include incestuous relationships, sex before undergoing puberty rites, impregnating a woman without performing the marriage rites, and adultery.[13] Sexual taboos as part of the moral code help to keep the sanctity of sexual relationships and unions, and are strictly enforced and sanctioned. There are anecdotes and cultural knowledge found in songs and rituals among cultures in Ghana that are used as informal social control mechanisms, particularly around sexual practices. Among the Ewes of southeastern Ghana, for example, some men engage in various sexual rituals such as the use of *fia te kli*— chastity hex to ensure their female partner's sexual fidelity.[14] Because of the presence and widespread perceptions of these rituals and their implications on the individual and to the community, such as calamity/misfortunes/illness and death, they instill fear and a sense of responsibility in women in such cultures.[15] In this regard, responsibility is an important aspect of the upbringing of children especially concerning the sexual fidelity of women.

For younger women, sexual training includes not appearing too easily wooed by men, distrusting men,[16] and protecting one's self-dignity and the family image. They are also encouraged to get to know the background of a possible suitor, to introduce them to one's parents/family as soon as possible, and not to disclose too much about oneself or family background to a stranger. Therefore, being exposed to sex and engaging in sex with a man on a first encounter is considered as *adwamammɔ* (Akan-Twi, "prostitution" or sex work), and this is taboo, (i.e., *akyiwade* or *mmusuo* in Akan). A deviation from the sexual training discussed above is thus normally met with commensurate punishment which could include ridicule, hooting, being laughed at, seclusion, and banishment from the community. On this note, men and boys are socialized to be patient (though adventurous) and gentle with girls and women since it is believed that women and girls do not easily accept men's sexual overtures due to their upbringing.[17]

For younger men, sexual training includes emphasizing methods of titillating women (described in Akan as *ɛmmaa aso mu yɛ wɔn dɛ*) and keeping them engaged in conversation. Ironically, men are also stereotyped as not trustworthy, and this is translated in Akan as *mmarima nka nokorɛ* (meaning men are liars). It is important to add, however, that these stereotypes and (mis)conceptions have seen changes in terms of the capacities and abilities of women based on lived experiences and the changing narratives in Ghanaian popular culture. It is a cultural norm or expectation for women to "lie" to men (i.e., tell men what they want to hear) in the first or early stages of a potentially "amorous"/dating relationship. The media, including print, audio, video, internet and art, and formal education also remain potent platforms that shape young women's sexuality and gender relations especially in ways that disrupt and (re)produce cultural and moral scripts.[18]

STUDY AREA

This chapter focuses on young Ghanaian adults' sexuality. Using 20 women and men aged 18–28 years, the researcher explored first sex on a dating experience as well as interrogated how young women's knowledge and perceptions of sex inform their dating behaviors and practices with young men. How do young Ghanaian adults construct sex and how does cultural knowledge inform their sexual experiences and health practices on a first date? This is a central question that grounds the analysis in the chapter. The study was conducted in urban Cape Coast (known locally as *Oguaa,* meaning "market" in Fante), one of the most urbanized municipalities in the Central Region of Ghana. Cape Coast has one of the highest rates of sexual activity among young adults in Ghana.[19] Urbanization generally shapes and influences social and gender relations in cities/towns. As such, many adults have a waning influence on young adults and this affords them the space to negotiate patriarchal and gerontocratic and authoritarian ways of upbringing.[20] Thus, compared to rural spaces where the sexuality of young adults is "policed" due to the presence of older folks and traditional norms, urban areas require upholding fundamental rights and freedoms although urbanization processes also have the potential for greater disparities that further marginalize and discriminate against those most in need. Therefore, for convenience, participants were drawn from Amamoma (heterogeneous, but majority Akan) and Duakor (largely homogenous and Ewe) located in an urban area of Cape Coast. Cape Coast is about 165 kilometers from Accra, the capital city of Ghana. It is heterogeneous, with several settlements including Duakor, Effutu, Ekon, Kokoado, Mpaesem, Ola, Pedu, Ankaful Village, and Amisano. The others are Abura, Akotokyire, Nkanfoa, Kotokoraba, Bakano, Amamoma, Apewosika, Kwawpro, and Essuekyir.

The selection of the study areas, near the University of Cape Coast, was intentional as it is an area with diverse sociodemographic characteristics. Amamoma largely engages in trading activities—women and men mostly engage in petty trading and skills work like hairdressing/barbering/dressmaking, catering services, and retail activities. A few young people are also engaged as laborers in cleaning and security work at the university. On the other hand, and because of its closeness to the sea, the major occupation and main source of livelihood for Duakor is fishing for the men, although some also work as laborers at the university. The women engage in fish mongering and petty trading.

DESIGN, POPULATION, AND PROCEDURE

The study is part of a larger project to understand young adults sexual behavior in Ghana. This initial exploratory study comprised 10 women and 10 men aged between 18–28 years. This research utilized in-depth interviews, informal conversations and group discussions, and field notes. As James Clifford observes, field notes embody vast activities including textual inscription, participation, observations, and rapport,[21] such as understanding "local" perceptions and behavior and an ability to speak the same language as interviewees.

Accidental and purposive sampling techniques with an oral vignette technique were used in recruiting participants. The accidental and purposive sampling techniques were used to expand recruitment due to the sensitive nature of the study. All interviews were conducted by the author from March 2016 to June 2017. The interviews occurred at a time that was convenient for the interviewees. Seven in-depth interviews (5 women and 2 men) were conducted along with 7 individual informal conversations (5 women and 2 men). There were 6 informal group discussions with 6 young men. Women were less willing to discuss their sexual experiences in groups; therefore, no group discussion was organized for the women.

Participation in the informal group discussion was voluntary and there were no specific criteria for recruiting. The research was response-driven, and all the interviewees identified themselves as heterosexual with interests in erotic sexual relationships. Men who wanted to talk about sex were eligible. The average age was 25 years. The discussions did not have any specific length of time because, although it was about sex, occasionally some participants would interject into the discussion football fixtures; the Union of European Football Associations Champions League and the English premier league, in particular, were often a topic of conversation. Not restricting the time allowed me to keep the discussion informal and free flowing. The men felt the issues we discussed were interesting and shared their personal experiences because I afforded them the space to do so—discussions did not end formally as people left one by one either to eat or watch football.

For the male participants, the discussion began with an oral vignette because it was a bit easier. I normally would introduce a controversial issue on women, men and sex. For example, I would say, "So, you fit fuck a woman on a first date [PG English, so can you have sex with a woman on a first date]?" Again, the approach depended on the demographic profiles of the men. For the younger men, the approach was more of sharing our personal experiences during a football match such as the English Premiership or Champions League or a fixture involving the Ghana Black Stars or even a top local league match involving two popular local clubs, for example, Accra Hearts of Oak versus Kumasi Asante Kotoko.

Informal conversations with women took place in and around the university campus and marketplaces in Cape Coast and were impromptu. I did not set out to find participants, but after discretely observing and eavesdropping on conversations, I introduced myself into the discussion based on the dominant language used. I began by introducing myself depending on my profiling of the woman in terms of friendliness, assertiveness, and willingness to talk and then attempted to build rapport by asking her name: *ɔhemaa, me pa wo kyεw yεfrε wo sεn?* meaning, "lady/queen, please what's your name?" Should that fail—because not all women were interested in me as a person or my conversation, and depending on the context—I made complimentary comments such as *ebei, ɔhemaa*, local parlance in Fante, "why, my lady/queen." Some women smiled and laughed based on the comments; others did not bother at all because their cultural ethos would not allow them to talk to strangers they meet in the streets. As part of the socialization in Ghana, people, especially younger women, are cautioned not to entertain people they do not know especially in the streets. These were some of the challenges I had to surmount in search of young female interviewees to talk about sex.

The central issues discussed were whether the interviewees had ever gone on a date. I also probed for the gender of the date and reasons for dating and frequency; their sexual activity, if any, on a first date and kind of sexual activity; and strategies utilized to have or not to have sex on a first date and the health practices adopted if any. I did not specifically ask the interviewees about being heterosexual, queer, gay, lesbian or trans, etc. The anthropological approach to research emphasizes that for a researcher to understand a phenomenon in a given culture, the culture needs to be understood first, and language is of critical essence.[22] This approach guided the choices I made in the data collection process. For instance, because I am fluent in six dominant languages in Ghana (i.e., English, Ewe, Twi, Ga, Hausa, and Pidgin English), the interviewees had the opportunity to express themselves without the possibility of being misunderstood and without the danger of not finding the appropriate words to express their feelings and meanings about their sexualities. My culture, background, and expertise in various local languages such as PG English and slang for example were instrumental in achieving the confidence and rapport this study required. My ability to communicate in multiple languages ensured that I was able to get people from diverse backgrounds to participate in the study.

I am aware that my methodology, such as blunt discussion of sex with strangers, could overstep the boundaries of what might normally constitute a sensitive research design, especially with the attendant assumptions in this study that culture can be empowering for women. In that regard, I am guided by the required ethical protocol as well as the standards of professionalism as dictated in the social sciences such as the principles of respect of persons, to minimize possible harm and to ensure responsible publication.[23] The conversations with the young men and women were based on their informed consent. The young men were more willing to share their experiences than the women partially because the men are socialized to showcase their masculinity of conquering women. On the other hand, some of the women were reluctant and felt that I was invading their privacy; a few were shy, and others did not want to show that they are "too exposed to sex" for fear of projecting what is known in local parlance as the "bad child" image. However, based on my experience as a researcher, my approach was to show humility in prefacing conversations such as *Me pa wo kyɛw,* Twi for "please," and being friendly and good-humored.

DATA ANALYSIS AND RESULTS

The transcribed narratives were analyzed thematically. The first step consisted of systematizing the information about the demographics of the interviewees with specific objectives. To control bias, I defined descriptions of thematic categories and resolved meaning discrepancies to ensure data consistency. Three main themes emerged from the narratives based on the questions explored, namely: constructions of sex, experiences of sex on a first date, and health beliefs and practices on a first date. The findings were organized in relation to specific objectives and the themes developed. This chapter only reports findings from the individual interviews conducted.

The interviewees were aged between 18–28 years. The age range can be attributed to the purposive technique adopted in sampling the interviewees. The research focused on persons who fall within the legal age of consenting to sexual union in Ghana, i.e.,, 16 years and above. This age group also falls within one of the sexually active groups reported in Cape Coast.[24] The interviewees were not married; some were in steady relationships and had at least a basic education.

CONSTRUCTIONS OF SEX

Overall, younger adults knew they had the power to choose between engaging in sex on the first date, or not. Family socialization such as teachings on the need to protect the family image, cultural/moral ethos, the school (secular and faith-based), and social media (in particular: Facebook, Twitter, Instagram, WhatsApp) were instrumental in informing young adults' knowledge of and perceptions about sexuality irrespective of the educational attainment. While knowledge about sex was not gendered, perceptions and attitudes toward sex were gendered. Several factors explained the gendered perceptions and attitudes about sex among younger adults. These included culture and religious ethos and upbringing, sexual awareness, and sexual experience. Younger women, irrespective of educational background, stressed the need for commitment before sex and had a preference for older men, i.e., men who were 5 to 10 years older. According to them, age is an important construct of sexual maturity and financial capabilities, i.e., a man's ability to provide for a woman's needs. Younger men preferred younger women, but they did not give any specific age although a few (three) preferred to marry women who were 5–15 years younger. They, however, believed that the term "commitment" is contestable and ambiguous. According to the men, commitment has multiple meanings; for instance, they raised questions such as what does it mean to be committed to someone? What does it take to be committed? How long should a person be committed to another person? And what are the trust issues associated with commitment?

On the issue of trust, some of the men claimed that "women cannot be predicted" because they could find better suitors during the relationship. According to the men, women are "complex" beings, meaning women are multifaceted. This is a dominant view across cultures in Ghana and although it has implications for gender mistrusts and misconceptions, it can function to promote women's agency and choices. The point is that because men believe they compete for women's love and affection, it affords women the space to negotiate male sexuality. Thus, the acknowledgment that women can betray trust is a social fact which is coercive to men and amounts to social capital for some women.

Men had interesting perspectives on women. Some emphasized that women are titillated by what they hear; others said that, culturally, women are financially dependent on men; therefore, men must be financially sound before expressing sexual overtures to a woman. According to the men, financial considerations were important to some women and they could easily be wooed by men who have more privileges in society, including economic/financial capabilities. Since some men think that they are more privileged than women and expect women to be dependent on them, women may see this concept as agentic and empowering. Empowerment has social, economic, and political dimensions which can be explored through agency. Agency is, thus, not only about the making of choices but about the processes by which choices are made and put into effect. Therefore, if cultural stereotypes and misconceptions inadvertently privilege the position of being a woman, it can be empowering for some women.

The interviewees, women and men, also noted that while family upbringing was instrumental in how they constructed sex in terms of liberal or conservative attitudes, they also acknowledged, as stated above, that the schools and media were instrumental in shaping their perceptions and attitudes about sex. They indicated that the emphasis on moral uprightness and turpitude formed a significant aspect of the training they have had which they felt was empowering to them even though they also acknowledged the conservative nature of the training.

Religion appeared as a common feature in the narratives of the interviewees. Religion emphasized the need for moral constraints and uprightness. These lessons were guided by religious texts and admonishments during attendance at church activities and the performance of religious rituals such as fasting and prayer, and communion for those who were Christians. Young women upheld higher commitments to religious values compared to young men because culture and religion expected them to do so. This was because of their constant referral to their cultural and religious and moral upbringing. Some of the narratives translated from the local dialect that formed the basis of this conclusion included comments such as, "That's how I was brought up," "My Christian teaching does not allow that," "My parents are strict," and "The scriptures [Bible] frown on that." As part of the cultural upbringing in Ghana, young women and men are socialized to abstain from sex until they are married; however, society is more liberal about boys'/men's sexuality than girls'/women's due to patriarchal norms that construct young women who are sexually active as "bad," "spoilt child" or "spoiled brat," i.e., a child, typically a girl, who is badly behaved and/or too exposed to sex. Thus, girls considered "spoiled" are those who can easily accept men's sexual overtures. A young man shared his experience about "bad girls":

> If you get the "bad" ones, it's easier. A 'spoilt girl' about 14 or 15 [years]. This is the right time. When you treat them well you can easily fuck them. When I was at Bogoso [a mining town in the Western Region], I was about 21, yeah, something like that or so. I took this girl to a hotel. The way she fucked me heh, hm. I told my friend about what the girl did to me and he also went to fuck her. The account [what he also told me afterward] was shocking. . . . It is not because you are old or have a big tummy. She is just a bad girl.[25]

Some of the young women commented on the "bad girl" label and suggested that the stereotype suppressed younger women's sexual expression, particularly the ability to give in to sex. According to the women, the reasons why some younger women do not give in easily to men's sexual overtures or postpone sex is partly because of a culture where young women are perceived or labeled as "bad" or "spoilt." One lady shared her perspective on the impact of the "bad girl" image on her sexual expression:

> Because of my training at home, I don't think that sex before marriage and sex on a first date is good. It's against my Islamic teachings. More so, I'm a virgin. I know these days; some don't mind having liberal attitude towards sex. I know right, but this [is] me. I'm a Dagaaba and for us, especially women, the belief is different. If a guy asks you for sex on a first encounter then you know, he is not serious. He is not a proper one. I'm not "two two" [prostitute/sex worker]. They will say you are a "bad" girl. More so, your parents will feel bad because everybody calls you a bad girl, which brings shame and dishonor to your family name and image. You don't want your parents to disown or curse you just because of some stupid guy who will not even care about you when you get pregnant. He will even tell his friends he slept with you on a first date and be calling you a spoilt girl.[26]

In addition to culture, religious, and moral values, the media offered another window through which young women and men situated the construction of sexuality. For example, one woman suggested that:

> What is that one too? You have sex with someone the first time you met? Fashion or what? It's the TV programmes they watch. . . .They say something is called "Kumkum Bhagya" [a Hindi-language Indian soap opera]. My father will "kill" you. There are all these "sakawa" [fraudster] guys. I got a video from WhatsApp where the lady met the guy through Facebook, and they started chatting and became friends. They met and had sex for the first time and what happened afterward. . . . hm. The guy is crazy. He raped her, tortured her, hm, and all that.[27]

Thus, in addition to sexual training, parental and religious guidance, the fear of encountering harm based on hearsay or misconceptions presented in media shape young adults' knowledge and perceptions about sex and willingness to engage in sex on a first date.

The following section discusses whether young adults have ever engaged in sex on a first date, willingness to do so, reasons for engaging in sex on a first date or not, and how they negotiate sex on a first date.

EXPERIENCES OF SEX ON THE FIRST DATE

Out of the 20 interviewees, 12 (7 women and 5 men) indicated that they never had sex on a first date. While the women indicated that their dates were with older men (ranging from 25 years to 40 years depending on their age), the men dated younger women.

The reasons for not engaging in sexual activities such as caressing, fondling, kissing and sexual intercourse on a first date were interwoven and gendered. On the part of the young women, the reasons ranged from cultural and moral ethos to personal, emotional, and safety reasons. For example, statements and sayings such as the "body [physical and spiritual] is the temple of God," "dignity of a woman," respect, responsibility, and fear of being labeled cheap, loose, promiscuous or a sex worker were some of the multiple reasons noted that influenced their decisions about whether to engage in sexual activity on a first date or not. There were also personal and emotional reasons that impacted the decision to engage in sexual activity on the first date. These include duration of and commitment in relationship, and readiness to have sex. Some of the specific narratives captured included, "It's too early," "I hardly know you," "Let's get to know each other," "Is this serious or real?," and "Let's postpone sex for now." Some women were cautious on a first date because of disappointment from previous relationships while others were concerned for their sexual health. For the latter group of women, fear of contracting a sexually transmitted infection (STI) and concern over the man's HIV status were ever-present considerations for their behavior on a first date. Still, other women were concerned about their physical safety in terms of rape.

One critical issue for women was the issue of "dignity" and "respect." According to some of the young women (three of them), if a man respects a woman, he will not ask for sex on a first date. This was a curt-email one of the young women showed me some few hours before going on a date:

Date (man): Babe, I luv u so much u know. We can spend the night together afterwards.

R11 (female interviewee): How do you mean? I tot you want us to have fun? You know what, let sleeping dogs lie.

Date: Oh, I only want you to prove your love for me.

R11: Prove what love? Is it not too early to be talking about love? You shdnt be asking for sex now, you know! We only met today Sir. At least value me if you could . . . please. Let's meet tonyt then we have fun, at the bar.[28]

The willingness to have sex on a first date had a gendered dimension. Younger men were more willing to have sex on a first date compared to younger women. One of the reasons for this is because young men perceive sex on a first date as an indication of masculinity and a declaration of power.[29] It appears young men's power is located within patriarchal/cultural privileges that relate to strategies of wooing a woman, i.e., men tend to try to persuade/flatter/cajole/coax women into sexual activity. This ability also includes sweet-talking a woman to make her feel special and drawing on her experience during a conversation. For instance, some young men indicated that it is quite easy to have sex with a woman on a first date if she has had a recent broken relationship. The three women who had sex on a first date listed emotional satisfaction due to disappointment from a previous relationship, financial reasons, the approach and strategy or demeanor of the date, location, and personal choice as factors that influenced their decisions to have sex on a first date.

In addition to financially induced reasons, such as the willingness to spend money on a woman on a first date, men stressed cultural upbringing and demeanor as both triggers and barriers to wooing a woman into sex. One man explained:

> I know they like the 3Cs—Cash, Crown, Car. But not all of them are like that. Some is the approach, the way you talk to them. Look, I know this girl, heh, if you approach her, she wants to know your . . . mind. Whether you are in for sex or [in for] commitment. If you pretend like you want to date her and start like rushing into sex, she will cut you off. . . . So, sometimes, to go fast, you need to go slow. Some girls also want to have fun but do not want to look stupid to a man. They [women] at the same time want to be friends and so immediately you propose to them they will leave you (quit the relationship). They will say they are not ready. [Interviewer: so, it means women are different.] Sir [referring to the interviewer], you can't understand them o. [Interviewer: Yeah! Even men are the same.] Women are complicated. You think they are this before you realize they are that.[30]

The views of women on the matter, particularly on emotional and financial vulnerability, did not differ from what men said although women also drew on these factors especially those related to cultural upbringing as agency. Women indicated that they know that they are vulnerable when they are brokenhearted. Hence, they will not engage in another relationship or a date immediately after a breakup. They said they would normally use their mantra "let's be friends" and would not share information about their past relationships or breakups on a first date. These suggestions form core components of upbringing in Ghana. The women, thus, knew the strategies of men and devised their own strategies to protect themselves. One woman remarked:

> You know men, right? Sometimes you just have [to] tell them what they want to hear. I think it's a thing about human beings. When you disclose everything about your past to them, they tend to use it against you. They will then know that you are like this or like that [will get to know your weakness].

Even for women who did not go on a date or had sex on a first date, strategies for refusing men's dating advances and/or overtures of friendship have been to lie and, in some cases, depending on the principles of the woman, be point-blank. And men know when women lie in this regard. One Muslim woman, 23 years old, narrated:

> Me, I don't just give out my number like that o. You can't see me day one *nɔɔ* [local parlance in Ga meaning soon] and just ask for ma number for me to just give you. I remember this guy in a "trotro" [commercial bus] heading to school one day. There was something like that and we ended up chatting and later when we got off, he was like, "Are we not forgetting something?" I was like "Forgetting what?" . . . [both laugh]. I know, right . . .? I knew he wanted us to exchange contact but I pretended I didn't understand him. Later he said, "Oh I mean how do we contact each other?" . . . I just told him, "I don't give my number to strangers." And that was it. I know some other ladies would lie like "My phone is spoilt" or something like that. For me, I will just tell you, "I don't feel comfortable giving my number out to strangers." That would mean I'm a whore just giving out my contact to every man like that. Guys know when you don't want to.[31]

Thus, in the narratives of women and men, close acquaintance with or knowledge of someone whether in a dating relationship or not is important for building the trustworthiness and willingness of women to engage in sexual activities with men. Culture, moral suasions, choice, and principles work together to structure women's agency regardless of education or age.

Men's understanding of how women conceptualize trustworthiness was not different from women's views. The men indicated that the approach is not to give women the impression that men are desperate for sex or sexual activities, e.g., kissing, fondling, caressing, etc. Rather, compassion, care, selflessness, appearance, and a listening ear could be effective for some men. A male artisan listed the following strategies:

> Don't rush and make it seem like [the date] is all about sex. It will come naturally. Try and enter her world and don't be too difficult and blunt on a first date. Be gentle and make her laugh. Be sensitive to what she says, I mean pay attention to her needs and feelings. Women easily trust "cute"/gentle guys you know. Don't make her feel your money can buy her. Some will go crazy if you do that. You know culturally, women are brought up not to have sex for money or fall in love with someone because of their possessions. That will be considered as "ashawo" or "two two."[32]

Another woman added:

Sometimes you can't tell, maybe it's just "sex" at first sight. Ei, I mean love at first sight. Some guys are just too gentle. They are just too sweet [take good care of women and are respectful]. So, sometimes when he wants it, you also wanna do it but because of our culture it's hard to sometimes do that because you don't want to be "cheap," you see o. They think you "spoil." We know guys oo. They are "bad." If they want sex, they will tell you all manner of things and be too sweet and nice or "yap" [slang, to deceive or make a woman fall in love]. As for me, if I have sex with you, it's because I feel like doing that and not what you do per se. But being gentle and respectful can do the magic too.[33]

In terms of location (i.e., one's own residence or paid for accommodations such as a guest house, hotel or motel), the women indicated that they would rarely invite a man they barely knew to their residence or have sex with them. Across narratives, while young men would invite women to their apartment, women would prefer neutral locations like restaurants, beer bars, food joints, movie theaters, lover's joints on university campuses, or the beach where they would feel comfortable and secure; hence, women choose the location of a date. Women, in general, indicated insecurity of visiting a man at his residence on a first date because that can send a wrong signal to the man that the woman had consented to the man's sexual advances including the potential to engage in sexual activity. The insecurity also included physical insecurity of suffering possible harm of forced sex. It was, therefore, not surprising that only one out of the five men indicated that sex on a first date took place at his residence.

HEALTH BELIEFS AND PRACTICES

This section focuses on interviewees who never had sex on a first date. It deals with how young adults perceive sexual risk and how their understanding of sex (knowledge, perceptions) feeds into healthy sexual experiences and practices.

The young women and men defined sexual risk to include both social and biomedical risks. Socially, young adults constructed risk as being dumped after sex and acting against their cultural/moral/religious/spiritual upbringing/beliefs. On the other hand, they constructed biomedical risks to include practices related to unplanned pregnancy, sexually transmitted infections (STIs), and sexual discomforts. The constructions of risks were found to be gendered; young women were more preoccupied with biomedical risks than the social risks and devised strategies to address them. Women participants used lack of contraceptives or menstrual "excuses" as a reason not to have sex. Out of the 5 men who had sex on a first date, 2 used contraceptives (male condoms, spermicides, and emergency contraception for their female partner). According to one man who used a condom, since he had not dated the partner for long and did not want her to doubt his intention, for example, the misconception of their HIV or STIs status, he had no choice but to use a condom. By using a condom, his date trusted him and did not deny him sex. For the women, all 3 who had sex on a first date indicated that they used contraceptives; all insisted on male condom use and one used an emergency oral contraceptive pill, even after using a condom. One of the women narrated a situation where a condom broke during sex. In that instance, she used an emergency contraceptive to forestall an unplanned pregnancy. Also, the woman stated that she also went to get voluntary counseling and testing at a health facility to be sure that she had not picked up any STIs from the act because she had fears.

While the reasons for using contraceptives depended on the willingness of a male partner, it was also influenced by the women's willingness to have sex. This is because they (men and women) noted that women's sexual interests hinged on several factors including mood and menstrual periods. While men and women indicated that some women are "turned-on" for sex during their menstrual period, be it a first date or not, others (both women and men) stressed that menses, often referred to as "flow," "visitor," or "red flags" by the interviewees, offer women the opportunity to deny men sex, in particular, first date sex as indicated in the narrative of one woman: "Oh, I will just give an excuse that I have my visitor and that ends it."

For the men who did not use contraceptives, two claimed that the sexual act was impromptu; they did not expect the woman to give in to sex—they "got lucky." The other two also noted that they just do not like using condoms; hence, they had no condom with them. When asked whether the willingness to use a condom influenced the women's refusal to have sex with them, they claimed that at some point they had to lie about their HIV status to the women who insisted on the use of condoms. A man aged 28 years said in pidgin,

> Once you know sey you fuck "raw" [without condom] and no sure of the "chick" you for take some antibiotics immediately. Why do you think that you can't determine that you are HIV positive until 6 months after your last sex? Waiting period dey where the initial infection go develop. So make you no wait till in [it] develop. Use strong antibiotics like sey Amoxicillin/Amoxiclav, doxycycline, etc. Yeah![34]

However, some young men acknowledged that women are aware about men's sexual escapades, in terms of the desire to put sexual pleasure ahead of safe sexual practices, and that for some women, no amount of money or strategy or "yap" can make them have sex on a first date without the use of a condom. A young man aged 27 years, for example, said in Pidgin,

> A kai sey some girlie be like that, I shock sef. See, she come dey ask me HIV status. The way a bore heh. As a tell am I do am, she come dey ask make in see am. Ah ma guy. . . . You wan[t] chop woman, see this idiot. Masa ino bi easy o. I talk am sey ma last test be two weeks ago. Oh, no she was just too inquisitive and wanted to check everything. She read any leaflets in my drawer. I had some used prescriptions in my drawer somewhere and she even wanted to take the paper away. I don't know for what? But I think she checked from her phone. The time wey I finally convince am sef be another wahala. She they ask me "What's that?" All these be before the game o, oh boy! You know guys always have our style. Buh, masa ino be easy. Some be wild. [Translation: I met a very difficult lady who would insist on knowing my HIV status before having sex. It took me a hell of a time to convince her. She read every detail of used medicine and prescriptions I had. She even checked from the internet using her phone. When I finally persuaded her, she was again curious about a scar on my penis and asked, "What's that?" I managed to convince her but it wasn't easy.][35]

As the above quote indicates, young women have knowledge and agency about sexually transmitted infections. The young women's agency about sexual risk, especially about a male partner's sexual escapades, infidelity and/ or trustworthiness may be premised on what men tell them; the findings point to a promising direction of understanding young women's healthy sexual practices from their conceptualization of sexual risk and sexual practices. It also shows that women know that men can have multiple sexual partners and that the decision to engage in sex with a man on a first date is based on choice and principle.

DISCUSSION AND CONCLUSION

This chapter discussed young adults' perceptions and experiences of sex on a first date and highlighted their sexual negotiation strategies in sex decision-making on a first date. A male sex sociologist-turned anthropologist, I engaged in frequent reflexive discussions with my interlocutors and took care to reflect on the potential influence of personal experience on any feelings aroused by the data. I maintained focus on the interviewees' knowledge and construction of meaning and events and endeavored to understand the experiences from their perspectives. I am cautious not to oversimplify the sexuality of young adults using the narratives of 20 interviewees. However, the exploration of the narratives of young adults from the suburbs of Cape

Coast presents insights into the ways that heterosexual demands and certain gender codes intersect to empower the sexuality of young women in Ghana.

I found that knowledge and experiences of sex, including the decision to engage in sex, whether on a first date or not, were influenced by several outlets including family training/socialization, religious beliefs, the media, and formal education. The family and the church were instrumental in socializing young adults about their sexuality. The reasons offered for not engaging in sex on a first date were gendered. Women stressed five main concerns when confronted with the prospect of engaging in sexual activity: namely, family upbringing, religious beliefs (e.g., issues around fornication, spirituality), choice (e.g., decision to postpone sex, respect for womanhood, not appearing "cheap" to a man), perceptions/experiences (e.g., gender mistrusts: "men cannot be trusted"), and safety (secrecy, STIs and unplanned pregnancy). Men, on the other hand, stated two main factors that impacted their decisions: safety reasons (possibility of being infected with an STI) and women's mistrust as critical dimensions in their inability to have sex on a first date.

Regardless of the demographic profile, the women preferred male partners who were slightly older than they were. Therefore, in terms of sexual experiences, young women would date men who were older while younger men would normally date younger women. The findings support cultural expectations of adolescents' age preferences for dating partners in Ghana and can also be interpreted to mean that younger women are exposed to a sexual relationship and/or sexual activities at early ages compared to younger men.[36]

The reasons offered for engaging in sex on a first date were a complex blend of emotional and financial reasons and strategies and skills of a partner. For those who engaged in sex on a first date, the findings show troubling issues relating to the abuse of drugs among young men. The phenomenon of self-prescription of drugs based on previous knowledge and experiences of using a drug has negative implications for young men's sexual health. Women's understanding of risk was a complex blend of concern about contracting STIs, privacy/secrecy about sex and unplanned pregnancy. Although young adults had concerns about sexual risks, especially those related to having sex on a first date or with someone they do not know well, it appears young women were more preoccupied with biomedical risks such as unplanned pregnancy and contracting STIs than young men. The sources of risks were based on knowledge of mistrusts about men's sexual escapades. Young adults were aware of sexual risks and modern contraceptives and used them based on perceived risk assessment. They suggested it was "too early" or they were still "getting to know a partner" and wanted to wait before engaging in sex. Although this study reveals that young women's use of oral contraceptives was risky because it did not protect them from HIV, they did, however, perceive it as agency against the risk of unplanned pregnancy. Indeed, the findings support previous studies conducted by Fiaveh et al. as well as Yeboah and Appai that suggest that knowledge of modern contraceptives and sexually transmitted infections affect contraceptive use and sexual behavior.[37] The men's reasons for using contraceptives depended on the willingness of a woman to have sex and a woman's choice of contraceptives. This means that young men were at risk because they relied on young women to make the contraceptive decision. Culture in this regard may be harmful to young men because of the licentious attitude toward them. Culturally, men are expected to woo women for love and in sex even if some women contest cultural scripts.[38] These findings thus call for the need to educate young men about the implications of living risky sexual lives using the media, pharmaceuticals, and regulation.

Young women were constructed as agents in negotiating sexuality with men. Women knew that men have misconceptions about women's sexuality and devised strategies to deal with those misconceptions. For example, while some women would cite cultural and moral ethos not to engage in sex on a first date, some will simply ask men to postpone sex to prove love to them. The study thus supports the view postulated by scholars such as Bochow and Meyers that cultural and moral ethos that stress the chastity of young women can be empowering for young women's sexuality depending on how women draw on these teachings. While suggesting that cultural reproduction and social reproduction can be empowering for women, I am also aware of work conducted by other researchers like Bourdieu and some gender activists in Africa such as Stella Naynzi and colleagues who may argue the contrary. Synchronizing both perspectives, culture, then, can be both restrictive or repressive and empowering depending upon how agency is utilized.

In conclusion, this chapter has provided a discussion about the complexities of knowledge, attitudes, perceptions, and culture as tools for empowerment in social, economic, and political agency in relation to young adults' sexual decisions. Examples were provided which demonstrate that culture per se is not as disempowering to young women's sexuality as popular knowledge makes it appear. Thus, while the study agrees with scholars who have suggested that cultural and religious attitudes about sexuality can be negative, this study adds that women draw on cultural arguments as an agentic tool. Indeed, consistent with other studies, this study demonstrated that cultural and religious ethos shape understanding about sex, although in the Ghanaian situation, culture is both a suppressor and an agentic tool for women. It will also be useful to engage young adults about comprehensive sexuality education and sexual health needs to highlight discourses that promote women's agency in Africa. Indeed, as some earlier scholars have indicated, in designing interventions and programs for young women in Africa, there is a need to pay close attention to the dynamics of African societies and cultures. The intersection of culture and agency speaks to the complex and complicated ways in which some women negotiate sexuality.

NOTES

1. Margaret Mead, *Coming of Age in Samoa: A Study of Adolescence and Sex in Primitive Societies* (London: Penguin books, 1943).

2. Michel Foucault, *The History of Sexuality: Vol. I.* An Introduction, Trans. R. Hurley (New York: Pantheon, 1978).

3. Diana T. Meyers, *Gender in the Mirror: Cultural Imagery and Women's Agency* (Oxford University Press, 2002).

4. Meyers, *Gender in the Mirror.*

5. Margarita Lia Delgado-Infante and Mira Alexis P. Ofreneo, "Maintaining a 'Good Girl' Position: Young Filipina Women Constructing Sexual Agency in First Sex within Catholicism," *Feminism & Psychology* 24, no. 3 (2014): 390–407.

6. Pierre Bourdieu and Jean-Claude Passeron, *Reproduction in Education, Society and Culture*, 2nd ed. Trans. Richard Nice (Thousand Oaks, CA: Sage, 1990).

7. Patricia Hill Collins, *Black Feminist Thought: Knowledge, Consciousness, and the Politics of Empowerment,* 2nd ed. (New York: Routledge, 2000).

8. Patricia Hill Collins, *Black Sexual Politics: African Americans, Gender, and the New Racism* (New York: Routledge, 2005).

9. The society affords boys and men more sexual options than girls and women.

10. Daniel Yaw Fiaveh, "Daddy, Today We Have a Match!" Women's Agentic Strategies in Initiating Sexual Intercourse in an Urban Ghanaian Community, in *Research on Gender and Sexualities in Africa,* ed. Jane Bennett and Sylvia Tamale (Dakar: CODESRIA, 2017), 89–103.

11. Daniel Yaw Fiaveh, Michael P. K. Okyerefo, and Clara K. Fayorsey, "Women's Experiences of Sexual Pleasure in Ghana," *Sexuality & Culture* 19, no. 4 (2015b): 697–714.

12. John Kwasi Anarfi and Adobea Yaa Owusu, "The Making of a Sexual Being in Ghana: The State, Religion and the Influence of Society as Agents of Sexual Socialization," *Sexuality & Culture* 15, no. 1 (2011): 1–18.

13. Peter Sarpong, *Girls' Nubility Rites in Ashanti* (Tema: Ghana Publishing Corporation, 1977).

14. Chris Abotchie, *Social Control in Traditional Southern Eweland of Ghana. Relevance for Modern Crime Prevention* (Accra: Ghana Universities Press, 1997).

15. Abotchie, *Social Control in Southern Eweland.*

16. Daniel Yaw Fiaveh, "Phallocentricism, Female Penile Choices, and the Use of Sex Toys in Ghana," *Sexualities* 22, no. 7–8 (2019a): 1127–1144.

17. Daniel Yaw Fiaveh, Chimaraoke O. Izugbara, Michael P. K. Okyerefo, Fenneke Reysoo, and Clara K. Fayorsey, "Constructions of Masculinity and Femininity and

Sexual Risk Negotiation Practices among Women in Urban Ghana," *Culture, Health & Sexuality* 17, no. 5 (2015a): 650–662.

18. Astrid Bochow, "Let's Talk About Sex: Reflections on Conversations About Love and Sexuality in Kumasi and Endwa, Ghana," *Culture, Health & Sexuality* 14, sup1 (2012): S15–S26.

19. GSS, *Ghana Demographic and Health Survey.*

20. Mamadou Diouf, "Young adults and Public Space in Africa: Past and Present," in *The Palgrave Handbook of African Colonial and Postcolonial History*, eds. Martin S. Shanguhyia and Toyin Falola (New York: Palgrave Macmillan, 2018), 1157.

21. James Clifford, "Notes on (Field)notes," Chapter II, in *Fieldnotes: The Making of Anthropology*, ed. Roger Sanjek (New York: Cornell University Press, 1990), 47–70.

22. Clifford, *Notes on (Field)notes.*

23. Daniel Yaw Fiaveh, "Understanding Sexuality in Sub-Saharan Africa: A Manual Approach to Thematic Analysis of In-depth Interviews" (*SAGE Research Methods Datasets,* 2019b), http://dx.doi.org/10.4135/9781526474841.

24. Ghana Statistical Service (GSS), "*2010 Population and Housing Census: District Analytical Report. Cape Coast Municipality*," Accra: Ghana Statistical Service, October 2014), http://www.statsghana.gov.gh/docfiles/2010_District_ Report/Central/Cape%20Coast.pdf.

25. R16: 26 years, Christian, higher education.

26. R10: 23 years, Muslim, high school.

27. R13: 28 years, Christian, higher education.

28. R11: 21 years, Christian, secondary education.

29. Fiaveh, *Use of Aphrodisiacs in Ghana.*

30. R16: 26 years, Christian, higher education.

31. R10: high school.

32. R2: 28 years, Christian, higher education.

33. R6: 25 years, Christian, in school.

34. R 13: Christian, 28 years, higher education.

35. R18, Muslim, basic education.

36. GSS, *Ghana Demographic and Health Survey.*

37. Fiaveh, Izugbara, Okyerefo, Reysoo, and Fayorsey, *Sexual Risk Negotiation Practices among Women.*

38. Fiaveh, *Women's Agentic Strategies in Initiating Sex.*

BIBLIOGRAPHY

Abotchie, Chris. *Social Control in Traditional Southern Eweland of Ghana. Relevance for Modern Crime Prevention.* Accra: Ghana Universities Press, 1997.

Anarfi, John. *Universities and HIV/AIDS in Sub-Saharan Africa: A Case Study of the University of Ghana, Legon.* Institute of Statistical, Social and Economic Research, University of Ghana, Legon: ADEA Working Group on Higher Education, New York City: The World Bank; October 2000.

Anarfi, John Kwasi, and Adobea Yaa Owusu. "The Making of a Sexual Being in Ghana: The State, Religion and the Influence of Society as Agents of Sexual Socialization," *Sexuality & Culture* 15, no. 1 (2011): 1–18.

Awusabo-Asare, Kofi, Ann Biddlecom, Akwasi Kumi-Kyereme, and Kate Patterson. "Adolescent Sexual and Reproductive Health in Ghana: Results from the 2004 National Survey of Adolescents." *Occasional Report* 22. New York: Guttmacher Institute, June 2006.

Bernard, H. Russell. *Research Methods in Anthropology: Qualitative and Quantitative Approaches,* 4th ed. New York: Rowman & Littlefield, 2017.

Bochow, Astrid. "Let's Talk About Sex: Reflections on Conversations About Love and Sexuality in Kumasi and Endwa, Ghana," *Culture, Health & Sexuality* 14, sup1 (2012): S15–S26.

Bourdieu, Pierre. "Cultural Reproduction and Social Reproduction." In *Power and Ideology in Education*, edited by Jerome Karabel and A. H. Halsey, 487–511. New York: Oxford University Press, 1977.

Bourdieu, Pierre, and Jean-Claude Passeron. *Reproduction in Education, Society and Culture,* 2nd ed. Translated by Richard Nice. Thousand Oaks, CA: Sage, 1990.

Brownmiller, Susan. "Making Female Bodies the Battlefield." In *Rape and Society: Readings on the Problem of Sexual Assault*, edited by Patricia Searles and Ronald J. Berger, 171–173. New York: Routledge, 2018.

Butler, Judith. *Gender Trouble: Feminism and the Subversion of Identity*. New York: Routledge, 2011.

Clifford, James. "Notes on (Field)notes." In *Fieldnotes: The Making of Anthropology*, edited by Roger Sanjek, 47–70. New York: Cornell University Press, 1990.

Collins, Patricia Hill. *Black Feminist Thought: Knowledge, Consciousness, and the Politics of Empowerment,* 2nd ed. New York: Routledge, 2000.

Collins, Patricia Hill. *Black Sexual Politics: African Americans, Gender, and the New Racism*. New York: Routledge, 2005.

Connell, Raewyn. "Margin Becoming Centre: For a World-Centred Rethinking of Masculinities," *NORMA: International Journal for Masculinity Studies* 9, no. 4 (2014): 217–231.

Delgado-Infante, Margarita Lia, and Mira Alexis P. Ofreneo. "Maintaining a 'Good Girl' Position: Young Filipina Women Constructing Sexual Agency in First Sex within Catholicism," *Feminism & Psychology* 24, no. 3 (2014): 390–407.

Diouf, Mamadou. "Young People and Public Space in Africa: Past and Present." In *The Palgrave Handbook of African Colonial and Postcolonial History*, edited by Martin S. Shanguhyia and Toyin Falola, 1155-1173. New York: Palgrave Macmillan, 2018.

Evans-Pritchard, Edward Evan. "Sexual Inversion among the Azande," *American Anthropologist* 72, no. 6 (1970): 1428–1434.

Fainzang, Sylvie. *An anthropology of lying: information in the doctor-patient relationship.* Farnham: Ashgate, 2015.

Fiaveh, Daniel Yaw, and Michael P. K. Okyerefo. "Femininity, Sexual Positions and Choice." *Sexualities* 22, nos. 1 & 2 (2019): 131–147.

Fiaveh, Daniel Yaw. "Daddy, today we have a match!" Women's agentic strategies in initiating sexual intercourse in an urban Ghanaian community. In *Research on gender and sexualities in Africa,* edited by Jane Bennett and Sylvia Tamale. Dakar: CODESRIA, 2017.

Fiaveh, Daniel Yaw. "Phallocentricism, Female Penile Choices, and the Use of Sex Toys in Ghana," *Sexualities* 22, nos. 7–8 (2019): 1127–1144.

Fiaveh, Daniel Yaw. Understanding Sexuality in Sub-Saharan Africa: A Manual Approach to Thematic Analysis of In-depth Interviews. *SAGE Research Methods Datasets*, 2019.

Fiaveh, Daniel Yaw, Chimaraoke O. Izugbara, Michael P. K. Okyerefo, Fenneke Reysoo, and Clara K. Fayorsey. "Constructions of Masculinity and Femininity and Sexual Risk Negotiation Practices among Women in Urban Ghana," *Culture, Health & Sexuality* 17, no. 5 (2015): 650–662.

Fiaveh, Daniel Yaw, Michael P. K. Okyerefo, and Clara K. Fayorsey. "Women's Experiences of Sexual Pleasure in Ghana," *Sexuality & Culture* 19, no. 4 (2015): 697–714.

Fiaveh, Daniel Yaw. "Masculinity, Male Sexual Virility, and Use of Aphrodisiacs in Ghana," *The Journal of Men's Studies* 28, no. 2 (2020): 165–182.

Fiaveh, Daniel Yaw. Cultural Sensitivities: A Case Study of Sexual Pleasure in Ghana. Sage Research Methods Cases, 2018. http://dx.doi.org/10.4135/9781526429780.

Foucault, Michel. *The History of Sexuality: Vol. I.* An Introduction (R. Hurley, Trans). New York: Pantheon, 1978.

Ghana Statistical Service (GSS). *"2010 Population and Housing Census: District Analytical Report. Cape Coast Municipality."* Accra: Ghana Statistical Service, October 2014. http://www.statsghana.gov.gh/docfiles/2010_District_Report/Central/Cape%20Coast.pdf.

Ghana Statistical Service (GSS). *Ghana demographic and health survey 2014.* GSS, Ghana Health Service and ICF International, Rockville, 2015.

Haire, Norman. *Sex Problems of Today.* Sydney: Angus & Robertson, 1943.

Howson Richard. *Challenging hegemonic masculinity.* New York: Routledge, 2006.

Izugbara, Chimaraoke, Frederick Wekesah, Caroline W. Kabiru, Joshua Amo-Adjei, Zacharie Tsala Dimbuene, and Jacques Emina. *Young People in West and Central Africa: Health, Demographic, Education, and Socioeconomic Indicators.* African Population and Health Research Center (APHRC), Nairobi, Kenya, 2017. https://www.researchgate.net/publication/321062035_Young_People_in_West_and_Central_Africa_Health_Demographic_Education_and_Socioeconomic_Indicators.

Kimmel, Michael S. and M. Mahler. "Adolescent masculinity, homophobia, and violence: random school shootings, 1982–2001." *American Behavioral Scientist* 46, no. 10 (2003): 1439–1458.

Kimmel, Michael S., Jeff Hearn, and Robert W. Connell, eds. *Handbook of Studies on Men and Masculinities.* Thousand Oaks, CA: Sage, 2004.

Kinsman, John, Stella Nyanzi, and Robert Pool. "Socializing Influences and the Value of Sex: The Experience of Adolescent School Girls in Rural Masaka, Uganda." *Culture, Health & Sexuality* 2, no. 2 (2000): 151–166.

Kwankye, Stephen O., and Eric Augustt. "Media Exposure and Reproductive Health Behaviour among Young Females in Ghana." *African Population Studies* 22, no. 2 (2007): 79–108.

Licht, Hans. *Sexual Life in Ancient Greece.* London: Routledge, 1932.

Malinowski, Bronislaw. 1927 [2013]. *Sex and Repression in Savage Society, Vol. IV.* New York: Routledge.

Marcus, Steven. 1964 [2017]. *The Other Victorians: A Study of Sexuality and Pornography in Mid-Nineteenth Century England.* London: Routledge.

Mead, Margaret. *Coming of Age in Samoa: A Study of Adolescence and Sex in Primitive Societies.* London: Penguin Books, 1943.

Meyers, Diana T. *Gender in the Mirror: Cultural Imagery and Women's Agency.* London: Oxford University Press, 2002.

Miedema, Esther, and Georgina Yaa Oduro. "Sexuality Education in Ghana and Mozambique: An Examination of Colonising Assemblages Informing School-Based Sexuality Education Initiatives." In *The Palgrave Handbook of Sexuality Education*, edited by Louisa Allen and Mary Louise Rasmussen, 69–93. London, Buckingham: Palgrave Macmillan, London, 2004.

Neale, Jonathan. "Starting from Below: Fieldwork, Gender and Imperialism Now." In *Taking Sides: Ethics, Politics and Fieldwork in Anthropology*, edited by Heidi Armbruster and Anna Laerke, 217–255. New York: Berghahn Books, 2010.

Nukunya, Godwin Kwaku. *Tradition and Change in Ghana: An Introduction to Sociology,* 3rd Edition. Accra: Ghana Universities Press, 2014.

Patton, George C., Susan M. Sawyer, John S. Santelli, David A. Ross, Rima Afifi, Nicholas B. Allen, and Monika Arora. "Our Future: A Lancet Commission on Adolescent Health and Wellbeing," *The Lancet* 387, no. 10036 (June 2016): 2423–2478.

Sarpong, Peter. *Girls' Nubility Rites in Ashanti.* Tema: Ghana Publishing Corporation, 1977.

Spielmann, Stephanie S., Geoff MacDonald, Samantha Joel, and Emily A. Impett. "Longing for ex-partners out of fear of being single," *Journal of personality* 84 no. 6 (2016): 799–808.

Spronk, Rachel. "Female Sexuality in Nairobi: Flawed or Favoured?" *Culture, Health & Sexuality* 7, no. 3 (2005): 267–277.

Spronk, Rachel. "Sexuality and Subjectivity: Erotic Practices and the Question of Bodily Sensations." *Social Anthropology* 22, no. 1 (2014): 3–21.

Tamale, Sylvia. "The Right to Culture and The Culture of Rights: A Critical Perspective on Women's Sexual Rights in Africa." In *Old Wineskins, New Wine: Readings in Sexuality in Sub-Saharan Africa,* edited by Izugbara, Chimaraoke O., Chi-Chi Undie, and Jennifer Wanjiku Khamasi, 53–69. New York: Nova Science Publishers, 2010.

The United Nations Children's Fund (UNICEF). Young people in changing societies: the MONEE project, CEE/CIS/Baltics, Regional Monitoring Report No. 7 (Florence, UNICEF Innocenti Research Centre, 2000). http://www.un.org/esa/socdev/unyin/documents/ch04.pdf.

Van der Geugten, Jolien, Berno van Meijel, Marion H. G. den Uyl, and Nanne K. de Vries. "Protected or Unprotected Sex: The Conceptions and Attitudes of the Youth in Bolgatanga Municipality, Ghana," *Sexuality & Culture* 21, no. 4 (2017): 1040–1061.

Van der Geugten, Jolien, Berno Van Meijel, Marion HG den Uyl, and Nanne K. de Vries. "Virginity, Sex, Money and Desire: Premarital Sexual Behaviour of Youths in Bolgatanga Municipality, Ghana," *African Journal of Reproductive Health* 17, no. 4 (2013): 93–106.

Vanwesenbeeck, Ine, Judith Westeneng, Thilly de Boer, Jo Reinders, and Ruth van Zorge. "Lessons Learned from a Decade Implementing Comprehensive Sexuality Education in Resource Poor Settings: The World Starts with Me," *Sex Education* 16, no. 5 (2016): 471–486.

World Health Organization. Programming for Male Involvement in Reproductive Health. Report of the meeting of WHO Regional Advisers in Reproductive Health WHO/PAHO, Washington, DC, USA, 5-7 September 2001. Geneva: World Health Organization. https://apps.who.int/iris/bitstream/handle/10665/67409/WHO_FCH_RHR_02.3.pdf;jsessionid=AE13B11F2483AADE9898271B618D766B?sequence=1.

Yeboah, Thomas, and Thomas Padi Appai. "Does Knowledge of Modern Contraceptives and Sexually Transmitted Infections Affect Contraceptive Use and Sexual Behaviour? Evidence from senior high school girls in the Akuapem North Municipality, Ghana." *GeoJournal* 82, (2017): 9–21. https://doi.org/10.1007/s10708-015-9667-x.

Chapter 5

The Economic Impact of Divorce on Women in Ghana

Naa Adjeley Suta Alakija-Sekyi

Divorce has been one area of nuptiality that has attracted little scholarly attention in Ghana, despite the academic popularity of the subject in other parts of Africa and other regions of the world. The literature demonstrates that increasing rates of divorce are a global phenomenon. Several studies in Africa show that Nigeria, Malawi, and Ethiopia are the leading nations with high rates of divorce on the continent.[1] In *The Marriage-Go-Round*, Andrew J. Cherlin posits that marital instability characterized the last half of the twentieth century in the United States.[2] Other scholars suggest that the rate of divorce among older couples and military couples increases every year because of the likelihood of those people marrying at an early age.[3] In Europe, the findings vary across countries and yet results show that divorce is common. Regardless of the location, there is a great deal of resemblance in the causes and consequences of marriage dissolution across countries in Europe.[4] Although these works have proved the rising rate and causes of divorce globally, there is little on how most divorcees, especially women, can reconfigure their lives following divorce. Thus, there is a gap in the literature on the experiences of divorcees waiting to be filled. This chapter examines the ramifications of marriage dissolution on women in Ghana in hopes of bringing insights into the experiences of Ghanaian women. It explores the hardships Ghanaian women are likely to face if they do not possess the economic and financial capital to facilitate their transition from being married to being single women.

Marriage dissolution has both instantaneous and long-term effects on divorcees and their children (if any) as well as extended family members.

Scholars like Paul R. Amato posit that divorce turns out to be one of the most distressing situations with far-reaching ramifications for families. He notes that many divorcees go through dejection, neglect, isolation, heartache, defeat, disloyalty, and disappointment.[5] These negative impacts are differentiated by gender, and women in particular tend to experience the negative effects of divorce to a greater extent than men. Some scholars suggest that there exists a negative relationship between divorce and the median age of women. Divorce adversely affects urbanized and employed women more because of the young age at which they marry. Divorce currently has a positive effect on women who focus on their education and marry later in life. Most women who are older when they marry have stable marriages compared to those who marry at younger ages.[6]

There are several scholarly works on divorce in Africa that show rising rates reflected in an increase in the divorce rate from 22 percent in 1961 to 29 percent in 1988. The 7 percentage point increase over 27 years also correlated with a rise in female headship of households.[7] Other studies posit that increasing divorce rates result from changes in society brought on by modernization, the decline in kinship bonds, the increase in educational and job opportunities for women and the increasing individualism as a way of life.[8] These societal changes may offer positive post-divorce experiences for some women while others may go through poverty, hunger, diseases, and the inability to educate and provide shelter and clothing for dependent children.[9] Sylvia Chant, economist and critic of the expression "feminization of poverty," has argued that although female headship of households has been used to explain women's poverty, this argument does not take into account the fact that heading families can be empowering for women. She states that "women may actively choose headship as a means by which they can enhance the well-being of their households and/or exert more control over their own lives."[10] Since some women become heads of households due to divorce, it follows that divorce can be a good thing, even if in a limited sense, for some women.

Constance R. Ahrons has noted that divorce that happens unexpectedly has more devastating effects on mothers and children than when divorce happens in a long, drawn-out process.[11] Divorce is a significant social force whose gendered ramifications give insights into women's social lives as wives, mothers, workers, and members of extended family units. Against that backdrop, this chapter answers questions specific to women's post-divorce economic conditions in Ghana. It utilizes an Akan saying, *me nwe aboɔ* (literally, "I won't eat stones") to interrogate traditional responses to stressful familial situations, in this case, divorce, on women. What traditional expectations undergird women's economic contributions in marital situations? How do women execute these expectations once they are married? What does it mean when divorced women say that they will not eat stones? These questions are examined in the sections below.

THEORETICAL FRAMEWORK

The ABC-X model of family stress and coping was first developed by Reuben Hill in 1949 which he further refined in 1958. Hill developed the model to explain "the crisis-proneness and freedom from crisis among families."[12] His model was the first to systematically describe what might be anticipated when a family goes through a period of stress, and what factors influence their stress response. According to Manijeh Daneshpour, Hill's model "described the interactions of a set of variables to explain the events leading up to a family crisis."[13] Hill used the model to analyze stress and the coping mechanism of families. In Hill's model, A represents the crisis precipitating event or stressor event that interacts with B, which denotes resources available to a family. The C variable denotes the family's perceptions of the stressor, and X represents the result of interactions among A, B, and C.[14] The variables B and C determine whether the stressor event A results in crisis or not.

  Relating the model to the financial situations of divorced women in Ghana allows us to grasp the impact of stress on a family following divorce. "A" represented the divorce situation and "B" the kind of coping strategies that individual women adopted to survive financially. Variable C denotes the interpretation the women gave to the divorce situation which determined the kind of strategy to adopt and finally producing X, which represents the kind of divorce experience, that is whether a positive or negative experience, thus its name. Mainly, variable A represents the family stressor, which in this case is the divorce, and X represents the crisis that followed, what this study termed "chewing stones" or "not chewing stones." The impact of the stress can be cushioned by the two defensive factors, B and C, of which B constitutes the internal resources adopted by the divorcee, that is, the financial resources women had available and made use of. The variable C denotes individual perception, appraisal, or meaning, in other words, the interpretation given to the experience. These two defending factors are interconnected with the stressor, which in this case is the divorce. Thus, when the result is adaptive, implying that there are factors like savings, investments, extra ways of making money, it will ensure that women are not chewing stones. It also means that divorced women will experience manageable levels of stress, and so the ensuing outcome may not be negative. However, if the subsequent outcome is maladaptive, which implies that the divorce has a heavy toll on women's finances such that they must go through challenging times to survive and thus chewing stones, it means divorced women experience high levels of financial crisis.[15]

CULTURAL PERCEPTIONS THAT
UNDERGIRD DIVORCE

There is an Akan proverb that speaks to financial security post-divorce, "*se wo gyae me a, me nnwe aboɔ,*" which is translated as "I will not eat stones if you divorce me." This proverb stands in stark contrast to popular media conceptions of the financial fate of women post-divorce and the constant admonitions to women to stay in marriages for their financial security and the security of their children. "I will not eat stones" suggests two possibilities: one positive and confident and the other resigned but hopeful. Women who utilize the saying in the former sense may hurt emotionally but not financially. The patriarchal nature of Ghanaian society encourages male dominance and female subordination. As a result, in the past, more males were encouraged to go to school than females. This gave men more power over women because education exposed men to more employment opportunities and allowed them to be able to care for their dependents. Women, on the other hand, were encouraged to learn home science from home or if they were lucky, they were able to attend a vocational school. Women were encouraged to build up their domestic skills with the hopes that a rich, hardworking man would marry them. Women were, therefore, groomed to be submissive and obedient so they could have successful marriages. It is not surprising that a traditional leader from one of the regions in Ghana attributed the increasing rate of divorce to lack of submission of women and low level of grooming by modern parents.[16] Nana Ogyedum Tsetsewa I, a queen mother, further reiterated that most marriages are ending because young couples seek marital advice from the wrong people on social media. She claimed that "these self-acclaimed social media marriage counselors are feminists, divorcees, lesbian and inexperience (*sic*) people."[17] It is telling that the queen mother identified feminists, divorcees and lesbians as false social media counselors, people who are also women, without recognizing the changes occurring in society that go beyond social media. She rather admonished parents to groom their children, ergo daughters, well on the traditional norms and values which will help in the preservation of marriages.

What the queen mother and others who think like her did not address is that contemporary Ghanaian society is a society in flux. Women are increasingly educated, are working and are also earning incomes like men. Some are successful businesswomen who are more than capable of providing, even for their husbands. Many women, who have not received a formal education, build economic and social capital. For example, women dominate petty trading and also earn income as subsistence farmers by selling extra produce. The days are coming to an end when Akan men were told during marriage ceremonies that if a wife acquired wealth, she would take it to her family but if she incurred a debt, it would be the husband's responsibility. That advice could reference the fact that a couple's children belonged to the wife's family, but the trend now is toward nuclear families which have rendered that aspect of Akan family life obsolete. That said, the traditional concept of male breadwinner and female homemaker remains the norm for most Ghanaian societies; thus, the power of the working woman is downplayed and her financial abilities are not regarded.

In Ghana, a wife is seen as dependent on her husband and does not have the right to file for divorce. The belief is that economically she will not be able to survive a divorce, especially if she has children. Given this, women are always advised by parents and society to take very good care of their husbands and to be submissive to them regardless of how bad or mean their husbands treat them. Although Ghanaian society has both matrilineal and patrilineal descent groups, men are often given a place of honor in relationships because men are valued as heads of households. Even within families with matrilineal backgrounds, the uncles are the ones responsible for the upkeep of their nieces and nephews (children of their sisters). However, women from matrilineal backgrounds are expected to be industrious and thus tend to be more economically resilient compared to women from the patrilineal background.[18] Based on the financial power they wield, the former, as well as other empowered and industrious women from different backgrounds, are more likely to file for divorce or boldly come out to tell husbands that "even if you divorce me, I will not eat stones."

Most societies and some media outlets in Ghana have on several occasions hyped the issue of post-divorce financial challenges for women and have, thus, had discussions on programs advising women to keep a good relationship with their husbands because of the financial distress they are most likely to experience after divorce. The discussions also give the impression that most street children are from divorced homes and are on the streets because mothers took them away from their fathers and could not take good care of them financially. Sylvia Chant referred to this view of women's post-divorce poverty as a way of implying that "when women are without men, their situation is worse!"[19] We hardly hear of discussions encouraging men to respect women or emphasizing the fact that when there is divorce, men equally suffer like women. Further still, there is little discussion or encouragement of women to walk out of distressing or abusive marriages. A typical example is a YouTube discussion between a popular Ghanaian actress by the name of Vicky Zugah and a media person by the name Zion Felix, published 24 March

2020. Their discussion focused on the fact that women should not allow themselves to be 'oppressed to death' in marriage. They encouraged women to be bold and to walk out of an abusive marriage.

Most Western literature on divorce suggests that women are worse off financially after divorce.[20] While generalizations can be problematic, the one about women's worsening financial situations post-divorce should be interrogated in the same way that Chant and others have challenged the general notion of the feminization of poverty without adequate substantiation. A contextual analysis that critically examines the causes of divorce can reveal nuances in women's post-divorce financial circumstances that will be lost in generalized analysis. Women stay in or out of relationships for complex reasons, often informed by personal choices framed by cultural expectations and norms. According to Joseph Osafo et al., there are six major causes of divorce in Ghana. These include infidelity, abuse, financial support/financial problems, intimacy, third-party intrusion, and gender-role ideology.[21] These factors have differential influences on women's and men's decisions to divorce; however, testimonies by women in other studies show that intimacy, lack of financial support, and sole responsibility for domestic chores ranked high on women's decisions to divorce.[22] But there is a class dimension in the ways the variables influence women as a group when they contemplate divorce. Women who are financially independent and/or reside in urban areas are more likely to act on their feelings as the basis for divorce than their poor counterparts, regardless of location. In her study of divorce among Ghanaian immigrants in Toronto, Martha Donkor reported that some women found their husbands' refusal to do housework while expecting their wives to contribute 50 percent to the family budget a major point of disagreement and conflict among couples.[23] She quoted one woman as saying,

> In Ghana, I did not hear my father insist that my mother should contribute part of the chop money. Mother did all the housework as her contribution toward the upkeep of the family. She was not obliged to contribute financially. That was the father's responsibility. In Canada, the dynamics have changed. Both husband and wife have to work. I have to contribute 50 percent of the family budget, so why must I do one hundred percent of the housework?[24]

On the other hand, anecdotes from music and proverbs point to men's fear of "high-maintenance women" and infidelity as top reasons for divorce. Titles of popular songs like "*obaa yi dee ope srade nnam*" (this woman likes fatty meats) and "*sokoo na emaa pe*" (women like good things) underscore men's apprehension of women who demand money and other expectations from their husbands. In Donkor's study, referred to above, a husband reacted to women's call for "fifty-fifty" in this manner: "Some of the women who have gone to school behave as if they have not come from Ghana. When they were in Ghana they did everything without complaining. Now they are in Canada and they want to behave like white women. I will not put up with any of those women!"[25] The fear is that women can be too powerful and will not submit to men's control. Similarly, sayings/proverbs like "*emaa nye*" (women are bad) and "*mempe etwe a ete brɔfo*" (I don't like a vagina that understands English) express men's frustration with a woman they cannot control and a reason for divorce. Some men often threaten women by saying "*megyae wo ama wo ho akyere wo* (I will divorce you to make your life difficult)," which elicits women's response of "*wogyae me a me nnwe aboɔ*" (I won't eat stones if you divorce me).

HAPPILY DIVORCED WOMEN

This part of the chapter uses material from a larger research study conducted by the author and others to examine women's post-divorce experiences. The focus here is on women's financial situations after divorce; women's narratives underscore the primacy of money and its distribution in the family in women's decisions to divorce. As we will see, although women may not be happy about getting a divorce or being divorced, they prepare themselves financially toward the post-divorce. A case in point is a lady who mentioned that she has developed "shock absorbers" to withstand all that her husband was doing and even though she was not happy he was divorcing her, she knew she will be better off without him. According to her, she performed both the breadwinner and homemaker roles during the marriage and so it prepared her for the divorce. Her husband had stopped giving her housekeeping money when he started misbehaving in the marriage. Another woman reported that she had just started enjoying the fruits of her labor knowing that she is working hard and enjoying what she has toiled for. She is currently able to save and invest in her children's education, unlike previously when she often had to borrow money from friends for the upkeep of her household. She started borrowing money from friends to supplement her income when her husband who earned a lot of money stopped contributing to the upkeep of the home. Thus, at the time of her divorce, she was already a responsible breadwinner. She did not necessarily need a man's financial support to make her feel fulfilled.

The concept of financial violence does not resonate with some people despite its unambiguous meaning. Financial violence occurs in a relationship when one partner uses money to hurt the other. It can be particularly painful in a single-earner marriage in which the breadwinner, often the husband, believes the money is exclusively theirs. Women in such marriages can be treated like children by their husbands. Women must ask for money and then justify what they need the money for. In conversations with women who were full-time homemakers when they were married, some revealed how humiliating it was to ask a husband for money and then to have him ask what the money was needed for. Such women felt they were reduced to the status of children when it came to dealing with money in their marriages. In rural communities where women cook daily, they usually get the housekeeping money in the late afternoon and then plan around the amount given. Often, the money the husband provides is used for meat and/or fish; women buy vegetables and the carbohydrate part of the meal if they are not subsistence farmers. Thus, women's ability to hold families together depends to a degree on the availability of money men provide. Stingy men and men who drink heavily or chase after other women may not provide enough money for housekeeping, may not provide money regularly or may cease to provide money altogether if they realize that wives would pick up the slack. Men who do such things engage in the "double hurt," that is, emotional and financial hurt. Women who do not believe that they should be financially responsible for men and who divert their money elsewhere tend to feel positive after divorce.

Women who divorce because of financial hurt often say that they feel liberated from financial challenges. An underlying issue with financial troubles in families is the tendency for couples to keep separate accounts. Superimposed on this tendency is the cultural expectation that husbands are financially responsible for wives and children. Thus, women generally enter marriages with the expectation that they will have access to their husbands' money. Even when husbands set their wives up in a trade in hopes that money coming from selling goods will be part of the family budget, as is the case in many communities from the North, some women may misconstrue the gesture and perceive the men as users. It is socially frowned upon for a man to depend on his wife financially, especially among the Akan. Hence, it is common to hear women complain that "*wo a wontua; kakra a ye de bebɔ yen ho ban no nso wo begye adi; aden?*" (You won't pay, meanwhile the little available for us to preserve and depend on, must you come for it and squander, what type of man are you?). In such instances, the saying that "*sokoo na emaa pe*" provides cultural meaning to the intersection of gender and class in nuanced ways. A divorced woman shares that she would have died of depression had she not divorced her husband. She felt she was working too hard to have her husband emjoy the fruits of her labor. It should be noted, however, that society frowns on a woman who walks away from a marriage because her husband fell ill or lost his source of income and could no longer be responsible financially. The ABC-X model asserts that divorce can be beneficial particularly for women because of the positive experiences it brings them. The participant has benefitted positively from the divorce because instead of experiencing financial constraints as most literature confirms for women, she rather has financial freedom which has even extended to her mum and her younger sisters whom she could not assist previously when she was still married. She confirmed not being able to assist her family during the period she was married because she did not have enough money to support them as she was burdened with providing for her marital home without support from her working husband. She consistently had misunderstandings with her husband anytime her family visited and so she deliberately stopped them from coming to her marital home during the period she was married.

A fifty-one-year-old banker from the Western Region also shared that her husband never paid a dime in the house in which they lived although the property was owned by the woman. She had to stop asking him for money because any time she did, it generated unnecessary arguments. Sometimes he would go and stay at his mom's house for a while and come home later. She stopped asking for his support because she was not comfortable with his attitude. She resorted to managing the financial issues single-handedly. Interestingly, at the point when he started feeling guilty, he sat her down and told her that he was saving his money to go toward a bigger house, on land also owned by the woman, so that they could move into that house in the future. This happened to be a lie; instead, he was finding ways and means of selling the property to abscond with the money. She quickly started working on filing for divorce upon the realization that her husband was only in the relationship to rip her off. Though she doesn't have money in excess because of the children's education, she is still better off than she was when married. At the heart of this script is the power of gender roles to sustain or disrupt a family. In ordinary day conversations, when a woman declares that her husband takes good care of her, she means that he bears (sole) responsibility for the family's financial needs. On the other hand, a man who feels taken care of usually expresses it in terms of the absence of starvation. Starvation means two things: lack of food and intimacy. And so, when a man says that his wife takes good care of him, he means good culinary and sexual service. For many couples, these roles are not easily negotiated. A strong reason for a wife to file for divorce is when a husband reneges on his role to provide money to maintain the family.

In a case similar to the banker's experience, a businesswoman who was married to a rich fisherman indicated that she never enjoyed any of her husband's wealth until their marriage finally ended on a sad note. According to her, although her husband was very rich—he owned a lot of boats and had employees working for him in his cold stores—he never paid his children's school fees let alone gave her money to buy food to cook for the family. Yet he always returned home from work expecting to find food on the dining table awaiting him. She said she never stopped providing for the family until she was informed that he had been sending money to his mum and sisters to the detriment of his wife and children. She shared an expression in Fante—"*emidzi minfa bɔge nyɛ swine*" (I don't tolerate nonsense)—which means that her husband saw another side of her when she found out. She left the marriage and is happier because she knew that she was a single woman taking care of her home and had no expectation from a "good for nothing husband and father." She said her children were doing great and had no reason to worry. The woman had single-handedly raised four children during her marriage and did not see any difference between being married and being divorced. She preferred being single to being married because she could save and invest in the upkeep of her four children.

FINANCIALLY STRESSED POST-DIVORCE WOMEN

For some women, the economic burden is stressful even though they feel some level of freedom in other aspects of their lives after divorce. Financial stress happens when ex-husbands renege on their responsibility to care for their children. Divorced women can take husbands who refuse to take care of their children to the Department of Social Welfare for redress; however, many women are apprehensive about taking advantage of that service either through stigma, ignorance, or wanting to avoid further confrontation with ex-husbands. Women who face such situations strategize by engaging in other money-generating opportunities to be able to overcome the financial burden. As the narratives of some divorced women demonstrate, they experienced difficulty and stress caused primarily by lack of financial support or access to resources.

A forty-nine-year-old from the Central Region who was married for fourteen years without financial freedom until she divorced said she never benefited from the investment she put up for her family. Her ex-husband was, instead, misusing the proceeds from the investment because he took her for a fool. Her husband, who was more educated than she was, managed the finances without her input or knowledge even though she contributed a greater chunk of the investment package. As a businesswoman, she recalled that when they got married and moved into a new neighborhood, she realized that there were no stores in the neighborhood that sold electrical gadgets and appliances. She thought that such a shop would be lucrative. She took money out of her business account to set up this shop for her husband to manage because of his training in electrical engineering. After investing in the shop for the family's financial security, her husband left her for another woman who would enjoy her hard-earned investment. She did not fight him when he opted for a divorce because she realized he did not love her. She has moved on and is doing even better than her ex-husband, after the divorce.

She admitted that the divorce was difficult and stressful because she loved her husband and wanted to spend the rest of her life with him. However, he was not interested in her happiness. Love is many-sided and so it becomes difficult for adults to discuss it in their marriages. It is a problematic thing to handle even during couples' therapy. It is quite normal for a spouse to fall out of love and is sometimes the basis for which some marriages dissolve. Falling out of love is difficult to change because once the person says he or she has fallen out of love, there is nothing counselors can do about it.

Another participant expressed frustration with her financial situation after divorce and shared that she wished she could turn back the hands of time. When she was married, she would receive money from her husband to support the family. For this participant, divorce is not a pleasant experience because she must bear the brunt of expenses such as school fees and other living expenses. Although it was unpleasant, she was conflicted about the divorce to the extent that sometimes she wished she had stayed in the marriage. Her husband had started seeing another woman who had children. The participant has experienced much regret and anguish about an argument she had with her ex-husband when she found out that he was cheating on her. Out of anger and frustration, she made certain utterances she wishes to take back. She promised her ex-husband that she and the children would never come back to him for a dime, a statement she wishes she could take back. She wants to apologize to the ex-husband who had responded that he would hold her to her words. He would tolerate neither her return nor any request for support. In divorcing, she prioritized the needs of her children, and even though she has no problem making them happy, she feels that she should also be happy and not be stressed about it. Despite the challenges, she managed to find a way to care for the children and made sure that they were doing well.

Another participant maintained she understands why some divorced women insult their children when they think of their ex-husbands. When she feels burdened financially, all she thinks of is insults, especially words that can hurt her ex-husband. Her ex-husband provides little support and when she thinks of how much she is spending on the family, which under normal circumstances would have been less, it makes her furious. She then takes it out on the children by insulting them. While the insults are aimed at their father, the children bear the brunt of her frustrations. Emotionally, she claims to be happy but shares that the financial responsibility of ensuring her children stay in school and live comfortable lives makes her furious, particularly because she has had to pause her building project. The participant shared that she rushed into marriage because she saw her husband as a rich young man. She only realized he was not rich after they got married, but she endured until she finally asked for the divorce because the marriage was just not working. She now advises young people who are yet to marry to be patient and make sure they make the right choices. Her reason is that if one makes the mistake of choosing wrongly and becomes a single parent along the way, one may not like the financial challenges associated with the situation. She mentioned that apart from engaging in other activities to make extra money, she has ended up liquidating almost all her investments for the sake of the upkeep of her children.

One of the divorced women wonders if she is the same person who was so happily divorced at the beginning of the breakup. She confessed that while she was happy at the beginning of the divorce, as time passed, she began to envy her married friends. She compared herself to them and noticed how happy they were together. She felt they were better off than her, partly because of the financial burden she was handling alone. Sometimes she deliberately avoided them. Her financial burden was heavy. Although she was operating a grocery shop, there were times when she could not afford to buy goods for the shop. The participant emphasized that she had a very genuine case for divorce: her husband was from a different ethnic group and his family was always interfering in their marriage because they didn't like her. Her family was also not in favor of the marriage. Since she was gainfully employed, she never anticipated any financial challenges after the divorce. Now that she knows and understands the realities of single parenting, she doesn't take it for granted. Irrespective of her resilience, the experience of this participant and the others discussed above confirm the conclusion drawn in studies on divorce, that even though divorce is a normal occurrence within contemporary societies, it is still very traumatic to the people who experience it.

FINANCIAL BOOSTING FACTORS

Apart from the discretionary income they received post-divorce, the participants engaged in two major strategies to earn extra income: improve their earnings in the formal sector and take on additional jobs in the informal sector. These helped with their adaptive experiences post-divorce as the ABC-X model posits.

Scholars have explored the association between financial distress and marital breakups. Previous research shows that women's post-divorce financial welfare is subject to the social resources available to them at the time of divorce[26] According to Amato these social resources could be a skill, aid, or support that can be willingly applied when needed.[27] These comprise individual (such as education and skills), interpersonal (for example, kin support, and remarriage) and structural (for instance, welfare, alimony and child support) resources. There is therefore a direct link between individual resources and improved circumstances as Amato points out.[28] The participants who had formal education and some money were able to upgrade their skills by going back to school after divorce. They were subsequently promoted with accompanying higher salaries which allowed for a better standard of living for themselves and their children. This example aligns with studies that show that for highly educated and high-income women divorce may have a positive impact since it gives women the opportunity to gain a sense of control over their financial management.[29] Indeed, these women reported that divorce had a positive impact on their lives because they are happy, particularly because they now have full control over their finances and other properties, which before the divorce they did not have control over. The majority of the participants who were working in the formal sector furthered their education with hopes of getting a promotion. Promotion often would mean an increase in their monthly earnings, and, therefore, a better quality of life for the family.

A participant pointed out that she is very happy now because she has been promoted at her workplace and now earns more than enough to take care of her children, whose father was not contributing financially to the care of the children. The participant had supported her husband financially so he could further his education in hopes that he could increase his salary. After he had completed his education, when she expressed interest in going back to school, he refused to support her. Due to the lack of support she received, she divorced him for a better life for herself and the children. Similarly, another participant said that she was grateful to God for helping her to successfully further her education as well as granting her the promotion she deserved. This has made her very happy because of the higher increments in her monthly earnings. She invests in businesses and facilities, which she enjoys doing. She says her life is more comfortable without her ex-husband. To boost her financial stability, one woman who refused to let her dreams be destroyed, pursued a master's program at a university. This helped her cope with the stress of the divorce. After completion of her studies, she was promoted into a headmistress position at one of the senior high schools. Within a short period, she was transferred to the district education office with a higher promotion. She indicates that she is well paid and contributes to the children's school fees. And although her ex-husband sometimes refuses to contribute to the caring of the children, it does not negatively impact the children's education. These three cases demonstrate that some years after a divorce, women employ strategies such as furthering their education to increase their earning power.

ADDING INFORMAL EMPLOYMENT
TO FORMAL SECTOR JOBS

The interviewees also shared the various strategies they employed to increase their income. To live more comfortably and to have financial freedom, some of the women in this study who were employed in the formal sector also engaged in other businesses to raise additional money to ensure that they were financially secure. These individuals indicated that they wanted to break the cycle of poverty associated with divorced women. They all reported that their friends, family and church members discouraged them from getting a divorce because, apart from the fact that Ghanaian society frowns on it, divorce can lead to poverty among female divorcees.[30] To ensure financial security, they took on additional jobs.

One participant attests that if she had not established a business in addition to teaching, people in her community would have laughed at her. Many felt that her ex-husband's irregular contributions, although insufficient, were better than nothing. Additionally, they felt that after the divorce, he may not provide money for food or living expenses to assist with caring for the children and that would increase her burden. The participant indicated that she already had a grocery shop which was doing very well until her husband started taking stuff from it and never paying back. As a result, the store collapsed and she decided to start a new business by selling cement and other building materials a few months after the divorce was finalized. The participant shared that the new business has helped in diverse ways, including granting her the opportunity to purchase land on which she has already started building a house.

Similarly, another participant has also taken an additional job in the informal sector to help her care for the children and fulfill her dreams. She, therefore, decided to start a company and started doing door-to-door businesses. She initially started supplying goods to friends and church members on request. Though it was not easy combining this with her formal sector job, she gradually has been able to balance her time. She is happy, particularly when she thinks about her achievements and successes after the dissolution of her marriage. The experience of another participant is comparable to the narratives above. Her husband warned her that if she took the children, he would not pay their school fees. Although scared, she ignored him and took custody of the children knowing that she would have to work hard to take care of them. Looking at the financial challenges she faced, she quickly started to supply goods to her colleagues at her workplace for extra money. The money she earned not only paid the school fees, but she was also able to invest some of it toward the future of her two children. After she started supplying basic needs to her colleagues at work, they encouraged her to get a shop where they could go shopping for supplies. She verifies that she is overjoyed and that although she started small, the business is now successful. She was able to build a house for herself and her children. These examples challenge findings by researchers such as Amato and others who argue that marriage dissolution holds negative financial consequences for women as opposed to men.[31] In the examples above, expenses increased; however, participants' strategies of adjustment saved them from post-divorce poverty. This confirms the ABC-X model's level of a crisis being adaptive due to the resources available to the divorcee.

CONCLUSION

Considering the above discussion, this research contributes to the literature on the financial impact of divorce on women in Ghana. The participants in this study, unlike the traditional Ghanaian families they originated from where men were the financial mainstay of the family, broke tradition and contributed to the upkeep of the home without considering it as an anomaly. When their marriage failed, the women used a number of strategies to survive and were in a better financial position compared to when they were married.

As discussed above, during their marriage the majority of the participants were responsible for the financial upkeep of their homes with little support from their husbands. As such, after divorce, very little has changed for them financially. This finding suggests that the discourse about women's poorer financial circumstances post-divorce is simplistic and requires nuance. Certainly, a woman's financial circumstances post-divorce may be worse, particularly if children are involved and the husband contributed to the financial upkeep of the home during the marriage. However, if a woman played the dual role of homemaker and breadwinner during a marriage, she found she was in a better financial situation after divorce. Thus, a financially stable woman was more likely to have a positive financial experience after divorce. Though divorce is not viewed positively in Ghana based on the stigma associated with divorce, for the women in this study, divorce provided them with a sense of financial freedom. One of the most important conclusions for this study is that exiting a bad marriage leads to a better situation post-divorce.

NOTES

1. Baffour K. Takyi and Christopher I. Broughton, "Marital Stability in Sub-Saharan Africa: Do Women's Autonomy and Socioeconomic Situation Matter?" *Journal of*

Family and Economic Issues 27, no. 1 (2006): 113–132; Anastasia J. Brandon-Gage, "The polygyny-divorce relationship: A case study of Nigeria," *Journal of Marriage and the Family* (1992): 285–292; Monica J. Grant and Erica Soler-Hampejsek, "HIV risk perceptions, the transition to marriage, and divorce in Southern Malawi," *Studies in family planning* 45, no. 3 (2014): 315–337.

2. Andrew J. Cherlin, *The Marriage-Go-Round: The State of Marriage and the Family in America Today* (New York: First Vintage Books, 2010).

3. Jennifer Hickes Lundquist, "A comparison of societal divorce rates to those of enlisted families," *Journal of Political and Military Sociology* 35, no. 2 (2007): 199.

4. Paul R. Amato, "The consequences of divorce for adults and children," *Journal of marriage and family* 62, no. 4 (2000): 1259.

5. Paul R. Amato, "The consequences of divorce for adults and children," *Journal of marriage and family* 62, no. 4 (2000): 1259.

6. Shelley Clark and Sarah Brauner-Otto, "Divorce in sub-Saharan Africa: Are unions becoming less stable?" *Population and Development Review* 41, no. 4 (2015): 583–605.

7. D. S. Boateng, "The changing family and national development in Ghana," in *The changing family in Ghana*, ed., Elizabeth Ardayfio-Schandorf (Accra: Ghana Universities Press, 1996): 1–4.

8. William Josiah Goode, *World changes in divorce patterns* (New Haven, CT: Yale University Press, 1993).

9. Baffour K. Takyi, "Marital instability in an African society: Exploring the factors that influence divorce processes in Ghana," *Sociological focus* 34, no. 1 (2001): 77–96.

10. Sylvia Chant, "Re-Thinking the 'Feminization of Poverty' in relation to Aggregate Gender Indices," *Journal of Human Development* 7, no. 2 (July 2006): 206.

11. Constance R. Ahrons, "Divorce: An unscheduled family transition," *The expanded family life cycle* (1999): 381–398.

12. Reuben Hill, "Generic features of families under stress," *Social Casework* 49 (1958): 143.

13. Manijeh Daneshpour, "Examining Family Stress: Theory and Research," *Quarterly of Clinical Psychology Studies* 7, no. 28 (Fall 2017): 2.

14. Reuben Hill, *Families under stress: adjustment to the crises of war separation and return* (New York: Harper & Brothers, 1949), 265.

15. Yan Xu and Brant R. Burleson, "Effects of sex, culture, and support type on perceptions of spousal social support: An assessment of the 'support gap' hypothesis in early marriage," *Human Communication Research* 27, no. 4 (2001): 550.

16. Ghana News Agency, "Lack of submission in marriages leads to rampant divorce—Nana Ogyedum Tsetsewa I," reproduced on Ghanaweb on March 20, 2021 at https://www.ghanaweb.com/GhanaHomePage/NewsArchive/Lack-of-submission-in-marriages-leads-to-rampant-divorce-Nana-Ogyedum-Tsetsewa-I-1209838?audio=1.

17. GNA, "Lack of submission in marriages leads to divorce."

18. Jean M. Allman and Victoria B. Tashjian, *I will not eat stone: A women's history of colonial Asante* (Portsmouth: James Curry, 2000).

19. Chant, "Re-Thinking the feminization of poverty," 206.

20. Karen C. Holden and Pamela J. Smock, "The economic costs of marital dissolution: Why do women bear a disproportionate cost?" *Annual review of sociology* 17, no. 1 (1991): 51–78.

21. Joseph Osafo et al., "Factors Contributing to Divorce in Ghana: An Exploratory Analysis of Evidence from Court Suits," *Journal of Divorce & Remarriage*, 62, no. 4 (2021): 312–326; see also Kwaku Oppong Asante, Joseph Osafo, and Georgina K. Nyamekye, "An Exploratory Study of Factors Contributing to Divorce Among Married Couples in Accra, Ghana: A Qualitative Approach," *Journal of Divorce & Remarriage,* 55 no. 1 (2014): 16–32, DOI: 10.1080/10502556.2013.837715.

22. Kwaku Oppong Asante, Joseph Osafo, and Georgina K. Nyamekye, "An Exploratory Study of Factors Contributing to Divorce Among Married Couples in Accra, Ghana: A Qualitative Approach," *Journal of Divorce & Remarriage* 55 no. 1 (2014): 25–27.

23. Martha Donkor, "I'm Divorcing because I Drank Lake Ontario": Marital Breakdown in Ghanaian Immigrant Families in Toronto," *Southern Journal of Canadian Studies* 5, nos. 1–2 (December 2012): 241–254.

24. Donkor, "I'm divorcing because I drank Lake Ontario, 250.

25. Donkor, "I'm divorcing because I drank Lake Ontario, 249.

26. Paul R. Amato, "The consequences of divorce for adults and children," *Journal of marriage and family* 62, no. 4 (2000): 1259.

27. Amato, "The consequences of divorce for adults and children," (2000), 1259.

28. Amato, "The consequences of divorce for adults and children," (2000), 1259.

29. Van Eeden-Moorefield et al., "From divorce to remarriage: Financial management and security among remarried women," *Journal of Divorce and Remarriage* 47, no. 3–4 (2007): 21–42.

30. Abankwah Amoakohene, "Relationship between single parenting and academic performance of adolescents in senior high schools: A case study of Afigya Sekyere district in Ashanti region." PhD diss., 2013; Amato, "The consequences of divorce for adults and children," 2000, 1259.

31. Amato, "The consequences of divorce for adults and children," 2000, 1259; Duncan and Hoffman 1985, 485–497; Richard R. Peterson, "Statistical errors, faulty conclusions, misguided policy: reply to Weitzman," *American Sociological Review* 61, no. 3 (1996): 539.

BIBLIOGRAPHY

Ahrons, Constance. R. "Divorce: An unscheduled family transition." In *The Expanded Family Life Cycle: Individual, Family, and Social Perspectives*, 4th ed., edited by Monica McGoldrick, Betty Carter, Nydia Garcia-Preto, 381–398. Boston: Allyn and Bacon,1999.

Allman, Jean M., and Victoria B. Tashjian. *I will not eat stone: A women's history of colonial Asante*. Portsmouth: James Curry, 2000.

Amato, Paul R. "The consequences of divorce for adults and children." *Journal of marriage and family* 62, no. 4 (2000): 1269–1287.

Amato, Paul R. "Research on divorce: Continuing trends and new developments." *Journal of Marriage and Family* 72, no. 3 (2010): 650–666.

Amato, Paul R., and Spencer James. "Divorce in Europe and the United States: Commonalities and differences across nations." *Family Science* 1, no. 1 (2010): 2–13.

Amoakohene, Abankwah. "Relationship between Single Parenting and Academic Performance of adolescents in senior high schools: A case study of Afigya Sekyere district in Ashanti region." PhD diss., 2013.

Boateng, D. S. "The changing family and national development in Ghana." In *The changing family in Ghana,* edited by Elizabeth Ardayfio-Schandorf, 1-4. University of Ghana, Legon, 1996.

Boss, Pauline E., and Carol Mulligan, eds. *Family stress: Classic and contemporary readings.* Sage, 2003.

Braver, Sanford L., Jenessa R. Shapiro, and Matthew R. Goodman. "Consequences of divorce for parents." *Handbook of divorce and relationship dissolution* (2006): 313–337.

Chant, Sylvia. "Re-Thinking the 'Feminization of Poverty' in relation to Aggregate Gender Indices." *Journal of Human Development* 7, no. 2, (July 2006): 201–229.

Cherlin, Andrew J. *The Marriage-Go-Round: The State of Marriage and the Family in America Today.* New York: First Vintage Books, 2010.

Clark, Shelley, and Sarah Brauner-Otto. "Divorce in sub-Saharan Africa: Are unions becoming less stable?" *Population and Development Review* 41, no. 4 (2015): 583–605.

Daneshpour, Manijeh. "Examining Family Stress: Theory and Research." *Quarterly of Clinical Psychology Studies* 7, no. 28 (Fall 2017): 1–7.

Donkor, Martha. "I'm Divorcing because I Drank Lake Ontario": Marital Breakdown in Ghanaian Immigrant Families in Toronto." *Southern Journal of Canadian Studies* 5, nos. 1–2 (December 2012): 241–254.

Duncan, Greg J., and Saul D. Hoffman. "A reconsideration of the economic consequences of marital dissolution." *Demography* 22, no. 4 (1985): 485–497.

Gage, Anastasia J., and Wamucii E. Njogu. *Gender Inequalities and Demographic Behavior: Ghana/Kenya.* Population Council. New York, 1994.

Gage-Brandon, Anastasia J. "The polygyny-divorce relationship: A case study of Nigeria." *Journal of Marriage and the Family* (1992): 285–292.

Ghana News Agency. "Lack of submission in marriages leads to rampant divorce— Nana Ogyedum Tsetsewa I." March 20, 2021. https://www.ghanaweb.com/ GhanaHomePage/NewsArchive/Lack-of-submission-in-marriages-leads-to-rampant-divorce-Nana-Ogyedum-Tsetsewa-I-1209838?audio=1.

Ghana News Agency. "Lack of submission in marriages leads to rampant divorce— Nana Ogyedum Tsetsewa I." March 20, 2021. https://www.ghanaweb.com/ GhanaHomePage/NewsArchive/Lack-of-submission-in-marriages-leads-to-rampant-divorce-Nana-Ogyedum-Tsetsewa-I-1209838?audio=1.

Goode, William Josiah. *World changes in divorce patterns.* New Haven, CT: Yale University Press, 1993.

Grant, Monica J., and Erica Soler-Hampejsek. "HIV risk perceptions, the transition to marriage, and divorce in Southern Malawi." *Studies in family planning* 45, no. 3 (2014): 315–337.

Hill, Reuben. "Generic features of families under stress." *Social Casework* 49 (1958): 139–150.

Hill, Reuben. *Families under stress: adjustment to the crises of war separation and return*. New York: Harper & Brothers, 1949.

Holden, Karen C., and Pamela J. Smock. "The economic costs of marital dissolution: Why do women bear a disproportionate cost?" *Annual review of sociology* 17, no. 1 (1991): 51–78.

Lloyd, Cynthia B., and Anastasia J. Gage-Brandon. "Women's role in maintaining households: family welfare and sexual inequality in Ghana." *Population Studies* 47, no. 1 (1993): 115–131.

Lundquist, Jennifer Hickes. "A comparison of societal divorce rates to those of enlisted families." *Journal of Political and Military Sociology* 35, no. 2 (2007): 199–217.

McCubbin, Hamilton I., and Joan M. Patterson. "The family stress process: The double ABCX model of adjustment and adaptation." *Marriage & family review* 6, no. 1–2 (1983): 7–37.

Oppong Asante, Kwaku, Joseph Osafo, and Georgina K. Nyamekye. "An Exploratory Study of Factors Contributing to Divorce Among Married Couples in Accra, Ghana: A Qualitative Approach." *Journal of Divorce and Remarriage* 55 no. 1 (2014): 16–32, DOI: 10.1080/10502556.2013.837715.

Osafo, Joseph, Kwaku Oppong Asante, Charlotte Asantewaa Ampomah, and Annabella Osei-Tutu. "Factors Contributing to Divorce in Ghana: An Exploratory Analysis of Evidence from Court Suits." *Journal of Divorce & Remarriage* 62, no. 4 (2021): 312–326.

Peterson, Richard R. "Statistical errors, faulty conclusions, misguided policy: reply to Weitzman." *American Sociological Review* 61, no. 3 (1996): 539.

Powers, Sally I., Paula R. Pietromonaco, Meredith Gunlicks, and Aline Sayer. "Dating couples' attachment styles and patterns of cortisol reactivity and recovery in response to a relationship conflict." *Journal of personality and social psychology* 90, no. 4 (2006): 613.

Spradley, James P. *Participant observation*. Long Grove, IL: Waveland Press, 2016.

Takyi, Baffour K. "Marital instability in an African society: Exploring the factors that influence divorce processes in Ghana." *Sociological focus* 34, no. 1 (2001): 77–96.

Takyi, Baffour K., and Stephen Obeng Gyimah. "Matrilineal family ties and marital dissolution in Ghana." *Journal of Family Issues* 28, no. 5 (2007): 682–705.

Van Eeden-Moorefield, Brad, Kay Pasley, Elizabeth M. Dolan, and Margorie Engel. "From divorce to remarriage: Financial management and security among remarried women." *Journal of Divorce & Remarriage* 47, no. 3–4 (2007): 21–42.

Xu, Yan, and Brant R. Burleson. "Effects of sex, culture, and support type on perceptions of spousal social support: An assessment of the 'support gap' hypothesis in early marriage." *Human Communication Research* 27, no. 4 (2001): 535–566.

Chapter 6

Mothers, Daughters, and Queens: Motherwork as Pedagogy

Shemariah J. Arki

This interdisciplinary course is an academic/cultural opportunity designed to explore the contemporary "way of life" of a modern West African society. This is a 10–14-day experiential sojourn that will introduce participants to the "real Africa." The course will address topics in public health, education, sociology, public policy, and government. Students from varying disciplines and community-based professionals will have the opportunity to think critically about both the commonalities and the differences between their lives in the United States in comparison to what they will see in Ghana. Program members will be required to observe and/or participate in cultural, academic and service-learning activities.[1]

This is the course description for Ghana: The Real Africa. Offered as a study abroad opportunity for all upperclassmen at Kent State University, the two-week pilgrimage is not for the faint of heart. Touting an abundance of happenings, the itinerary consists of activities such as welcome receptions, beachfront lunches, and visits to a palace to meet the paramount chief and queen mother. These diplomatic activities were sandwiched between visits to museums, national landmarks, and, of course, a tour of the slave dungeons of Cape Coast and Elmina Castles. The castles were the main attraction for many visitors to Ghana during the maiden *Year of Return* events in 2019. According to the website yearofreturn.com,

The "Year of Return, Ghana 2019" is a major landmark [and] spiritual and birth-right journey inviting the Global African family, home and abroad, to mark 400 years of the arrival of the first enslaved Africans in Jamestown, Virginia. The arrival of enslaved Africans marked a sordid and sad period when our kith and kin were forcefully taken away from Africa into years of deprivation, humiliation and torture. While August 2019 marks 400 years since enslaved Africans arrived in the United States, "The Year of Return, Ghana 2019" celebrates the cumulative resilience of all the victims of the Trans-Atlantic slave trade who were scattered and displaced through the world in North America, South America, the Caribbean, Europe and Asia.[2]

The group of seven students and four professors from Kent State University who went to Ghana had only two male-identified folks, initially skewing the results of this ethnographic study based on gender identity and expression, which is deeply impacted by a colonized perspective on social norms rooted in the amalgamation of biological sex and political power. As an intersectional feminist scholar, the fact that our travel group was mostly female identified excited me greatly as I began to think of how identity/expression could be an unapologetic central theme of the study abroad. At the onset, I failed to consider the colonial and imperialistic implications of those who identified as women on the continent and how gaps in knowledge and experience between Africans in the Diaspora and Africans on the continent would further differentiate the results of our study. Also, I failed to interrogate my assumptions about gender, specifically around the roles of mother and queen. This chapter conflates the five tenets of Black Feminist Thought (BFT) with a sociopolitical recitation of what it means to identify as a US-born, Black woman who was enstooled as a Ghanaian queen mother. The research presented here seeks to juxtapose the sociopoliticized concept of queen mother with the academic theory and frame of BFT to provide an inclusive and intersectional pedagogy that centers Black girls and positions classrooms as spaces of radical transformation.

According to Marijke Steegstra, the role of queen mother remains an integral role in traditional Ghanaian villages and towns and their accompanying government structures.[3] Rooted in the traditional African religion, the most significant role a queen mother participated in was the grooming and selection of the next chief. Often referred to as "sisters of the chief," queen mothers of the Akan and Krobo traditions were political leaders, providing wisdom, knowledge and understanding of complex village issues directly to the chief so that he would be able to make sound and equitable decisions. As Ghana gained its independence and began to create new systems of government, the role of the queen mother shifted. Based on geographic location and proximity to traditional religion, the role of queen mother has been influenced greatly by modernization and colonization while adapting and remaining vital to the modern world.[4]

The role of gender and the framing of it through a Eurocentric lens gives us further insight into the historical and sociopolitical role of the queen mother in today's Ghanaian society. Steegtra maintains that one of the current roles of the queen mother is to serve as a broker between the government and community, noting that colonialism and other missionary activities are important factors in this change of perception.[5] Colonial and postcolonial governmental structures, laced with patriarchal iterations, began to relegate queen mothers to an inferior position, making a distinct point of demarcation in the traditional and contemporary roles of Ghanaian queen mothers. Admin explains further that,

> For West Africa, one aspect remains consistent: the African people have a very different approach to power among women than the traditional western conception implies. When people in the West consider the concept of equality between the sexes, they think of men and women sharing equal roles in society. However, in traditional West African culture, power actually lies in the dynamic differences between the roles of men and women. It is within these unique characteristics that are distinctively male or female that the power emerges.[6]

Despite these facts, queen mothers in Ghana have managed to circumvent gender norms and stereotypes to remain an integral part of communities and governments alike, providing assistance, support, and wise counsel that centers the most marginalized by reinforcing group identity and solidarity across lines of difference.[7]

BLACK FEMINIST THOUGHT AS WAYS OF KNOWING

In the US, Black women were historically overlooked and underrepresented in social, economic, and political interactions. As a result of the interlocking nature of oppression produced by the European colonization and imperialism of Black, Indigenous and People of Color (BIPOC) across the globe, strategies like double consciousness[8]—often referred to today as intersectionality[9]—became tools for enslaved Africans, and free Black folks, to create agency in the pursuit of their liberation. As the news of the end of the Civil War reached Black communities in the rural South and Reconstruction began, a limited quest for equality and access was only made available to Black men, leaving Black women to strategize for themselves and their community.

Throughout the abolition and suffrage movements, Black women began to articulate a radical consciousness born out of their oppressive historical experiences. According to Shemariah Arki, "The very nature of what it meant to identify as a Black womxn, an enslaved African female in the colonial United States, creates agency and fuels resistance in the persons identified as such."[10] Named "race women" by the dominant power structure at the time, Sojourner Truth, Anna Julia Cooper and Ida B. Wells are just a few examples of the women who were able to articulate this consciousness of resistance and demanded to be treated as equals. Like many Ghanaian women, Black women in the US had a unique standpoint because of their material reality.

As gender constructs and gender roles were woven into the very fabric of the US Constitution, Black women produced an alternative epistemology to survive, contoured by their most salient identities of race, class and gender. Contemporary Black feminist identity and the epistemologies and ontologies they privilege, are rooted in the sociopolitical contradictions of minoritized, intersectional identities for those who identify as Black women. To survive, many Black feminists find themselves in a constant state of knowing and becoming. This juxtaposition of identities and the negotiation of them provides the social construction for the introduction of Black feminist thought (BFT) as a research framework for this project.

The theory and methods originated by Patricia Hill Collins as BFT are: (1) lived experience as the concrete criterion for meaning, (2) using dialogue to assess knowledge claims, (3) the ethic of caring, and (4) the ethic of responsibility.[11] Very similar to the role of the queen mother, BFT is a framework based on the material realities and lived experiences of Black women; that is, BFT recognizes that Black women do the work that builds and sustains their communities. Their labor is often in opposition to the colonial and imperialist narrative that relegates Black women to the margin and disrupt their ways of being, a very similar narrative to the evolution of the role of the queen mother in Ghana, upon the arrival of Eurocentric and Christian principles. At the center of BFT is the love and labor of Black women—their "enslavement to this country, to suffrage, to civil rights, and family rights."[12]

In her work, *We Can Speak for Ourselves: Parent Involvement and Ideologies of Black Mothers in Chicago,* Billye Sankofa Waters advances Hill Collins's idea of motherwork as theory and method. Like the construct of the queen mother, motherwork "blurs discipline lines towards a collective experience."[13] Therefore, motherwork, which is an output of BFT, can be viewed as a parallel westernized praxis of a Ghanaian queen mother.

MOTHERWORK: THE WESTERNIZED
PRAXIS OF A QUEEN MOTHER

The very nature of what it meant to be an enslaved African woman has the potential to create agency and fuel resistance. Harriet Jacobs illuminates the story of Margaret Garner, an enslaved African woman who escaped, with her children, from her northern Kentucky plantation.[14] Garner, when recaptured, chose to behead her oldest daughter and proclaimed to her mother-in-law: "Mother, before my children be taken back to Kentucky I will kill every one of them!" As an enslaved African, Garner had very little autonomy over her children. What she knew, in her mind and her heart, was that if her babies were to ever be free, it was her responsibility to make it happen. That inherent responsibility, with the tenacity to move forward by any means necessary, can be identified as a performance of motherwork. Sankofa Waters, in her exploration of the work of Hill Collins, tells us that motherwork is that which "can be done on behalf of one's biological children, or for the children of ones' racial-ethnic community, or to preserve the earth for those children who are yet unborn."[15] In previous writing, Hill Collins posits the following 5 pillars of motherwork: bloodmother, othermothers and women-centered networks (WCN); mothers, daughters and socialization for society; community othermothers and political activism; motherhood as a symbol of power; and the view from the inside: the personal meaning of mothering.[16] These pillars are also embedded in the ideation and work of the queen mother—African women who generally hold leadership roles in the community and/or government and who work toward increasing development and providing basic needs to women, children and other oppressed populations.[17]

Before colonization, the role of a queen mother was an important political figure who often ruled autonomously. In the Akan tradition, queen mothers rule *with* the chief and are considered the spiritual leaders and keepers of the genealogical history of all families in the village. One of the more traditional duties of the queen mother is to aid in the selection of the next chief, which is someone in her family, as chieftaincy is a matrilineal process.[18] Colonizers minimized the importance of the role of queen mother, often dismissing and/ or diminishing their roles, and addressed them as "sisters" of the chiefs.[19] Even today, gender roles, which empower men, are still used in colonialist government structures to diminish the extremely important role of mothers and motherwork in Ghanaian communities. Today in Ghana, various queen mother associations organize to reposition the queens as the title of queen mother has been diminished in value relative to the title of chief. To be influential queen mothers, they must organize themselves in regional and national networks to ensure their communities' needs are met.

BLOODMOTHERS, OTHERMOTHERS, AND WOMEN CENTERED NETWORKS (WCN)

Bloodmothers, Othermothers and Women Centered Networks (WCN) are built and sustained by women with a strong connection to their matriarchal ancestors and an intrinsic connection to the feminine divine.[20] According to Sankofa Waters, "WCN's are described as a community of mothers, grandmothers, sisters, aunts, cousins [or neighbors] responsible for taking care of the children."[21] As communities of women who share the responsibility of child-rearing, these networks operate as a family, either birth or chosen, and remain just as dynamic as its women, as many identify with multiple oppressed identities.[22] While removed from the direct trauma of slavery, Black women are still directly affected by its impact, as the US continues to create laws and policies that perpetually leave Black girls, women and femmes as the unpaid laborers of American life. The legacy and impact of inherited, multigenerational trauma is often observed through the mere presence of othermothers and WCNs. These networks are a direct derivative of slavery, as families were intentionally separated to maintain slavery as the economic engine of the American South. Othermothers often replaced bloodmothers in familial units and provided the chosen family with the physical health and spiritual healing to live another day as an enslaved African in the US. While this trauma is scientifically proven to be passed from mother to child in utero, it also serves as an important catalyst for motherwork. Newman et al. confirmed the importance of mitochondrial DNA (mtDNA) in determining African identity and agency in the descendants of the transatlantic slave trade.[23] Newman et al. further state that mothers play a significant role in child-rearing, family organization, and, thus, in the transfer of cultural beliefs systems and practices to their offspring.[24] Among Ghanaians, the practice of kin fostering ensures that children who lose their bloodmothers or whose bloodmothers are not in a position to care for them are not bereft of motherly care. Indeed, the idea that children, regardless of age, must have parents partly explains why Akans have a system of succession and inheritance.

MOTHERS, DAUGHTERS AND
SOCIALIZATION FOR SOCIETY

Black mothers and daughters often find themselves in the space between theory and practice, creating dynamic spaces of teaching and learning through their daily interactions with one another and with the world. Evans-Winters, author of *Black Feminism in Qualitative Inquiry,* uses the concept of "daughtering" to further conceptualize this concept.[25] In line with motherwork, daughtering is fostered by an inherited communal, ontological, and spiritual-cultural responsibility. This term represents the myriad of roles and responsibilities Black girls play within their families, communities, and society. Evan-Winters explains the role of a Black daughter is to support the household and also to model the ways of active citizenship by standing up for other minoritized populations.[26] In line with the outputs of mtDNA, daughtering is also present in the keeping of the culture through activities like witnessing and testifying, a long-used tool of the Black literary aesthetic that includes the listener as an active participant in storytelling, encouraging active participation, both physically and verbally.

Daughters then have the important task of being better and going farther than their mother; nevertheless, many mothers shield and protect their daughters from the ugly parts of their past to keep them safe. This shielding is often at the root of many mother-daughter melees. This emotional destruction highlights the pragmatism of Black women's motherwork. For many daughters, it's through realization and acceptance of their mother's identity as a woman first, often through their own participation in a WCN, that they ascertain and transcend the goals they have set for themselves. Wallace said it best, "Now that I know my mother better, I know that her sense of powerlessness made it all the more essential to her that she take radical action."[27]

COMMUNITY OTHERMOTHERS
AND POLITICAL ACTIVISM

Community othermothers often speak as a part of a collective, standing on the shoulders of ancestors and at the front lines with fellow othermothers and activists, shouldering the fight for freedom. Black women's community activism is often realized through the example of their othermothers, paired with the contention that their "worldly accomplishments" must be used for the betterment of their people. Navigating the identity politics of what it means to be a Black college-educated and second-generation free-born Black woman, activist and organizer, Ella Baker was heavily influenced by the racial uplift and social responsibility present in her own family values system. Known as the midwife of the civil rights movement, Baker's Black feminist practice and display of motherwork helped to birth Black women leaders on today's frontlines, including Alicia Garza, Patrice Cullors and Opal Tometi—the founders of #BlackLivesMatter. Baker's stance on humanities and service functioned as the precursor to future generations of women who educate, agitate and organize grassroots movements in their communities. Like the process of becoming a queen mother, her moral formation, social and religious influences proved foundational as her identity was constructed into the icon we know her as today.

Manye Esther, a Ghanaian queen mother in the Manya Krobo Queen Mother Association (MKQMA), is the essence of motherwork, given her service on the Ghana AIDS Commission. Manye Esther recognizes her role in the chain of queen mothers, bloodmothers and othermothers as she provides supportive services to families, orphans and people living with HIV/AIDS. Before her work with the HIV/AIDS community, she was part of the 31st December Women's Movement, one of Ghana's largest political organizations that seeks to aid women in improving their living standards, both economically and socially.[28] The founder of the movement, former first lady and leader of the National Democratic Party, Nana Konadu Agyemang-Rawlings, has worked with queen mothers and nongovernmental organizations to advance the well-being of women and girls in the country. People affectionately call Agyemang-Rawlings "Mama" to denote her role as former mother of the state. Both Manye Esther and Nana Konadu place mother caring as central to the ethos of Ghanaian community.

MOTHERHOOD AS A SYMBOL OF POWER

In the US, community othermothers have long been seen as middle-class Black women's political activism. However, the labor imparted by many othermothers to move their community forward is often shouldered by many whose names and faces are unknown. These "strong Black women" are the ethos of the continual development of the Black family, the Black community and the Black radical tradition. This intrinsic sense of care and power can be traced back to various aspects of African cultural values found in social practices and affirmations such as Sankofa. Sankofa, the Ghanaian principle that translates to "return and fetch it" (back to the roots), is spoken or referred to by many Black women in the US as an affirmation of their duty as a bloodmother and othermother. Maternal politics often include acting on such feelings of power when viewed through the sociopolitical context of the times. Motherhood as power most often occurs when a Black woman has, and chooses to, put forward their privileged identity. By negotiating their identities, Black women can position themselves, and those who enter with them, at the center, shifting the focus from the margin and demanding the necessary tools and resources needed to improve their communities. This position can also be taken up by those who care about Black women, nodding to the role of motherwork as pedagogy.

THE VIEW FROM THE INSIDE: THE
PERSONAL MEANING OF MOTHERING

To serve in the capacity of mother is one of the highest honors. Through the practice of motherwork, Black women shine. This shine often comes after settling the internal dissonance around the responsibilities and the pressures of practicing motherwork, which in American culture can be viewed as a contradictory institution based on the Western concepts of gender, which remain in stark contrast to the role of mother and othermother in an African context. Many Black feminist writers posit that birthing and/or raising children can serve as catalysts for mothers as they begin their work of identity development. What cannot be overlooked in this process is the radical love that children give their mothers and othermothers in a world that consistently shows them the opposite. Love serves as an affirmation that exists in the place of failed relationships with Black men and strained sisterhood with other Black women. This agape and unconditional love from child to mother affirms the importance of Black motherhood as an institution "in a society plagued by the sexual politics of Black womanhood."[29]

While the earliest versions of queen mothers were identified through lineage and family, today's queen mothers are selected, appointed and/or enstooled based on their display and commitment to each of the tenets of motherwork, independent of the biological affiliation to the chief or chieftaincy.[30] While the needs of each community are different, the manifestations of colonialism and imperialism and their impacts on the lives of Ghanaians are what helps to drive the motherwork. On the continent or in the US, mothers and othermothers have a role to play in keeping the culture, which is vital to the cultural survival of Black folk on the continent and in the diaspora.

MOTHERWORK AS PEDAGOGY

As an early career educator, I ran out-of-school programs for middle and high school students that focused on diversity (identity), leadership (activism) and service (community organizing). I saw myself as an othermother—in the same path as those fierce educational activists who came before me to lay the foundation and open the way. As my identity shifted to include becoming a bloodmother to two Black boys, my other identities also shifted in such a way to privilege the role of mother, specifically in an epistemological and ontological manner. Therefore, my research, teaching and praxis became equally informed by my intersectional identities—a US-born, working-class, Black, Queer single mom, creating a unique blueprint to center the lived experience of other folks at this same intersection.

In addition to my identity shifts, the sociopolitical context had also shifted. The research I have conducted has been in the wake of #BlackLivesMatter, an implicitly conceptualized and explicitly manifested intersectional liberation movement that centers Black lives. Serving alongside mothers who had lost their children to state violence to assist them in amplifying their message became, unbeknownst to me, the training I needed to become enstooled as a Ghanaian queen mother.

As a graduate student, I founded the Ellipsis Institute for Womxn[31] of Color in the Academy, curated to bring people together across lines of difference in the pursuit of a common goal: gender equity for all womxn in all roles. Grounded in Black Feminist Thought, Ellipsis Institute became the place where I could amalgamate my identity intersections and my interdisciplinary research to create this unique tool of praxis that centers the most marginalized while employing critical and radical methodologies. As queen mother Bonyi Bofor Akosua Kalesea of the Igbaba lineage, I am honored to continue the tradition of development—amplifying the voices of Black girls, women and femmes who experience oppression because of their intersecting identities. Through the following programming initiatives, Ellipsis Institute has been able to intentionally create space for womxn of color students, staff, and faculty by providing tools and resources to successfully produce advocacy actions on campus. Ellipsis Institute provides connections and relationships that build a support network, help navigate barriers to access, and inspire co-conspirators in one's journey toward gender equity.

In 2018, our theme, *#SeizeTheNarrative*, came from Damita Frazier of the Combahee River Collective, 40 years after its founding. Frazier empowers us to seize our voice and occupy our legacy in our collective quest for liberation, which is increasingly relevant in the wake of #BlackLivesMatter. Building on this, our 2019 theme was *Womxn of Color on the Line: Our Bodies Are Borders*. By positioning the classroom as spaces of radical transformation for womxn of color, our bodies serve as the primary medium to effectively enact our pedagogy. Thus, our performance of self emerges as an integral element in our collective liberation. In 2020, the threat to us as womxn and femmes of color—and all oppressed people—was arguably the highest we've experienced in our collective lifetime, being targeted via legal policies, media outlets, and even systems, institutions, and individuals who are expected to represent, serve, protect, and care for us. Our 2020 conference theme, *If They Come in The Morning . . . ,* is taken from the inmate communication between two of the most iconic activists of our time: James Baldwin and Angela Davis. Used as a salutation in a letter penned to Davis while incarcerated, Baldwin eloquently calls us all to collective action: "If we know, we must fight for your life as though it were our own—which it is—and render impassable with our bodies the corridor to the gas chamber. For, if they take you in the morning, they will be coming for us that night."[32]

After being enstooled as queen mother in the village of Akpafu-Todzi in the Volta region of Ghana, it was clear that my mission was to bring the work of the Ellipsis Institute to the motherland to serve the same population as we serve in the US: Black girls, women, and femmes in educational settings. Upon seeing the success of the 21st Century Village concept in the village of Antonkwa on my first trip to Ghana, I am energized to join and become active in the variety of Pan African organizations, founded by queen mothers, representing over 20 countries to center child protection through education and economic development efforts.[33] It is here that I can employ my BFT frames and methods in curating spaces of teaching and learning for girls and femmes in an attempt to prepare them for today's rapidly changing global society. Situated outside of the Eurocentric gaze of gender and intentionally subversive to the dominant narrative about who Black girls and Black Queens should be, Ellipsis International seeks to provide dynamic spaces of teaching and learning that center the most marginalized and that operate as a space of radical transformation for Black girls. Through my role as Queen Mother, I am validated by village leaders and supported by ancestors to move forward in the same sense as Nana Yaa Asantewaa, the Ashanti queen mother who exercised her motherwork to help defend her kingdom from the British. When the British colonial governor of the Gold Coast demanded the Golden Stool, the symbol of Asante power, Nana Yaa Asantewaa stood up to him and declared war on the British. In remembrance of her bravery in the face of British aggression and her mother work on behalf of the Asante kingdom, Nana Yaa Asantewaa has been eulogized in song, art, and education. Yaa Asantewaa Girls Senior High School in Kumasi, the capital of Ashanti Region, is a permanent monument to her mother work. A popular song titled *Koo koo hin koo, Yaa Asantewaa ee*[34] is often evoked at important gatherings of the Ashanti to remind themselves of their history and thank her for her bravery as the epitome of Asante power.

NOTES

1. Kent State University Department of Pan African Studies "Ghana Study Abroad," Brochure, Kent State University Department of Pan African Studies, 2019.

2. The Year of Return, Ghana 2019, "About Year of Return." https://www.yearofreturn.com/about/.

3. Marijke Steegstra, "Krobo Queen Mothers: Gender, Power, and Contemporary Female Traditional Authority in Ghana," *Africa Today* 55, no. 3 (2009): 105–123. http://www.jstor.org/stable/27666987.

4. Steegstra, "Krobo Queen Mothers," 106.

5. Steegstra, "Krobo Queen Mothers," 112.

6. Admin. "The Power of Women in West Africa: Queen Mothers." http://rainqueensofafrica.com/2011/03/the-power-of-women-in-west-africa-queen-mothers/.

7. Admin, "The Power of Women."

8. In his book, *The Souls of Black Folk*, W.E.B. DuBois introduces double consciousness: "It is a peculiar sensation, this double-consciousness, this sense of always looking at one's self through the eyes of others, of measuring one's soul by the tape of a world that looks on in amused contempt and pity. One ever feels his two-ness—an American, a Negro; two souls, two thoughts, two unreconciled strivings; two warring ideals in one dark body, whose dogged strength alone keeps it from being torn asunder. The history of the American Negro is the history of this strife—this longing to attain self-conscious manhood, to merge his double self into a better and truer self.

In this merging he wishes neither of the older selves to be lost. He does not wish to Africanize America, for America has too much to teach the world and Africa. He wouldn't bleach his Negro blood in a flood of white Americanism, for he knows that Negro blood has a message for the world. He simply wishes to make it possible for a man to be both a Negro and an American without being cursed and spit upon by his fellows, without having the doors of opportunity closed roughly in his face."

9. According to legal scholar Kimberle Crenshaw, intersectional theory asserts that people are often disadvantaged by multiple sources of oppression: their race, class, gender identity, sexual orientation, religion, and other identity markers. Intersectionality recognizes that identity markers (e.g., "woman" and "Black") do not exist independently of each other and that each informs the others, often creating a complex matrix of oppression.

10. Shemariah Arki, *Who Are Black Girls? An Intersectional Herstory of Feminism.* (Thousand Oaks: Sage, 2021), 204–209.

11. Patricia Hill Collins, *Black Feminist Thought: Knowledge, Consciousness and the Politics of Empowerment* (Boston: Unwin Hyman, 1990), 29.

12. Sankofa Waters, Billye, *We Can Speak for Ourselves: Parent Involvement and Ideologies of Black Mothers in Chicago* (Rotterdam: Sense Publishers, 2015), 13.

13. Sankofa Waters, *We Can Speak*, 13.

14. Steven Weisenburger, *Modern Madea* (New York: Hill and Wang, 1998).

15. Sankofa Waters, *We Can Speak*, 14.

16. Patricia Hill Collins, "Shifting the Center: Race, Class and Feminist Theorizing About Motherhood," in *Mothering Ideology, Experience and Agency*, edited by Evelyn Nakano Glenn, Grace Chang, and Linda Rennie Forcey (New York: Routledge, 1994).

17. Admin, "The Power of Women."

18. Admin, "The Power of Women."

19. Steegstra, "Krobo Queen Mothers," 109

20. Sankofa Waters, *We Can Speak*.

21. Sankofa Waters, *We Can Speak*, 14.

22. Hill Collins, *Black Feminist Thought*; Hill Collins, "Shifting the Center."

23. Simon P. Newman et al., "The West African Ethnicity of the Enslaved in Jamaica," *Slavery & Abolition* 34, no. 3 (2013): 376–400.

24. Newman et al., "West African Ethnicity," 376

25. Evans-Winters, Venus E. *Black Feminism in Qualitative Inquiry: A Mosaic for Writing Our Daughter's Body* (Abington: Routledge, 2019).

26. Evans-Winters, *Black Feminism*.

27. Michelle Wallace, *Black Macho and the Myth of the Superwoman* (Brooklyn, NY: Verso, 1979), 98.

28. Steegstra, "Krobo Queen Mothers."

29. Hill Collins, *Black Feminist Thought*, 215

30. Steegstra, "Krobo Queen Mothers."

31. The political term "woman of color" surfaced in the violence against women movement in the late 1970s to unify all women experiencing multiple layers of marginalization with race and ethnicity as a common issue. In today's sociopolitical

context, the use of womxn is inclusive of those who identify as cisgender, gender queer, gender-nonconforming, transgender and/or femme—people who may use she/her pronouns. Womxn is often used by those who identify as part of the intersectional feminist movement and written with the "x" to be intentionally subversive to the Eurocentric and patriarchal dominant narrative and to intentionally transcend social constructs and to unite, by relationship, those womxn with the following shared global experiences: culture appropriation; economic disenfranchisement; genocide; loss of autonomy; militarism, targets of war and police states; physical displacement (eminent domain, gentrification); race, class, gender-based oppression and all intersections; stolen legacy.

32. James Baldwin, "An Open Letter to My Sister, Angela Davis." In *If They Come in the Morning: Voices of Resistance,* edited by Angela Y. Davis (London: Verso, 1971).

33. Steegstra, "Krobo Queen Mothers."

34. Chanelle Denton and Deolu King, "Yaa Asantewaa," I Am History. April 1, 2021. https://www.iamhistory.co.uk/yaaasantewaa.

BIBLIOGRAPHY

Admin. "The Power of Women in West Africa: Queen Mothers." Accessed March 1, 2021. http://rainqueensofafrica.com/2011/03/the-power-of-women-in-west-africa-queen-mothers/.

Arki, Shemariah. "Who Are Black Girls? An Intersectional Herstory of Feminism." In *Teaching Beautiful Brilliant Black Girls,* edited by Omobolade Delano-Oriaran, Marguerite W. Penick, Shemariah J. Arki, Ali Michael, Orinthia Swindell, and Eddie Moore, Jr., 204–209. Thousand Oaks: Sage, 2021.

Baldwin, James. "An Open Letter To My Sister, Angela Davis." In *If They Come In The Morning . . . Voices of Resistance,* edited by Angela Y. Davis, 13–16. London: Verso, 1971.

Denton, Chanelle and Deolu King. "Yea Asantewa." I Am History. April 1, 2021. https://www.iamhistory.co.uk/yaaasantewaa.

Evans-Winters, Venus E. *Black Feminism in Qualitative Inquiry: A Mosaic for Writing Our Daughter's Body.* Abington: Routledge, 2019.

Hill Collins, Patricia. "Shifting The Center: Race, Class and Feminist Theorizing About Motherhood." In *Mothering: Ideology, Experience and Agency*, edited by Evelyn Nakano Glenn, Grace Chang, and Linda Rennie Forcey, 45–66. New York: Routledge, 1994.

Hill Collins, Patricia. Black Feminist Thought: Knowledge, Consciousness and the Politics of Empowerment. Boston: Unwin Hyman, 1990. https://www-tandfonline.com.ezproxy.neu.edu/doi/full/10.1080/0144039X.2012.734054.

Kent State University Department of Pan African Studies "Ghana Study Abroad." Brochure, Kent State University Department of Pan African Studies, 2019.

Ladson-Billings, Gloria. "Just What Is Critical Race Theory and What's It Doing In a Nice Field Like Education?" In *Race Is . . . Race Isn't: Critical Race Theory and*

Qualitative Studies in Education, edited by Lawrence Parker, Donna Deyhle and Sofia Villenas, 7–30. Boulder, CO: Westview Press, 1999.

Newman, Simon P., Michael L. Deason, Yannis P. Pitsiladis, Antonio Salas, and Vincent A. Macaulay, "The West African Ethnicity of the Enslaved in Jamaica." *Slavery & Abolition* 34, 3 (2013): 376–400.

Sankofa Waters, Billye. *We Can Speak For Ourselves: Parent Involvement and Ideologies of Black Mothers in Chicago.* Rotterdam: Sense Publishers, 2015.

Steegstra, Marijke. "Krobo Queen Mothers: Gender, Power, and Contemporary Female Traditional Authority in Ghana." *Africa Today* 55, no. 3 (2009): 105–123.

The Year of Return Ghana 2019. "About Year of Return." https://www.yearofreturn. com/about/.

Wallace, Michelle. *Black Macho and the Myth of the Superwoman.* Brooklyn, NY: Verso, 1979.

Weisenburger, Steven. *Modern Madea.* New York: Hill and Wang, 1998.

Epilogue

Amoaba Gooden

Our desire to write a book, primarily by Ghanaian scholars, on gender and sexuality(s) in Ghana was driven by our quest (1) to add to the growing literature on gender and sexuality in Africa and (2) to bring together in one place, a select body of multi- and interdisciplinary literature that critically analyzes the intersection of gender and sexuality in a multiethnic and multicultural patriarchal country. Ensuring that the majority of the authors are Ghanaian also supported our need to establish that individuals within a particular culture can be experts of their own experiences. The authors have underscored how contemporary Ghanaian scholars have understood the dynamics of gender and power in the current social arrangements regarding sexuality.

While scholarship has increasingly engaged the discourse on gender and sexuality across the African continent, Ghanaian spaces remain largely underexplored. Consequently, not much is known about the multiple ways in which gender and sexuality present and influence various identities, cosmoses, and cultures in the country. According to Yeboah, Ampofo and Brobbey, it was not until the 1980s that gender issues began to take up space in institutions of higher learning in Ghana.[1] The authors point out that the early 1990s saw the development of academic programs in Ghana designed to study gender with a focus primarily on the gendered experiences of women and men, feminist frameworks and the dynamics of culture and power. Research and scholarship did not focus on sexuality. Signe Arnfred in *Re-Thinking Sexualities in African* notes this silence on issues of sexuality in African feminist writings.[2]

As indicated in the introduction, the initial intention of this book was to provide a broad overview of gender and sexuality(s) in Ghana, however, there are noted gaps. For example, there are no chapters on LGBTQI+ experiences, class and sexuality, masculinity, femininity, or disability. While this epilogue will not address all the gaps, it will briefly focus on some aspects and experiences of the LGBTQ+ communities in Ghana. Unfortunately, as of the writing of the book, many African countries, including Ghana, continue to criminalize same-sex intimacies and relationships, a carryover of colonial laws that European colonial administrations put in place to control the sexuality of their colonial subjects. According to Human Rights Watch, prosecutions for same-sex intimacies in Ghana are rare, but that is not true for other African countries. Even so, members of the LGBTQ+ communities in Ghana continue to be socially and politically persecuted.[3] Many African heads of state, including Ghanaian leaders, claim same-sex practices to be "Western imports," and laws remain unchanged or are enacted to regulate "how, when and with whom adults have consensual sex."[4] However, Arnfred and other researchers and activists have pushed back against this idea that same-sex relationships were introduced into African spaces by Europeans (see, for example, work by Sylvia Tamale, Stephen O. Murray and Will Roscoe as well as work by Essien and Aderinto).[5] In Ghana and elsewhere, homophobia and transphobia are common, thus making heterosexism and its antecedent, heteronormativity, common practices. As Essien and Aderinto remind us,

> the presence or absence of homosexuality in Africa is still generating serious debate among scholars and commentators of different ideological persuasions. Contemporary commentators and authors tend to freely borrow from the ideas of earlier counterparts, who saw African sexuality as predominantly heterosexual and devoid of the so-called "negative" influence of homosexual behavior and fantasies.[6]

Early in 2020, Ghana was caught in a fierce public debate over a planned LGBTQ+ conference in the country. The conference was billed as a continental event that would bring activists, performers, and LGBTQ+ individuals together in July 2020. Politicians and religious leaders denounced the proposed conference as demonic and antithetical to Ghanaian cultural values. In a rare show of solidarity, the chief imam of Kumasi, Ghana's second-largest city, called on all religious groups—Christian, Islamic and Traditional—to come together to stop the conference. And they did. The vitriol that ensued was enough to move some civil rights organizations to denounce the public outcry and to argue for the human rights of LGBTQ+ citizens of Ghana and Africa, in general, to be respected. We cannot tell what would have happened to the conference had there not been a sudden spread of Covid-19 and subsequent lockdown of various African countries, including Ghana.

The coronavirus pandemic has not stopped the Ghanaian public from persecuting members of the LGBTQ+. In February 2021, Al Jazeera reported that an LGBTQ office in Accra, the capital city, was raided and closed.[7] In the report, the minister-designate for gender and social protection is quoted as saying that "the issue of the criminality of LGBT is non-negotiable and our cultural practices also frown on it." The minister-designate was wrong in one aspect of her observation. The constitution of Ghana does not criminalize homosexuality per se, even if the public frowns on it. What the constitution criminalizes is what it terms "unnatural carnal knowledge" for which offenders can be jailed for a maximum of 25 years.[8] Without a clear definition of "unnatural" in sex, coupled with heteronormativity, homophobia and transphobia, the constitution ends up exposing members of LGBTQ+ communities to vulnerabilities that infringe upon their rights as citizens of Ghana

A CONTESTED SPACE

The general topic of gender and sexuality is still a much-contested discourse in contemporary Ghana. For example, the proposed Ministry of Education Comprehensive Sexuality Education (CSE) program, a collaborative effort between the Ghanaian government and the United Nations, excludes topics on gender and sexuality. The CSE program is a curriculum-based program of the International Planned Federation (IPPF) and advocates for the "sexual and reproductive health and rights for all." The program provides students with the skills and knowledge to make healthy personal and sexual choices, ultimately aiming to prevent sexually transmitted diseases and reduce unplanned pregnancies. Additionally, the program promotes sexual abstinence and offers self-esteem programs with the hopes of decreased violence against women and girls.[9] However, as we point out in the introduction, religious groups, parents, and opposition political parties used various media outlets to condemn the government for attempting to introduce sex to children. According to one columnist, the CSE proposed curriculum would "sexualize children, and destroy sexual sanctity of the future generation of the country."[10] The columnist then argued that same-sex relations were "unnatural, and offends the culture, traditions and faith of the people of Ghana."[11] In a public statement, the government assured the public that the program did not support LGBTQI+ causes and assured the country that they would revise the content of the initiative.

As discussed in the introduction, gender and sexuality are socially constructed and are interlinked. We cannot understand sexuality and sexual behavior without first understanding aspects of gender, sex and sexual identity. Many Ghanaians often conflate sex and sexual identity with gender. However, sex and sexual identity just give shape to gender, and, as Tamale points out, they are not the same.[12] We are assigned a sex at birth; we are either assigned male or female or intersex. Gender identity is linked to the way we are socialized to think about masculinity and femininity and is related to gender in terms of how one thinks about appearance and for some, how one feels about one's gender. When one identifies, for example, as woman, man, transgender, genderqueer, nonbinary, bigender, gender nonconforming, or gender fluid, one is claiming a particular gender identity. Sexual identity refers to how we see ourselves and therefore how we identify as straight/ heterosexual, asexual, queer, pansexual, lesbian, gay, celibate, etc. Like patriarchal societies elsewhere, Ghana recognizes only two genders—women and men—and ascribes to them only one form of sexual expression, heterosexuality, one that occurs only between women and men. There is irony in the view that "natural" sex occurs only between women and men. For example, heterosexual couples use sex toys and/or have anal sex; however, will such a couple be prosecuted and jailed if they are caught? We do not have an answer to this question, but we pose them to draw attention to the power of heteronormativity, homophobia and transphobia, which privileges the lives of some people while demonizing others.

LBGTQI+ SILENCES

One cannot generalize sexualities in Ghana, a vast, complex and diverse country. There are, however, "different types of silences" at play that influence what we know about LGBTQI+ experiences in Ghana.[13] According to Currier and Migraine-George, African "sexualities have largely been shaped by silence and secrecy, oppression and repression, uncertain definitions and varying situational practices."[14] We do want to note that these silences should not be viewed, as both Arnfred and Tamale point out, through Western eyes, but through an African cultural or ethnic lens.[15] In the text *Rethinking Sexualities in Africa*, Arnfred pushes back against the notion of silences as powerlessness within colonial and post-colonial frameworks of understanding sexuality in Africa. Instead, Arnfred suggests that researchers should not only deconstruct previous analysis but also reconstruct knowledge about African sexualities by developing new and alternative lines of inquiry.[16] Tamale supports Arnfred's position by pointing us to research which demonstrates that African cultural silences can be as empowering as speech and are not always silences of the powerless.

These silences are, furthermore, influenced to some degree by the absence of research/discourse in the academy. As a relatively new field of study in Africa, sexuality studies is still emerging and "located at the moving junction of various disciplinary formations—ethnographic case studies and literary and visual studies."[17] According to Currier and Migraine-George, since the early twenty-first-century, scholars and activists have "worked on debunking the myth" that same-sex relationships are un-African.[18] These "scholars have also documented Africans' same-sex sexual practices before, during, and after colonialism," ultimately foregrounding their work in an African-centered queer perspective that honors "African modes of blending, bending, and breaking gender boundaries."[19] Tamale points out that the bulk of studies on African sexuality have been conducted by scholars in Western institutions of higher learning.[20] Accordingly then, continental scholars are wary and mindful of using a Western voice to look at sexual identity within the African context.

While the literature on the African LGBTQI+ experiences is growing, the scholarship that focuses specifically on Ghana is still relatively small. Essien and Aderinto argue that Africanists did not put the study of LGBTQI+ issues on the academic agenda in West Africa.[21] However, even though more research and scholarship is needed in this area to increase our understanding of the experiences of those who are part of the LGBTQI+ Ghanaian community, there is some outstanding research that explores sexualities in Africa and they provide insight into experiences, opportunities and challenges of the LGBTQI+ Ghanaian community. The literature below, although not an exhaustive list, gives us a glimpse into the life experiences of Ghana's LGBTQI+ communities.

Serena Dankwa's article, "'It's a silent trade': Female same-sex intimacies in post-colonial Ghana," picks up on Arnfred's concept of "different types of silences" to explore types of "sexual sociality" among women who love women in Ghana. Dankwa argues that there is a female same-sex culture that thrives in Ghana. She confirms that there is a "covertness of female same-sex intimacy in post-colonial Ghana and this constructed space is where women voice and practice their passions and desires beyond the public eye." *African Sexualities: A Reader*, while not focusing on Ghana specifically nor only on LGBTQI+ sexualities, contextualizes gender and sexuality broadly, reminding the reader that African sexuality is plural and diverse and must be understood within specific African context. *African Sexualities* also includes an excellent chapter by Ampofo and Boateng, "Multiple Meanings of Manhood Among Boys in Ghana," which explores the masculinity among boys, 11–15 years of age. The authors push back against the hegemonic construction of masculinity and suggest the creation of "safe spaces" where boys can unlearn patriarchal and heteronormative ways of being.[22] In "'Cutting the head of the roaring monster': Homosexuality and repression in Africa," Essien and Aderinto explore how the 2006 planning of an LGBTQI+ conference by the Gay and Lesbian Association of Ghana (GALAG) increased discrimination and created a "new wave of homophobic expression," which was supported by government and religious leaders. Similarly, *Human rights violations against lesbian, gay, bisexual, and transgender (LGBT) people in Ghana: A shadow report* illustrates the increased violence that members of the LGBTQI+ communities face.[23]

The Queer African Youth Networking (QAYN) has published *Struggling alone: The lived realities of women who have sex with women in Burkina Faso, Ghana and Nigeria,* which documents the lived experiences of lesbians, bisexuals, queer and transgender women in West Africa who have sex with women.[24] *Struggling alone* reminds us that Ghana's oppressive penal code, which is tied to political and religious authorities, criminalizes same-sex relationships and largely influences these silences as well as provides a lens through which to see how the public discourse on LGBTQI+ is driven by political, religious, and social influences by highlighting policies and laws such as the Ghanaian Criminal Code Amendment Act of 1992, which outlaws same-sex sexual activities and refers to such intimacies as "unnatural carnal knowledge." Activists have noted that although this law has primarily been used against men who have sex with men, strong Ghanaian Christian and Muslim influences and other sociocultural values have led to large-scale discrimination against LGBTQI+ individuals. As a result, members of the LGBTQI+ community are marginalized and face "severe discrimination [. . .] at the hands of their families and the larger community."[25] These "acts of discrimination and harassment are often justified and condoned by the state . . . [and] the level and layers of discrimination are so pervasive that [LGBTQI+ individuals] are unable to effectively actualize their identity and sexuality safely and experience their sexual rights freely."[26] For example, in July 2011, Paul Aidoo, who serves as the Ghanaian Western Region Minister, urged the police to arrest those who identified as gay. He also urged members of the public to notify the police if they suspected anyone of being gay.[27] His actions are supported by the majority of Ghanaians. According to the Africa Center for International Law and Accountability, 87 percent of the population supports a ban on LGBTQI+ public meetings, and 75 percent support homophobic statements made by government and religious figures.[28] As members of the LGBTQI+ community advocated for their well-being and rights, violence against LGBTQI+ individuals increased such that by 2013, according to *Human rights violations against lesbian, gay, bisexual, and transgender (lgbt) people in Ghana: A shadow report,* Amnesty International reported on this increased violence as well.[29] In 2020, another fierce public debate emerged over a planned LGBTQ conference that was to occur in Ghana. The conference, organized by the Pan African International Lesbian, Gay, Bisexual, Trans and Intersex Association, sought to bring scholars and activists from around the African continent together to discuss the development of strategies to improve the rights of LGBTQI+ individuals across the continent of Africa.[30] However, as we pointed out in the introduction, politicians and religious leaders alike denounced the proposed conference as antithetical to Ghanaian and African cultural values. Sheikh Dr. Usumanu Nuhu Sharubutu, who serves as the National Chief Imam, urged all religious groups to work together to end the conference. The Chief Iman also urged the government to criminalize same-sex relationships.[31]

Again, in January 2021, after activists from the LGBTQI+ community opened up a community space in Accra where they can come together in a safe space to plan, advocate and socialize; politicians, religious leaders and members of the general public called for its closure and the arrest of the organization's members and allies. Police officers raided and closed down the community space approximately a month after it opened.[32] A year later, on March 30, 2022, approximately 22 individuals were arrested in Kwahu-Obomeng, a town located in the Eastern Region of Ghana, for participating in what was thought to be a lesbian wedding ceremony.[33] The comments on social media were homophobic and violent. Posts included comments such as, "Gays and lesbians has no respect or dignity in their own families, workplace and the society as a whole" and "Well done Ghana police, but is my wish if you kill all of them, please. Kill them. They are more than animals." One individual even wished death on the couple saying, "These are animals and should be slaughtered. I bet animals have brains to think because they chase the opposite-sex partner. They are animals period."[34] Not all comments were discriminatory. Members of the LGBTQI+ community and their allies also responded with supportive statements such as, "Why don't they go fight real crime and stop harassing people and their private lives?" and "What sort of nonsense is this? Your politicians are busy stealing from you and we are busy here jailing adults over their sexuality? What you people refuse to see is that not everybody subscribes to your religious beliefs and if we are going by the current law of the land then almost everyone will be in jail because men . . . wives and women . . . boyfriends and husbands are equally committing an act of carnal knowledge!"[35]

The above are examples of how homophobia and heteronormative privileges are played out through social media. It is within this context we turn now to the two known openly transgender women in Ghana: Angela Coleman and Angel Maxine.[36] While there is a lack of research focusing on transgender populations in Ghana specifically and Africa generally, the experiences of Coleman and Maxine shed light on the experiences of this community in Ghana. While the majority of transgender Ghanaians live their lives in secret because of issues of safety, both Coleman and Maxine risked their safety to share their stories and are working to raise awareness of the transgender experience by telling their stories. Maxine, a 35-year-old musician in Ghana has participated in several interviews. She says, "I am a transgender . . . that is how I feel. From a childhood that is how I felt, I battled with myself for so many years to fully understand myself to become who I am today. And I love the way I am, I'm happy. This is what I wanted and this is who I am."[37]

The writer of the news report, located on *Ghanaweb*, refused to recognize Maxine's gender identity and referred to her as "he" throughout the report, showing his heteronormative and homophobic thinking.[38]

Coleman is a self-employed hairstylist with a booming business and shares that life has also been difficult as she was often discriminated against. In an interview with host Celly, on BrutallyUncensored.com, Coleman says that she has identified as female from a very young age.[39] While she was accepted for who she was by her family, she was often discriminated against by members of her community and targeted because of such things as her voice and her walk. She was not safe to go to the market or the store. However, Coleman feels that her community has grown to accept her for who she is. She shared that,

> I was initially scared because I was receiving death threats just because people thought I was gay but now I don't think there is someone out there who hates me so I feel proud and free-spirited and my family is okay with who I have become. I completely feel like a woman and would have killed myself if I hadn't undergone the surgery.[40]

She does admit that threats and messages of rape or murder were sometimes left on her voice mail. And while Coleman has become somewhat of a celebrity in Ghana, her notoriety is based on her objectification and her treatment as a spectacle. For example, throughout the entire interview with Celly, there were numerous times in which Coleman was objectified. Celly referred to Coleman as "what" a few times, even asking "What are you?" at one point during the interview and asked very intimate questions about Coleman's sexual history and activity.[41] Celly, confused about gender identity and conflating gender with sexuality, asked Ms. Coleman time and again if she was sexually active. This objectification continued throughout the entire interview. At the end of the interview, the host shared that she was no longer fearful of Coleman because she was not scary and seemed "human."[42] In other interviews, Coleman is often degraded and treated as a specimen. For instance, there was the prodding of her breasts by a male TV host as mentioned in the introduction, and the lengthy discussion by another host as to whether Ms. Coleman should be leading a praise service in the church, intimating that she was not god-like or praiseworthy and that the church had lost its way for supporting Coleman. The life experiences of both Ms. Coleman and Ms. Maxine reflect current understandings of gender and sexuality in Ghana, where gender is binary, fixed and immutable. Their marginalization and harassment reflect the heteronormative and homophobia embedded in national understandings of gender and sexuality.

NOTES

1. Abena Animwaa Yeboah, Akosua Adomako Ampofo and Maame Kyerewaa Brobbey, "Women's and Gender Studies in Ghana," in *Changing Perspectives on the Social Sciences in Ghana, eds. Samuel Agyei-Mensah, Joseph Atsu Ayee and Abena D. Oduro (Hekmatfar, Springer, 2014), 285–312.

2. Signe Arnfred, "'African Sexuality'/Sexuality in Africa: Tales and Silences," in *Re-Thinking Sexualities in African*, ed. Arnfred Signe. (Sweden, Almqvist and Wiksell Tryckeri Ab, 2005), 59–76.

3. See "Here's why Ghana's sex education program is controversial," *African News*, October 3, 2019, https://www.africanews.com/2019/10/03/here-s-why-ghana-s-sex-education-program-is-controversial//.

4. Arnfred, "African Sexuality/Sexuality in Africa," 2005, 73; see also Sylvia Tamale, *African Sexualities: A Reader* (Istanbul, Turkey: Mega Print, 2011).

5. Kwame Essien and Saheed Aderinto, "Cutting The Head Of The Roaring Monster": Homo-Sexuality And Repression in Africa, " *African Study Monographs*, 30.3 (2009):121–135; Stephen O. Murray and Will Roscoe, *Boy Wives and Female Husbands: Studies in African Homosexualities* (State University of New York Press: Albany, 1998); see also Arnfred, "African Sexuality/Sexuality in Africa," 2005, 73; Tamale, *African Sexualities,* 2011.

6. Essien and Aderinto, "Cutting The Head Of The Roaring Monster," 121–135.

7. Al Jazeera, "Ghana security forces shut down LGBTQ office: Rights group," https://www.aljazeera.com/news/2021/2/24/ghana-shuts-down-lgbt-office-rights-group.

8. Ghana Criminal Code 1960, (Act 29) Sec 104 (2), https://www.wipo.int/edocs/lexdocs/laws/en/gh/gh010en.pdf.

9. "Everyone's Right to Know Delivering Comprehensive Sexuality Education for all Young People," International Planned Parenthood Federation, March 2019. https://www.ippf.org/sites/default/files/2016-05/ippf_cse_report_eng_web.pdf.

10. Sylvanus Akorsu, "Comprehensive Sexuality Education Implementation in Ghana—Concepts, Context and Content," Modern Ghana, November 22, 2019. https://www.modernghana.com/news/969233/comprehensive-sexuality-education-implementation.html.

11. Akorsu, "Comprehensive Sexuality Education Implementation in Ghana." https://www.modernghana.com/news/969233/comprehensive-sexuality-education-implementation.html (Nov. 22, 2019).

12. Tamale, *African sexualities, 11–12.*

13. Signe, "'African sexuality'/sexuality in Africa," 2005, 73.

14. Ashley Currier and Thérèse Migraine-George, "'Lesbian'/female same-sex sexualities in Africa," *Journal of Lesbian Studies,* 21, no. 2 (2017): 133–150.

15. Signe, "'African sexuality'/sexuality in Africa," 2005, 73; Tamale, *African sexualities, 27.*

16. Signe, "'African sexuality'/sexuality in Africa," 2005, 8.

17. Currier and Migraine-George, "'Lesbian'/female same-sex sexualities in Africa," 133.

18. Currier and Migraine-George, "'Lesbian'/female same-sex sexualities in Africa," 133

19. Currier and Migraine-George, "'Lesbian'/female same-sex sexualities in Africa,"134.

20. Tamale, *African sexualities*, 12.

21. Essien and Aderinto, "Cutting the head of the roaring monster," 121.

22. Akosua Adomako Ampofo and John Boateng, "Multiple meanings of manhood among boys in Ghana," in *African sexualities*: *A reader*, ed. Sylvia Tamale, (Pambazuka Press: Kindle Edition, 2011), 420–436.

23. "Human rights violations against lesbian, gay, bisexual, and transgender (lgbt) people in Ghana: A shadow report," Solace Brothers Foundation, The Initiative for Equal Rights, Center for International Human Rights of Northwestern Pritzker School of Law, and Heartland Alliance for Human Needs & Human Rights Global Initiatives for Human Rights, May 2016. https://tbinternet.ohchr.org/Treaties/CCPR/Shared%20 Documents/GHA/INT_CCPR_CSS_GHA_24149_E.pdf.

24. Kehinde Okanlawon, Akudo Oguaghamba, Caroline Kouassiaman and Mariam Armisen, *Struggling alone: The lived realities of women who have sex with women in Burkina Faso, Ghana and Nigeria, (QAYN,* April 2012), 1–46. http://static1. squarespace.com/static/54191049e4b0677471aa06c9/t/559ab41ee4b0e9796cd26 3fa/1436202014978/QAYN-LBTQWSW-Publication.pdf.

25. Okanlawon, Oguaghamba, Kouassiaman and Armisen, *Struggling alone*, 14.

26. Okanlawon, Oguaghamba, Kouassiaman and Armisen, *Struggling alone*, 14.

27. Okanlawon, Oguaghamba, Kouassiaman and Armisen, *Struggling alone*, 14.

28. "Ghana's emerging lgbt movement battles with hostility," France 24, March 8, 2021. https://www.france24.com/en/live-news/20210308-ghana-s-emerging-lgbt-movement-battles-with-hostility.

29. "Human rights violations against lesbian," https://tbinternet.ohchr.org/Treaties/ CCPR/Shared%20Documents/GHA/INT_CCPR_CSS_GHA_24149_E.pdf.

30. Lily Wakefield, "A history-making lgbt+ rights conference in Ghana has been banned and, no, it's not because of coronavirus," *Pink News*, March 13, 2020. https://www.pinknews.co.uk/2020/03/13/ghana-lgbt-rights-conference-coronavirus-pan-africa-ilga-nana-akufo-addo/.

31. Kweku Eshun "Review laws to criminalise homosexuality—Chief Imam," TalksGhana. https://talksghana.com/review-laws-to-criminalise-homosexuality-chief-imam/.

32. Al Jazeera, "Ghana security forces shut down LGBTQ office: Rights group," February 24, 2021, https://www.aljazeera.com/news/2021/2/24/ ghana-shuts-down-lgbt-office-rights-group.

33. "22 arrested by Mpraeso police over alleged lesbian wedding," *Ghana Web*, March 29, 2021. https://www.ghanaweb.com/GhanaHomePage/regional/22-arrested-by-Mpraeso-police-over-alleged-lesbian-wedding-1218046.

34. Comment Section, *Ghana Web.* https://www.ghanaweb.com/GhanaHomePage/ NewsArchive/artikel.php?ID=1218046&comment=0#com.

35. Comment Section, *Ghana Web.* https://www.ghanaweb.com/GhanaHomePage/ NewsArchive/artikel.php?ID=1218046&comment=0#com.

36. Cine Krom, "I don't regret being a transgender in Ghana: An Interview with Angel Maxine," December 9, 2019, 26.6 minutes. https://www.youtube.com/watch?v=TGvlIteLOoo. See also "My mind feeling tell me i am female not male," *Ghana Web*. https://www.ghanaweb.com/GhanaHomePage/NewsArchive/My-mind-feelings-tell-me-I-m-a-female-not-male-35-year-old-transgender-803961. Ms. Coleman has been nicknamed Madina Broni—Madina is a suburb of Accra where she lives and Broni (also oburoni) is the Akan word for a white person—because Ms. Coleman used creams to lighten her complexion.

37. "My Mind Feeling Tell me I am Female not Male," Ghana Web, https://www.ghanaweb.com/GhanaHomePage/NewsArchive/My-mind-feelings-tell-me-I-m-a-female-not-male-35-year-old-transgender-803961#.

38. "My Mind Feeling Tell me I am Female not Male," Ghana Web, https://www.ghanaweb.com/GhanaHomePage/NewsArchive/My-mind-feelings-tell-me-I-m-a-female-not-male-35-year-old-transgender-803961#.

39. "Inside Out: an Exclusive Inerivew with Ghana's Only Open Transgender, Madina Broni," *Brutally Uncensored*, January 13, 2018. http://brutallyuncensored.com/inside-exclusive-interview-ghanas-open-transgender-angela-coleman-aka-madina-brono/.

40. Audrey Osabutey, "Video: Transgender woman in Ghana set to marry her pastor fiancé," Occupy.com, May 10, 2019. https://occupygh.com/transgender-woman-ghana-marry-pastor-fiance

41. "Ghana's First Transgender Madina Broni now Born again? Spotted singing at Church," Ghafricnews.com, April 4, 2019, https://www.youtube.com/watch?v=XE_7FQiq8Co.

42. Brutallyuncensored.com, "INSIDE OUT: An Exclusive Interview with Ghana's Only Open Transgender-Angela Coleman Aka Madina Broni," n. d, https://www.facebook.com/BrutallyUncensored/videos/interview-with-ghanas-only-open-transgender-angela-coleman-aka-madina-brono/1709168005809313/.

BIBLIOGRAPHY

Adomako Ampofo, Akosua, and John Boateng. "Multiple meanings of manhood among boys in Ghana." In *African sexualities*: *A reader*, edited by Sylvia Tamale, 420–436. Pambazuka Press: Kindle Edition, 2011.

Akorsu, Sylvanus. "Comprehensive Sexuality Education Implementation in Ghana—Concepts, Context and Content." *Modern Ghana*, November 22, 2019. https://www.modernghana.com/news/969233/comprehensive-sexuality-education-implementation.html.

Al Jazeera. "Ghana security forces shut down LGBTQ office: Rights group." https://www.aljazeera.com/news/2021/2/24/ghana-shuts-down-lgbt-office-rights-group.

Animwaa Yeboah, Abena, Akosua Adomako Ampofo and Maame Kyerewaa Brobbey. "Women's and Gender Studies in Ghana." In *Changing Perspectives on the Social Sciences in Ghana*, edited by Samuel Agyei-Mensah, Joseph Atsu Ayee and Abena D. Oduro, 285–312. Hekmatfar, Springer, 2014.

Arnfred, Signe. "'African Sexuality'/Sexuality in Africa: Tales and Silences." In *Re-Thinking Sexualities in African*, edited by Signe Arnfred, 59–76. Sweden, Almqvist and Wiksell Tryckeri Ab, 2005.

Brutallyuncensored.com. "INSIDE OUT: An Exclusive Interview with Ghana's Only Open Transgender-Angela Coleman Aka Madina Broni." N. d. https://www.facebook.com/BrutallyUncensored/videos/interview-with-ghanas-only-open-transgender-angela-coleman-aka-madina-brono/1709168005809313/.

Currier, Ashley, and Thérèse Migraine-George. "'Lesbian'/female same-sex sexualities in Africa." *Journal of Lesbian Studies* 21, no. 2 (2017): 133–150.

Eshun, Kweku. "Review laws to criminalise homosexuality—ChiefImam." TalksGhana. https://talksghana.com/review-laws-to-criminalise-homosexuality-chief-imam/.

Essien, Kwame, and Saheed Aderinto. "Cutting the Head of the Roaring Monster": Homo-Sexuality and Repression in Africa." *African Study Monographs* 30 no. 3 (2009): 121–135.

"Everyone's Right to Know Delivering Comprehensive Sexuality Education for all Young People." International Planned Parenthood Federation, March 2019. https://www.ippf.org/sites/default/files/2016-05/ippf_cse_report_eng_web.pdf

France 24. "Ghana's emerging lgbt movement battles with hostility." France 24, March 8, 2021. https://www.france24.com/en/live-news/20210308-ghana-s-emerging-lgbt-movement-battles-with-hostility.

Ghafricnews.com. "Ghana's First Transgender Madina Broni now Born again? Spotted singing at Church." Ghafricnews.com, April 4, 2019, https://www.youtube.com/watch?v=XE_7FQiq8Co.

Ghana Criminal Code 1960, (Act 29) Sec 104 (2). https://www.wipo.int/edocs/lexdocs/laws/en/gh/gh010en.pdf.

Ghanaweb.com. "22 arrested by Mpraeso police over alleged lesbian wedding." *Ghana Web*, March 29, 2021. https://www.ghanaweb.com/GhanaHomePage/regional/22-arrested-by-Mpraeso-police-over-alleged-lesbian-wedding-1218046.

Ghanaweb.com. "My Mind Feeling Tell me I am Female not Male." Ghana Web, https://www.ghanaweb.com/GhanaHomePage/NewsArchive/My-mind-feelings-tell-me-I-m-a-female-not-male-35-year-old-transgender-803961#.

"Heartland Alliance for Human Needs & Human Rights Global Initiatives for Human Rights." http://brutallyuncensored.com/inside-exclusive-interview-ghanas-open-transgender-angela-coleman-aka-madina-brono/1709168005809313/.

"Here's why Ghana's sex education program is controversial," *African News*, October 3, 2019. https://www.africanews.com/2019/10/03/here-s-why-ghana-s-sex-education-program-is-controversial//.

Krom, Cine. "I don't regret being a transgender in Ghana: An Interview with Angel Maxine." December 9, 2019, 26.6 minutes. https://www.youtube.com/watch?v=TGvlIteLOoo.

Murray, Stephen O., and Will Roscoe. *Boy Wives and Female Husbands: Studies in African Homosexualities*. State University of New York Press: Albany, 1998.

Okanlawon, Kehinde, Akudo Oguaghamba, Caroline Kouassiaman and Mariam Armisen. *Struggling alone: The lived realities of women who have sex with women in Burkina Faso, Ghana and Nigeria, (QAYN,* April 2012), 1–46. http://static1.

squarespace.com/static/54191049e4b0677471aa06c9/t/559ab41ee4b0e9796cd26
3fa/1436202014978/QAYN-LBTQWSW-Publication.pdf.

Osabutey, Audrey. "Video: Transgender woman in Ghana set to marry her pastor fiancé." Occupy.com, May 10, 2019. https://occupygh.com/transgender-woman-ghana-marry-pastor-fiance.

Solace Brothers Foundation. "Human rights violations against lesbian, gay, bisexual, and transgender (lgbt) people in Ghana: A shadow report." The Initiative for Equal Rights, Center for International Human Rights of Northwestern Pritzker School of Law, and Heartland Alliance for Human Needs & Human Rights Global Initiatives for Human Rights, May 2016. https://tbinternet.ohchr.org/Treaties/CCPR/Shared%20Documents/GHA/INT_CCPR_CSS_GHA_24149_E.pdf.

Tamale, Sylvia. *African Sexualities: A Reader.* Istanbul, Turkey: Mega Print, 2011.

Wakefield, Lily. "A history-making lgbt+ rights conference in Ghana has been banned and, no, it's not because of coronavirus." *Pink News*, March 13, 2020. https://www.pinknews.co.uk/2020/03/13/ghana-lgbt-rights-conference-coronavirus-pan-africa-ilga-nana-akufo-addo/.

Index

About the Contributors

Dr. Naa Adjeley Suta Alakija-Sekyi is a lecturer at the University of Cape Coast, Ghana. She holds a BA in Sociology and Economics, an MPhil in Sociology and an MA in Human Resource Development. She holds a PhD in Sociology with specialization in Gender and Family Studies. Dr. Alakija-Sekyi has expertise in Gender and Sexualities, Women and Development, Gender and Education, Media and Leadership, Ethnicity and Ethnic Relations, and Human Resource Development. She is a gender specialist and a gender consultant.

Shemariah J. Arki identifies as an educator, an activist and an organizer. Currently serving as a professor in the Department of Africana Studies and as the interim Director of the Center for Pan African Culture, both at Kent State University, she is an intersectional feminist scholar with expert knowledge and skills to develop, implement, facilitate and evaluate curricula that promote institutional equity, communication, and access for traditionally marginalized students and families.

Dr. Martha Donkor is a professor of women's and gender studies at West Chester University of Pennsylvania. She obtained her first degree in history from the University of Cape Coast and continued her education in Canada at the University of Guelph, where she obtained an MA in American history and then a PhD in women's history from the Ontario Institute for Studies in Education, University of Toronto. Dr. Donkor specializes in transnational feminism and focuses her research on women and education, work, and poverty. She is the author of *The Experiences of Ghanaian Live-in Caregivers in the United States* and *Child Rape in Ghana: Lifting the Veil*. Dr. Donkor is currently working on a manuscript on women and old age poverty in rural Ghana.

Dr. Amoaba Gooden is a professor of Pan-African Studies at Kent State University. Her ongoing research includes the study of African Canadian organizing, leadership and community building, and gender and sexuality. She is the editor of a special edition of the *Southern Journal of Canadian Studies*: Constructing Black Canada—Becoming Canadian. Her publications can also be found in *African Canadian Leadership: Perspectives on Continuity, Transition, and Transformation*; *S'TENISTOLW-Moving forward in Indigenous Higher Education*; in the *Journal of Black Studies*; *Journal of Pan-African Studies; Wagadu: Journal of Transnational Women's and Gender Studies;* and the *Canadian Woman Studies Journal*.

Dr. Daniel Yaw Fiaveh is a sex sociologist-turned anthropologist with primary research interests on men and sex studies, especially contestations around masculinities, representation of men and boys in popular cultures, understanding sexual cultures in postcolonial English West Africa, and social-cultural health. A senior lecturer in the Department of Sociology and Anthropology, University of Cape Coast, Ghana, he founded the Centre for Men's Health and Sex Studies, a not-for-profit establishment to promote research on men's health and sex studies.

Nana Afia Karikari has research interests and expertise in medical sociology, gender and sexuality, social policy, rural sociology and qualitative research methodology. Nana Afia holds an MPhil in Sociology from the University of Cape Coast, Ghana, and has several years of research experience. She has been involved in several collaborative research projects with the University of Sheffield, University of Western Australia, University for Development Studies (Ghana) and Carleton University. Her current research examines health behaviors of cervical cancer patients in Northern Ghana. Nana Afia has publications in *Gender and Behaviour*, *Geoform and Gender*, and *Place and Culture*.

Dr. Alex Somuah Obeng is a Doctor of Philosophy in Sociology and a senior lecturer at the Department of Sociology and Anthropology, University of Cape Coast, Ghana. His teaching centers on rural sociology, criminology, sociology of education, research methods, environmental sociology and conflict management and prevention. He has expertise in rural development, poverty, criminal justice, and gender issues.

Dr. Georgina Yaa Oduro is the Director of the Centre for Gender Research, Advocacy and Documentation (CEGRAD) at the University of Cape Coast, Ghana. She is also a senior lecturer in the Department of Sociology and Anthropology at the same university. Her research interests include gender, sexuality, youth cultures, popular culture, ocean heritage and marginalized populations. Dr. Oduro has written extensively on sexualities in Ghana. Some of her recent works have appeared in the *Palgrave Handbook for Sexuality Education* (2017), *Routledge International Handbook for Sex Industry Research* (2019), and *The Routledge Handbook for African Queer Studies* (2020).